Development of Chinese Church Leaders: A Study of Relational Leadership in Contemporary Chinese Churches

Otto Lui

Langham

MONOGRAPHS

© 2013 by Otto Lui

Published 2013 by Langham Monographs
an imprint of Langham Creative Projects

Langham Partnership
PO Box 296, Carlisle, Cumbria CA3 9WZ, UK
www.langham.org

ISBNs:
978-1-907713-46-0 Print
978-1-907713-47-7 Mobi
978-1-907713-48-4 ePub

Otto Lui has asserted his right under the Copyright, Designs and Patents Act, 1988 to be identified as the Author of this work.

All rights reserved. No part of this publication may be reproduced, stored in a retrieval system or transmitted, in any form or by any means, electronic, mechanical, photocopying, recording or otherwise, without the prior written permission of the publisher or the Copyright Licensing Agency.

Scriptures taken from the Holy Bible, New International Version®, NIV®. Copyright © 1973, 1978, 1984, 2011 by Biblica, Inc.™

Scriptures also taken from the New Revised Standard Version Bible, copyright 1989, Division of Christian Education of the National Council of the Churches of Christ in the United States of America. Used by permission. All rights reserved.

British Library Cataloguing in Publication Data
Langham Monographs
Otto Lui
Development of Chinese Church Leaders: A Study of Relational Leadership in Contemporary Chinese Churches.
 1. Christian leadership--China--History--21st century.
 2. China--Religion--21st century.
 I. Title
 262.1'0951-dc23
ISBN-13: 9781907713460

Cover & Book Design: projectluz.com

Langham Partnership actively supports theological dialogue and a scholars right to publish but does not necessarily endorse the views and opinions set forth, and works referenced within this publication or guarantee its technical and grammatical correctness. Langham Partnership does not accept any responsibility or liability to persons or property as a consequence of the reading, use or interpretation of its published content.

Dedication

To my wife, Yvonne
My daughters, Jurita and Jackie

Contents

Acknowledgments xiii
Abstract xv
   English Language Disclaimer xv
   Note on Romanization xvi
List of Abbreviations xvii
Introduction 1
   Background 1
   Purpose 6
   Goal 6
   Significance 6
   Central Research Issue 7
   Variables 8
   Research Questions 8
   Assumptions 8
   Definitions 9
   Delimitations 10
   Limitations 11
   Research Methodology 11
      Historiography in Chinese Church History 12
      Case Studies 13
      Life Stories/Oral History 14
      Ethnographic Interviewing 15
      Participant Observation 17
      Grounded Theory 18
   Overview of the Study 19

PART I: DIFFERENT CULTURAL PERSPECTIVES ON RELATIONAL LEADERSHIP

Chapter 1 23
Biblical Foundation on Relational Leadership
   Biblical Accounts of Leaders and Followers in the Gospels 25
      Leaders and Followers in the Graeco-Roman World 26
      Rabbi and Leader 27
      The Followers of Jesus 28

    The Selection of Potential Leaders..30
    Approaches of Jesus Christ in Developing Followers 31
        Team Approach 32
        Lifelong Approach 34
        Inner Life Approach..35
        Scripture-Saturation Approach...36
        Experiential Learning Approach...37
        Empowerment and Delegation Approach 39
    The Characteristics of Relational Leadership in the Gospels 41
        God-with-us Relationship...41
        Situational in Nature 42
        Lifelong Process 42
        Mutual Dependence 43
        Vision Driven 43
        Inner Life Development..44
        Empowerment 44
    Summary 45

Chapter 2 47
Theoretical Foundation of Relational Leadership
    Leadership Attributes and Leader-Centric Studies...........................49
        Traits, Great-man, and Leader-centric Studies.........................50
        Contributions and Application of Leadership Attributes.............50
        The Inadequacies of the Studies on Leadership Attributes...........52
    The Impact of Culture: A Wider Scope of Situational Theory 54
        The Early Models of Situational Theory..................................54
        The Leader-Followers-Situation Interactions 56
        Culture as an External Situation 58
        The Limitations in the Study of Organizational Culture 59
        Leadership in a Changing World 60
    Culture and Followership...63
        The Leader-centric Studies on Followership 63
        Culture and Followers' Expectations..65
        Paternalistic Culture and Leadership.......................................72
    Towards a Relational Leadership Model 75
    Summary 76

Chapter 3 79
Confucian Culture and Relational Leadership in China
    Confucianism, Wang Yangming and Leadership Development 80
    The Beginning of Leadership Development: Human Nature...............86

  Jen and *Liang Zhi* in Human Nature 87
  Principle and Truth in Human Nature 90
 The Goal of Leadership Development: The Sage 93
 The Process of Leadership Development: Self-Cultivation 96
  Acquisition of Principle 96
  The Unity of Knowing and Acting (*Zhi Xing He Yi* 知行合一) ... 98
  Self-Cultivation 100
 A Review of the Characteristics of Confucian Leadership 102
  An Idealized Human Being 102
  Moral Leadership 103
  Modeling 103
  Extension of a Family 104
  Paternalistic Leadership 104
  Inner Life Quality 105
  Pragmatic Culture 105
 A Summary 105

PART II: CHINESE THEOLOGICAL ROOTS OF RELATIONAL LEADERSHIP

Chapter 4 109
Situational Factors Influencing the Understandings and Expectations of Leaders and Leadership in China
  Impacts of Western Missions and Revival Movements 111
  Impacts of Fundamentalism 114
  Impacts of the Anti-Christian Movement 116
  Impacts of the Indigenization Movement 120
  Impacts of the Three-Self Patriotic Movement 124
  Summary 126

Chapter 5 129
Confucian Christian Theologians and Relational Leadership
 Wang Mingdao: A Confucian Pastor 135
  Personal Pursuit of Truth 137
  Ethical Expectations 139
  Direct Communication from God to the Human Conscience ... 140
  Pragmatism 141
  The Importance of Knowing and Acting 142
  Self-Reflection and Cultivation 143
  Faithfulness to the Mandate of Heaven 144
 Jia Yuming's "Perfect Leader" and "Christ–Human" State 146
  Sanctification Begins at Salvation 147

  Sanctification as a Process of Becoming a Leadership
    Role Model 151
  Victory as the Result of Sanctification 156
Yang Shaotang's Pastoral Mentoring 158
  Leadership Models and Pastoral Mentoring 160
  Leadership Models and Character Nurturing 165
  Pastoral Mentoring and Practical Training 170
A Further Reflection on Relational Leadership in Chinese Churches ... 172
  The Relationship with the Divine 173
  The Relationship with the Self 174
  The Relationship with Others 175
Summary 177
  The Implication of Situational Factors in Chinese Leadership
    Development 178
  The Implication of the Indigenous Approaches to Leadership
    Development 179
  The Implication of the Inadequacies 180

PART III: RELATIONAL LEADERSHIP IN CONTEMPORARY CHINESE CHURCHES

Chapter 6 185
Internal and External Situiations of Urumqi, Sanyuan and Fuzhou Churches
  General Information on the Churches in China in This Study 187
  Urumqi: An Expanding Church with a Harmonious
    Leadership Team 190
    Geographical and Political Background 190
    A Brief History of Christianity in Urumqi 191
    The Informants and Interviews 194
  Sanyuan: A Church Characterized by Family Relationships 197
    Geographical and Political Background 197
    A Brief Historical background of Sanyuan Churches 198
    The Informants and Interviews 199
  Fuzhou: A Church in Transition 203
    Geographical and Political Background 203
    A Brief Historical Background of the Zhong Zhou Church 203
    The Informants and the Interviews 206
  Summary 208

Chapter 7 211
Findings from the Case Studies
- The Historical Impacts from the Early Twentieth Century 212
  - Experiences of Suffering 212
  - Political Sensitivity 214
  - The Church Tradition 217
- The Cultural Impacts of Confucianism 219
  - Confucianism and Human Development 219
  - Collective Culture and Team Development 222
  - Community as the Extension of Family 226
  - Experiential Learning and Leadership Development 229
- Summary 244

Chapter 8 247
Missiological Implications of Relational Leadership in Chinese Churches
- The Characteristics of Relational Leadership 247
  - Relational Leadership is a Response to Situational Factors in Leadership Development 248
  - Relational Leadership Recognizes Leadership Development is a Process of Spiritual Growth 249
  - Developing Role Models is the Major Goal in Relational Leadership 249
  - Experiential Learning Is the Major Method in Developing Relational Leader 250
  - Relational Leadership Performs Well with Good Interpersonal Skills 251
  - Relational Leadership is Effective Leadership Team Development 252
- The Missiological Implications 253
  - The Encouragement of Developing Indigenous Approach in Leadership Development 254
  - An Affirmation of the Study of Leadership Attributes 254
  - A Possible Consensus on Human Nature 255
  - Awareness of the Negative Aspects of Relational Culture 257
  - A Balance between Theory and Practice in Leadership Development 257
  - The Compatibility of Relational Leadership with Other Theories 258
- Summary 259

PART IV: CONCLUSION

Chapter 9 263
   Conclusion
      Areas of Significance in this Research Study 263
      Reviews of Existing Practices in Leadership Development in Chinese
         Churches 264
         To Review the Existing Leadership Training Program in the
            Chinese Churches 264
         To Review the Existing Curriculum of the Seminary 266
         To Review the Recruitment and Internship Arrangement of
            Seminary Students 267
      Recommendations for Further Research 268
         Seminary Education and Leadership Development 268
         Possible Negative Aspects of the Old Pastors 269
         Ethnicity in the Leadership Development in Rural Churches 269
         The Gender Issue in Chinese Leadership Development 269
         Other Influences of Confucianism 270
         Liberal Traditions in the TSPM Churches 270
         The House Churches and the Third Churches 271
      A Summary and Final Conclusion 271

Appendix A 273
   Interview Guide for Old Pastors

Appendix B 275
   Interview Guide for Younger Church leaders

Appendix C 277
   The Life of Wang Mingdao

Appendix D 279
   The Life of Jia Yuming

Appendix E 281
   The Life of Yang Shaotang

Appendix F 283
   Major Life Events of Pastor HQZ

Appendix G 285
   Major Life Events of Pastor CXQ

Appendix H 287
   Major Life Events of Pastor ZGR

Appendix I 289
    Major Life Events of Pastor YZD
Glossary 291
Bibliography 295
Index 319
Vita 327

LIST OF FIGURES

FIGURE 1: The Relationship of Variables Used in Leadership Research 55
FIGURE 2: An Interactional Framework for Analyzing Leadership 57
FIGURE 3: Informants: Male and Female 188

LIST OF MAPS

MAP 1: Location of Urumqi, Xinjiang 191
MAP 2: Location of Sanyuan, Shaanxi 198
MAP 3: Location of Fuzhou, Fujian 203

LIST OF TABLES

TABLE 1: Great Faith Leaders of the Bible 154
TABLE 2: Interview Schedule 186
TABLE 3: Informants: Age Groups 189
TABLE 4: Positions of the Pastors in Urumqi TSPM/CCC Church 194
TABLE 5: Background of Theological Education of the
  Young Pastors in Urumqi 196
TABLE 6: The Major Responsibilities of the Church Leaders in
  Sanyuan and Fuping Churches 200
TABLE 7: The Major Responsibilities of the Church Leaders in
  Fuzhou Zhong Zhou Church 206

Acknowledgments

It is my pleasure and honor to learn from the professors at Fuller Theological Seminary. Special thanks to the patience, guidance, and prayers of Dr. C. Douglas McConnell, my mentor in the past four years. Dr. David D. Bundy, my committee member who enriches my scope of knowledge in historical survey. Dr. Jason Yeung and Dr. Ying Fuktsang in Hong Kong guided me on my tutorial studies on Confucianism and Chinese church history. The General Secretary Mr. Thomas Tang and the ministry team of Christian Communications Ltd in Hong Kong support my whole family through prayers, visits, fund raising, and field research coordination. My whole family is blessed by the pastors and church members of both the Yuen Long Lutheran Light Church in Hong Kong and the First Evangelical Church of San Gabriel Valley in Los Angeles. Without my wife, Yvonne, who gave up her career in Hong Kong to take care of the whole family during my years of study, it is not possible for me and our daughters to cope with the changes easily. More importantly, great thanks to our Lord who calls me to serve and provides everything we need.

Abstract

Under the strong impact of Confucianism, the Chinese churches today have their specific ways in developing church leaders. The study on the impact of cultural situations in affecting leadership development is necessary but not well developed in the previous studies on Chinese leadership. Therefore, this dissertation is an attempt to study and analyze the ways of developing followers in contemporary Chinese churches.

The primary purpose of this dissertation is to develop an indigenous approach in developing church leaders in contemporary China. The impact of Confucianism as a cultural force in affecting the perceptions and practices of the Chinese pastors is discovered in this study. Based on the theories and case studies of the churches in mainland China, relational leadership has proved to be an effective indigenous pattern of leadership development in contemporary China.

This dissertation is presented in four parts. Part I is a study of the understandings of relational leadership through different cultural perspectives. Part II is a study of the Chinese theological roots of relational leadership. Part III is the analysis of the field data which reflects the practice of relational leadership in contemporary Chinese churches, and part IV is the final conclusion and overall significance of this research.

English Language Disclaimer

As a non-native speaker of English, I am aware that my writing may at times lack clarity, though I have attempted to write as clearly as possible. Please note that the primary purpose of this work is to acknowledge a theory and to apply it to a particular context. I appreciate the editorial assistance I have received from various individuals but acknowledge that the responsibility for this work is entirely my own.

Note on Romanization

Chinese names are written with surname first. The names of people, places, and some philosophical terms have been romanized according to the *pinyin* system instead of the Wade-Giles romanization system. Exceptions appear only in quotations and with names and terms like *Jen* and *Taoism* that have been long known and widely used in English publications in their Wade-Giles romanized forms.

List of Abbreviations

ACSF	Anti-Christian Student Federation
BTJ	Back to Jerusalem Movement
BJEB	Back to Jerusalem Evangelism Band
CAH	Church Assembly Hall
CCC	China Christian Council
CCL	Christian Communications Ltd.
CIM	China Inland Mission
CPC	Communist Party of China
CPPCCC	Chinese People's Political Consultative Conference
CWWYM	Complete Works of Wang Yang Ming
EI	Ethnographic Interviewing
FMS	Finnish Missionary Society
IGL	Inquiry on the Great Learning
IPL	Instructions for Practical Living
KMT	Kuomingtang, the Chinese Nationalist Party
LET	Leadership Emergency Theory
MLQ	Multifactor Leadership Questionnaire
NSM	Northwest Spiritual Movement
PO	Participant Observation
PRC	People's Republic of China
RAB	Religious Affairs Bureau
TSPM	Three Self Patriot Movement

Introduction

In the twenty-first century we witness the growing influences of China in world politics and economics. At the same time, the Christian churches in mainland China are entering another stage of developing indigenous mission leaders. As a ministry worker serving the churches in mainland China for over fifteen years, I have witnessed the growth in quality is not balanced with the growth in quantity of the church members: even though the Christian population is still increasing, the inadequate number of trained pastors and Bible teachers cannot fulfill the requests of discipleship. It is therefore hard to mention about participating cross-cultural mission of the Chinese churches. Indigenous ways of developing church leaders are needed urgently. In this introductory chapter, I am going to present my personal background and passion on this research project. The main purpose of this research project and research methods will be discussed as well.

Background

I was born and raised in Hong Kong. During my childhood in the 1970s, I had only a negative impression of mainland China. The main reason was the Cultural Revolution (1966-1976),[1] a political, social, and cultural disaster, magnified some of the worst aspects of human sinfulness. Hong Kong was still a British colony; for that reason the Red Guards[2] could not attack

---

1. The beginning of the Cultural Revolution was signified by the posting of a "big letter poster" in Qing Hua University on June 2, 1966 (Shen 2004, 5).
2. Red Guards were formed by Mao Zedong, the chairman of China in the 1960s. They were different from the Red Army in the sense that they did not have formal military training and were composed mainly of teenagers. The only purpose for their existence

it directly. Nevertheless, it was so terrible to listen every day to the news that corpses floated from the Guangdong province of mainland China to Hong Kong. Because of my perception of the cultural inferiority of China, I grew up wondering why I was not born in the Western hemisphere where there were peace and prosperity.

My personal journey of faith was connected with the foreign missionary when I was a child. The first Christian I met was a Finnish missionary. I was also baptized by a Finnish pastor. The Finnish Missionary Society (FMS) had just started a church close to where I lived. I therefore came to know Christ when I was a teenager under the impact of the services provided by the missionaries. The FMS later gave all their ministries to the Evangelical Lutheran Church of Hong Kong before 1997 in a process of indigenization. My first encounter with the Finnish missionaries was a good experience and left an impression that Christianity and Western culture were good. I therefore asked myself, if I were not born in the West, was there a particular purpose for God to give me this "dual citizenship" of being Chinese as well as Christian (Kung and Ching 1989, 273-283)?

Right after the Tiananmen Square Incident in 1989, the Chinese government launched a series of propaganda campaigns through the media to cover up the number of people killed on June 3 and 4.[3] The "white lies" of the communist government were so obvious and overwhelming. I thought it was the failure to address the issue of human sinfulness in Chinese culture and religion that caused the tragedy. My goal became to search for the answer. I chose to study religion and philosophy in college in order to understand more about Christianity and Chinese culture. Since then, God has shaped my path, affording me opportunities to research the gaps between

---

at that time was to execute the orders of Mao and his wife Jiang Qing, to uphold the principle of "class struggle" and eliminate everything "old" and "feudal." The name "Red Guard" first appeared in public on May 25, 1966 on a poster in the subsidiary secondary school of Qing Hua University (Zhu 2001, 21).

3. The Tiananmen Square Incident refers to the suppression of the democratic movement of the students mainly in Beijing from April to June of 1989. As reported by the press and electronic media, an estimated 1,500 students and protesters were killed. However, according to the official announcement released on June 6, only twenty three people died on June 4th. According to an interview with a US news agency later the same month, the Chinese government denied killing any of the students (Ceng 1989, 49-50; N. Li 1989, 24-25).

Christianity and Chinese culture in college. I began my journey to search for a specific area and mission in which I could use my role in this "dual citizenship." This journey led me to join Christian Communications Ltd. (CCL) in 1995 as a ministry staff member in the China ministry.

During the last fifteen years in CCL, I have travelled across China to visit church pastors of different backgrounds and coordinated different kinds of ministries ranging from publishing to training, church building to Christian music. God has opened my eyes through the participation in the frontline ministries in China about the historical significance of the missionary works in the past. One noteworthy experience was in Southwestern China when I visited a church of the Bai ethnic group. The young pastor told me that the church building had belonged to another denomination, but no church members left since the expulsion of foreign missionaries in the early 1950s. All the members remaining in the church belonged to the China Inland Mission (CIM). The pastor told me that the CIM missionaries focused on Bible teaching and training of local church workers, which allowed the Christians to keep their faith through the years of hardship between the early 1950s and the late 1970s. Christians all over the world have witnessed the amazing church growth in China over the past 30 years. The CIM missionaries trained local pastors with the language and concepts they understood in Bible study classes. The strong faith developed by the missionaries through contextualized Bible teaching is one of the historical roots behind this church growth.

Different forms of ongoing inter-faith dialogues have taken place between Christianity and Chinese culture ever since Christianity came to China in the seventh century. However, most of the discussions have focused on philosophical and ideological aspects. The debates on the similarities and differences between the Confucian concept of Heaven and the Christian God have lasted over a century but still have not been able to any conclusion.[4]

---

4. For example, the contemporary Confucian scholar Liu Shuxian argues that "Heaven referred to a personal God in ancient China"(Liu 1972, 45). Another scholar, Tang Junyi, has strong resistance against this argument and believes that the Chinese concept of Heaven is distinctively different from a Christian God, and he believes such a comparison is a form of cultural invasion from the West (Tang 1974, 56).

In light of the tremendous growth in the number of Christians and the expansion of the churches in China in the last thirty years, the previous theological dialogues have made no significant impact to the development of Christianity in China. Many practical issues related to the contextualization of the Chinese churches need more attention: liturgy, Christian education, church management, church planting, and models of church growth.

Relationship is one of the key elements in Christianity when salvation is defined as the recovery of the broken relationship between God and human beings. In the meantime, relationship is a key to success in business in contemporary China. Are the relationships with God and with others similar? How about the practice of contemporary Chinese church on relationship in handling the leadership development issue? These questions are waiting to be discussed.

Leadership development is at the top among the list of the key issues which require further attention. In Christianity only God is perfect; all humans are sinners. In contrast, in the Chinese Confucian tradition, people look for a perfect leader, who is a "sage." How can Chinese Christians deal with these extreme expectations for leaders? Since the beginning of reform and open policy of the Chinese government in the late 1970s, numerous programs have been implemented to train church leaders. For instance, short-term pastoral training programs, training curricula, websites, and publications have been provided continuously by overseas Christians. However, the churches are still seeking improved systematic training for leaders. Although some research studies and writings about leadership training are available in China, there has not been much specific discussion of how to synthesize traditional Chinese teaching methods with Christian tradition.[5]

The problem of leadership transition is entering a critical stage in China. Because of the lack of trained pastors in China in the past decades, there is literally no retirement for the older generation of pastors. The churches

---

5. In fact, no research has been done in leadership development from an internal perspective. Brent Fulton has interviewed organizations which trained church leaders in 2007, but his work was an external views towards the typology and needs of the church leaders in China (2007, 6-9). The church leaders in mainland China did not have an opportunity to speak for themselves about their needs.

need the knowledge and experiences of the old pastors and the old pastors are more than willing to serve until they die. Many of the old pastors serve in the pulpit until they become physically unable to continue. Most of them are now over eighty years old. The younger generations of leaders are emerging with great difficulty. On the one hand, the more recent generations do not experience the same suffering as their predecessors. They are therefore not able to be qualified as spiritual leaders. On the other hand, there are always several options for leadership candidates within a given church. Those candidates received leadership training together. None of them are believed to be a better leader than the others. Not many churches have an undisputable successor to replace the leadership role of the old pastor. In many instances, churches split up because church members chose different leaders among themselves during the leadership transition period. Relationship is one of the major characteristics of Chinese culture. Good interpersonal relationships should be one of the strength of the Chinese churches. However, a good leadership team is not a common feature in the Chinese churches today.

The trainings the potential leaders received have provided only knowledge on how to be a leader but not much nurture for their inner life. They want to learn from foreign pastors but do not know how to work with their local colleagues and do not know how to appreciate what they have already achieved. I find the elements of life-coaching and mentoring are not new to either Christian or Chinese cultures, but they are not well-developed in the Chinese-Christian context either. More attention should be paid to this research area in order to rediscover and incorporate ways of leadership development that are both biblical and Chinese.

In addition, in 2003 the "Back to Jerusalem" (BTJ)[6] movement awakened the vision for cross-cultural mission among the Chinese churches.

---

6. "Back to Jerusalem" is a slogan originally used in mission among Chinese churches in the 1940s. The slogan was first announced by the church leaders in China during the Second World War. Several groups of church leaders claimed that they had a vision directly from God asking them to go west, to share the gospel until reaching the Jews in Jerusalem. In 2003, certain house church networks claimed that they wanted to take the baton of mission and evangelize the Muslims before the second coming of Christ (Aikman 2003, 193-205). In the past few years, many house church networks in mainland China have trained and sent missionaries to Middle Eastern countries in the name of BTJ. The slogan BTJ used in this research will refer to the cross-cultural mission movement in both periods.

Within a year, many unprepared missionaries had been sent from China. Since then many mission schools have been set up to train cross-cultural missionaries. In most cases, the missionaries from China received only three months of training and were sent to Middle Eastern countries without proper preparation. It is encouraging, on the one hand, to see Chinese churches wanting to take an active role in world missions, but on the other hand, the churches need more knowledge and preparation.

God has called me to serve as one of the bridges between Christianity and Chinese culture. I perceive a great need of research for contextualization in the pattern of developing leaders in Chinese culture in this new millennium. Through my doctoral studies, I hope to arrive at new but contextualized ways of developing mission leaders through the connections between the teachings and example of Jesus Christ and the Chinese culture of relationship. My goal is to propose an effective way to meet the critical need for leadership development in China.

Purpose

The purpose of this study is to explore the concept and role of relationship in both biblical and Chinese traditions in order to develop Chinese church leaders effectively.

Goal

The goal of this research is to develop culturally appropriate and applicable guidelines for the development of church leaders in mainland China.

Significance

Through this research, I hope to build a bridge for leadership development between Christianity and Chinese culture. Both Confucius and Jesus of Nazareth were great teachers. They both demonstrated effective examples for developing disciples. Chinese Christians need to learn biblical patterns of leadership development through the life and teachings of Christ and at the same time learn to incorporate the strength of Confucian culture in developing followers in the Chinese churches.

The churches in China are no longer only receivers of resources from the Western world, they are also developing into contributors of world mission. In recent years many African, Middle Eastern, and other Asian countries have begun to welcome Chinese labor workers and businessmen to work and invest in their countries. The churches in China have already perceived this welcoming atmosphere as a golden opportunity to send missionaries to plant churches. The development of culturally appropriate guidelines in equipping church leaders is an essential step in strengthening the growing Chinese churches. The stronger and healthier churches can in turn provide a more effective workforce to take part in world mission.

As a Chinese Christian based in Hong Kong, I have had good experiences of enjoying the strength and compatibility of both Western and Chinese cultures. Further exploration of the common areas between Christianity and the Confucian tradition will surely benefit the churches in Chinese cultural regions including mainland China, Hong Kong, Taiwan, Macau, and the North American Chinese churches. The introduction of the strength of Chinese tradition, assimilated into the framework of biblical principles on developing followers, also serves as an example for other Asian Christian churches to in leadership development. A successful incorporation of Confucian and Christian ways of equipping followers will bring cultural transformation regarding leadership development in Chinese churches.

Central Research Issue

The central research issue of this study is to compare and contrast Jesus' relationships with his disciples in the Gospels with the indigenous approaches to developing followers in Confucian China and to explore the relevance of such a comparison for contemporary Chinese churches.

Variables

   A. Jesus' leadership role in relation to his disciples in the Gospels.
   B. Indigenous approaches to developing followers in Confucian China.
   C. Context of leaders in contemporary Chinese churches.

Research Questions

   1. As reflected in the Gospels, in what ways did Jesus relate to his disciples, and how did he commission them to make disciples?
   2. What are the essential elements of developing followers in traditional Chinese culture as presented by Confucianism?
   3. To what extent are the recent leadership theories applicable to the cultural context of Chinese churches?
   4. What are the characteristics reflected in the life and teachings of Chinese pastors in pre-Cultural Revolution China in relation to followers' development?
   5. How are the followers in contemporary Chinese churches being equipped as church leaders?
   6. Are there missiological implications for mentoring as a way of developing Chinese church leaders?

Assumptions

   1. The relationship between Jesus and his disciples was a mentoring relationship. The way he lived and taught affected the lives of the disciples, which in turn shaped them as church leaders. One can read and interpret this relationship mainly in the Gospels and secondarily in other New Testament books.
   2. Confucianism is the dominant philosophy and culture in China. With a 2500-year history of Confucianism, the doctrines and practices have penetrated into everyday life of the Chinese people

all over the world. The Chinese churches are no exception.
3. The Han Chinese people represent the majority of the Chinese population and the Chinese churches. Confucianism is also originated among the Han Chinese. Other ethnic groups in China are regarded by Han Chinese as mission fields in different cultures. Therefore, this study is based on Han Chinese churches.
4. Some Chinese churches are willing to spend resources in developing leaders, and they are also ready to be developed as missionary-sending churches.

Definitions

China and the Chinese Churches: Although Hong Kong and Macau were returned to the People's Republic of China (PRC) in 1997 and 1999 respectively, I exclude them when referring to the PRC because the history and development of the churches in Hong Kong and Macau have more foreign cultural influences. I also use the term "mainland China" or "China" to refer to the PRC. The term "Chinese churches" refers to the churches located in mainland China, including the government registered churches that belong to the Three Self Patriotic Movement (TSPM), the independent registered churches, and the non-registered house churches. The Chinese churches located in Hong Kong, Macau, Taiwan, and other countries are called overseas Chinese churches.

Cross-cultural Mission: Mission is defined traditionally as having a "sending church" which sends missionaries to another culture to witness to the cross of Christ (Bosch 1991, 1). The purpose of cross-cultural mission includes evangelism, church planting, and other activities that witness about the love of God. When these activities go beyond a cultural boarder into an area with different languages, customs, or religions, they are referred to as cross-cultural mission.

Relational Leadership: Leadership is a relationship that involves a leader and his or her followers, which is a process of mutual influence (Wright 2004, 5). As defined by J. Robert Clinton (1993b, 21), the Christian leader exercises his or her influence over a period of time and uses his or her resources to impact the followers so as to accomplish the purpose of God. In this respect, Christian leadership involves the divine intervention into the human activities.

Cultural Revolution: Cultural Revolution in China refers to the political movement launched by Mao Zedong in 1966. The purpose of the Cultural Revolution was to uphold the principle of "class struggle" and to eliminate everything associated with capitalism and imperialism. Everything related to traditional beliefs, religions, and foreign countries had to be destroyed by the Red Guards. In a later stage, the Red Guards persecuted one another (Smart 1974, 19). In 1976, with the death of Mao Zedong and the arrest of the "gang of four," the Cultural Revolution came to an end.

Confucianism and Chinese Culture: Confucianism originated from the teachings of Confucius, who was born in 551 B.C. The core of his teachings concerns *jen* (仁), meaning benevolence or perfect virtue. *Jen* is realized in human society in the *junzi* (君子)—the gentleman or profound person (De Bary 1960). Although Confucianism does not have the term "leader," the concept of the perfect leader is *sheng ren* (聖人), which literally means a sage, who is developed from a *junzi*. With the abolition of all other ideologies and philosophies during the Han dynasty (206 B.C.-A.D. 20), Confucianism became the dominant ideology in China. Confucianism has therefore become the dominant cultural influence in China.

Delimitations

The scope of this study is on the one hand limited to the life and ministry of Jesus Christ and his relationship with his disciples. The study is based on the four Gospels and some specific texts selected from Acts and the Pauline letters, which indicate Jesus' relationship with his disciples. On the other hand, the research on the essential elements in Confucianism on leadership development is based on the philosophy of Wang Yangming (A.D. 1472-1529), the consolidator of Neo-Confucianism in the Ming dynasty (A.D. 1368-1644). This research cannot cover the entire 2500 years of Confucian tradition; however, Wang Yangming's understanding of human nature is developed from the teachings of Confucius (551-479 B.C.) and Mencius (471-298 B.C.).

The focus of this study is on the Confucian cultural impact on Chinese church leaders. The denominational background is less significant. In addition, the case studies and interviews are focused on the church leaders in government-registered TSPM churches. The influential pastors in this research study are restricted to those church leaders have lived and ministered in the twentieth century. The physical location of the church leaders and followers in major cities are selected as case studies.

Limitations

This research is limited by the degree of openness and willingness of the Chinese pastors to disclose their personal information and opinions. Typically, in Chinese culture, people will release personal information according to their relationship with the interviewer—the closer the relationship, the more detailed information they will provide. This need for a previous relationship with the pastors limit my choice of case studies. Further, the Chinese government still closely censors Christian activities, especially as they relate to Westerners and overseas Chinese people. The informants may not have been willing to provide politically sensitive information as requested. Due to the tradition of "giving face," leaders may be unwilling to share candid opinions, when those opinions may reflect negatively on their associates.

Research Methodology

In handling two major cultural heritages from the Eastern and Western hemispheres, a variety of methods should be employed in interpreting and analyzing classical texts, life stories, and case studies. In addition to the literature review and historiography of the Chinese church history, the inductive approach of qualitative research was the major approach adopted. Multiple methods were adopted in case study research, including life story/

oral history, ethnographic interviewing, and participant observation. After the collection of data, the data analysis and theory development method was based on grounded theory.

Historiography in Chinese Church History

Chapter 4 is a study and analysis of Chinese church history. The churches selected for the case study research require some understanding of their historical background. A threefold dialogue among the researcher, the historical texts, and historians is necessary. In contrast to the traditional Western model of "mission history" which studies China from a Western perspective, the viewpoint of this paper is from the inner development of Chinese history.

In studying Chinese church history of the nineteenth and twentieth century, many scholars have based their research on the biographies and testimonies of Western missionaries. The perspectives are therefore limited by the records and backgrounds of those missionaries. Kenneth Scott Latourette's *A History of Christian Missions in China* (1973) is one of the masterpieces of mission history (Y. Leung 2006, 12-13). Many scholars in the West are limited by the research resources available in English, therefore they cannot read and interpret events in China from the local Chinese perspective (Fairbank 1974, 4). Until the 1980s, under the direction of John K. Fairbank, the study of Chinese history shifted gradually from a Western missionary-centered perspective to a China-centered perspective (J. Li 2006, 23-24; Bays 1996, vii). Paul Cohen, a student of Fairbank, points out that the study of Chinese history should begin from the perspective of the Chinese people. While in some cases historical events may be caused by the West, the most valuable piece of information in this context is the experience of the Chinese people and their response to those events. Cohen states that the impacts of these historical events should be measured by Chinese people (Cohen 1984, 154; Ying 2006, 208-209). Chapter 4 therefore follows the Chinese perspective in studying and analyzing the impacts of the environment on the Chinese pastors.

Many Chinese scholars have written Chinese church history from a local Chinese perspective. For example, Wang Zhixin (1998) wrote the *History of Christianity in China* as early as the 1930s; Tang Qing (2001) published

The First Hundred Years of Protestant Mission in China in 1987. Both are pioneer works on Chinese church history. In the last two decades, a number of books on Chinese church history have been published from mainland China, Hong Kong, and Taiwan with different perspectives. Li Jinqiang has done a thorough summary in *A Study on Modern Chinese Church History* (2006, 13-59).

The historical survey and analysis in this dissertation is written from the perspective of the Chinese church leaders. Based on their interpretations of the situations they faced and the decisions they made, it is an analysis of the way the local pastors develop church leaders.

Case Studies

A case study is an approach to understand social phenomena. Multiple research methods were adopted in order to study the events or organizations more deeply through different perspectives; hence the validity and reliability of the findings were increased (Hamel, Dufour, and Fortin 1993, 34-38; Bloor and Wood 2006, 27-28; Woodside 2010, 6, 400). Through multiple research methods, the reality of the subject under study was reconstructed and triangulation was achieved (Denzin and Lincoln 2005, 5-6). The methods used in these cases were life story interviewing, ethnographic interviewing, and participation observation. The stories of the old pastors were collected from life story interviewing. The verbal communication with the old pastors brought a historical perspective which had not been recorded by the professional and official historians. Through ethnographic interviewing, an insider's perspective with the cultural and social contexts of the informants was collected. As I have personal connections with all the selected churches, a participant observation was therefore possible to help me bring an objective perspective into the research.

Multiple case studies were adopted in this research. To find the patterns and major elements of leadership development in the contemporary Chinese churches, a single case study is inadequate. It is hard to generalize and reflect on the cultural phenomena that has appeared in China. When more cases are studied, the time spent on each case may not be adequate enough to have a detailed investigation. This case study research is intended to explore a possible theory for leadership development in contemporary

Chinese churches. The final conclusion is expected to be a reference for those Chinese churches which face similar conditions. I have selected three churches as cases in this research project. All of them are Han Chinese churches but they are located in different parts of China: Xinjing, Shaanxi, and Fujian. I have studied the historical backgrounds of these churches. Through ethnographic interviews, participant observations, and life story interviews, twenty five long and short stories were collected.

The analysis of the research data began with a process of pattern matching. The special features and characteristics of each church under study were discovered. Through comparing and contrasting the data from all three cases, some common features were found. The aim at this stage was to find the literal replications among these cases, that is the common and repeated patterns in equipping leaders appeared in all three cases (Yin 2003, 4-5; 2009, 138-140). Some initial ideas of relational leadership in Chinese churches were discovered after the first case study. A further study and comparing of the findings from different cases were helpful in differentiating the core features of the leadership development patterns. In addition to the common features, some distinctive characteristics of each individual case were discovered as well. The process of refining data was essential in this stage. Causes and effects were analyzed in these cases as these are the explanatory case studies (Yin 2003, 5). The final result is an initial theory of leadership development in the contemporary Chinese churches based on the data of these three churches.

Life Stories/Oral History

Life story interviewing in the form of oral history is one of the three major research methods I used in collecting data in these cases. Oral history is an unwritten form of history collected through interviews or personal testimonies (Thompson 1998, 28; Bloor and Wood 2006, 125; Titon 2006, 135-138). The works of historians have provided some objective perspectives; however, through the narrations of the participants of events, the insiders' perspectives are also included. A combination of multiple methods was used to collect data from the old pastors, including life story interviewing, literature and document reviewing, informal interviewing with related people and participant observation (McKinney 2000, 179). Oral history is therefore a compliment to the written record of history (Allen and Montell 1981, 11-18; Portelli 1998, 66-69). It is especially important in studying the history of contemporary Chinese churches. The impacts of many significant historical events in China are not recorded due to the political unrest in the first half of the twentieth century.

I interviewed four old pastors who are over eighty years old. Their stories gave much valuable information, which has never been recorded officially as written history. According to Belgium anthropologist Jan Vansina (1985, 1965), eyewitness accounts, hearsay, visions and dreams are all important data in the process of reconstructing historical information through oral history. In the conversations with the old pastors, I listened and recorded every detail by computer. Finding the documents the old pastors mentioned during interviews were essential to verify the information collected. I even talked to some other people who were not in my original schedule of interviewing. In some occasions, I took pictures of the paintings, trees, rooms or whatever the informants mentioned as important. I paid special attention to their cultural contexts, including their family backgrounds, pilgrimages of faith, and major life events. Through these stories, the cultural impacts were discovered (Atkinson 1998, 5-7).

Some particular elements related to the leadership development process are found in the life stories. Church traditions, Confucian culture, and political and social environment are all important contributing factors which shaped the methods and patterns of the leadership development of these old pastors. Through life story interviews, the narrations of the old pastors are the major part of the data which supports these in-depth case studies.

Ethnographic Interviewing

The study of Chinese culture is an essential component of this research project. Apart from studying the philosophy of Confucianism, an ethnographic understanding of the perspectives of the Chinese pastors and church leaders in China is another key to unlock the indigenous patterns and methods on developing church leaders. By using the native language and concepts, the church leaders can speak for themselves through ethnographic interviewing (Spradley 1979, 3). Ethnographic interviewing is a way to understand the meaning of a culture through conversation with the informants. The research process emphasizes the perspectives of the targeted group which comes from their worldviews and cultural traditions (McKinney 2000, 10; Bloor and Wood 2006, 70).

Including the old pastors, I interviewed twenty five church leaders between 2008 and 2010. The selection of informants was based on my personal networks as well as connections through CCL's ministry partners. Due to the impact of Cultural Revolution, a whole generation of leaders between sixty and eighty years old is missing.[7] The old pastors I interviewed are therefore over eighty years old. The younger church leaders range from twenty to sixty years old. I personally have good relationships with the informants in two churches. The old pastors in Urumqi and Sanyang and I have known each other for almost ten years. In Fuzhou, I was introduced to the old pastor by a mutual friend. Because of the trust relationship, all the arrangement of interviews went smoothly and without difficulty.

I was accompanied by a local church leader who transcribed each interview. The interviews were arranged as semi-structured interviews (Bernard 2006, 212). Two different interview guides were used when interviewing the old pastors and the younger church leaders. Appendix A was used for the life story interviewing and appendix B was used for the ethnographic interviewing of the young leaders. The approach of interviewing I adopted was a combination of what James A. Holstein and Jaber F. Gubrium called "creative interviewing" and active interviewing (1995, 12, 76-77). Mutual trust between the interviewer and the informants is the key to success in collecting in-depth information in the interviewing process. In the interviewing process, the interviewers and interviewees exchanged one another's stories and pray as a group. The two ways communications created a relax and free sharing atmosphere (Portelli 1998, 70).

---

7. The most affected generation in the Cultural Revolution was the young people around fifteen to thirty five years old. They were either Red Guards or young intellectuals. The former were the diehard followers of Chairman Mao and the latter were sent to rural areas to experience the life of laborers. Anti-intellect was one of the common beliefs at that time; as a result, not many of the diehard followers of Mao went to school. After the Cultural Revolution, the ideal image of Mao and the Communist Party of China (CPC) collapsed. This group of young men and women became skeptical about all moral idealism, including Christianity. As a result, not many church members in this age group today were found, not to mention church leaders. This explanation comes from my personal conversations with more than a dozen pastors in China over the past fifteen years.

Participant Observation

While interviewing is the major activity between the researcher and the informants in the process of case study research, participant observation is a simultaneous activity of the researcher. Together with the semi-structured interviews, participant observation works well in a casual setting where the researcher performs the role of an observer so as to listen and watch the informants' verbal and nonverbal expressions (Spradley 1979, 32-33). I actively conducted all the life story interviews with the old pastors. Some of the interviews with the young leaders were conducted by the local interviewers while I was there to observe the responses of the informants.

Over the past fifteen years of my experience in serving Chinese churches, I have established ministry networks throughout the country. To some extent I am already an "insider" (emic perspective) to Chinese church culture because I know the language and culture of China. On the other hand, I am also an "outsider" (etic perspective) in that I can observe and interpret the phenomena objectively. David Fetterman suggests a "good ethnography requires both emic and etic perspectives" (1998, 22). Therefore (as an insider-outsider), I am uniquely situated to be an effective participant observer which increased the validity of this research. As Russell H. Bernard affirms, a participant observer who is familiar with the language, culture and background of the field under study has more confidence in making "strong statements about cultural facts" (Bernard 2006, 347-355). The internal and external validity are therefore increased.

As a participant-observer, I travelled to all the three selected churches and stayed for one to three weeks depending on the situation. Apart from interviews, my other purpose was to observe the interactions between the congregation and the leaders and their methods of teaching and training. In addition to my previous knowledge of the Chinese churches, I partially participated in the daily life of the pastors in order to collect multiple perspectives on the phenomena appearing in the selected churches. Participant observation is especially appropriate in the case study research which is exploratory and descriptive in nature (Jorgensen 1989, 13, 53-68). Through observation of their daily living, their attitudes, viewpoints and interpretation of events can be analyzed on site even during the data gathering process (Becker 2006, 367-368).

Grounded Theory

In this case study research, different methods served different purposes. Life stories and ethnographic interviewing were helpful in understanding the indigenous perspective on leadership development in Chinese churches. Participant observation was necessary to draw inferences from the various informants and situations (J. A. Maxwell 2005, 94). These methods are complimentary to one another. The final stage of this research was therefore to make use of the findings from various research methods in the leadership development of the Chinese churches. The process of generating theory from the data collected in field research without prior assumptions is called grounded theory. As defined by Barney G. Glaser, grounded theory is a research method to "generate an inductive theory about a substantive area" systematically (1992, 16). It is important to adopt grounded theory in this research because I found and developed new theory on leadership development in Chinese churches, but explained or verified an existing theory (Bartell 1982, 126).

Based on the methods of developing grounded theory by Barney G. Glaser (1992, 1994, 1995), Glaser and Anselm Strauss (1967; 1994), and Kathy Charmaz (1994, 2006), I have constructed an initial theory on relational leadership of the Chinese churches. After completing the field research on the first church, I begin an initial analysis of data. Some patterns and categories aroused from the field data through interviews and observations. Through careful analysis, the causal relations among the patterns were discovered. The process was therefore a process of constructing an explanation of the identified situation in the church. Using the terms of C. Baker, J. Wuest and P.N. Stern, the analysis of field data in grounded theory is used to identify and explain the "core process" (Baker, Wuest, and Stern 1992, 45). The continuous study of the second and third churches in case studies, further support and amendment of the initial theory was done.

After I analyzed all the field data from the three selected churches, many similar patterns appeared and I regarded this situation as saturation: adequate data was collected to support the initial theory of relational leadership (Glaser and Strauss 1967, 55). The basic conceptual framework was completed. There might always be another opportunity to revise this theory as the grounded theory is an "open ended approach to studying the empirical world" (Charmaz 2006, 23). New data can be collected if a fourth or fifth church is studied which may be the concern of future studies.

Overview of the Study

This dissertation is divided into four parts. Part 1 is a study of the understandings of relational leadership of different cultural perspectives. Chapter 1 gives a survey on the biblical perspective based on the life and work of Jesus of Nazareth. Chapter 2 argues for the existence of a root of relational leadership in Western leadership theories. Chapter 3 discusses the Chinese philosophical understanding of human development in relation to leadership development. Some common features among these cultures on relational leadership are reflected. Part 2 is a study of the Chinese theological roots of relational leadership. Chapter 4 argues from a historical perspective that the characteristics of Chinese church leadership are mostly affected by the situations in early twentieth-century China. Chapter 5 gives some in-depth analysis on the theology of the three most represented Chinese pastors and theologians, namely Wang Mingdao, Jia Yuming, and Yang Shaotang. Part 3 is the analysis of the field data which reflects the practice of relational leadership in contemporary Chinese churches. Chapter 6 gives a brief overview of the three churches in this research: in Urumqi, Sanyuan and Zhongzhou. Chapter 7 discusses the leadership development patterns disclosed by these case studies. Chapter 8 provides a complete analysis of the missiological implications for relational leadership in Chinese churches. Part 4 is the final conclusion and overall significance of this research.

In summary, I make the best use of my "dual citizenship" as a Chinese Christian when serving as a bridge between the two ancient traditions of culture and wisdom: Christianity and Confucianism. This research is based on both the life and teachings of Jesus Christ and the cultural foundation laid down by Confucius. This research helps to find the common elements in both biblical and Chinese approaches to leadership development. As I am based in Hong Kong, I have travelled extensively throughout many provinces of China to visit the church leaders from different backgrounds. The diversified ministry networks I established in the past can help me to understand the need of the church in a more objective way. Since I have a similar cultural background, I can communicate and collect information I need from the pastors with fewer obstacles. As both an outsider and an insider, I hope to establish a culturally sensitive approach to developing church leaders in China. The research will be significant on the Chinese churches by preparing them to participate in cross-cultural mission, and I hope it will serve as one of the pioneer studies on Chinese missions.

# Part I: Different Cultural Perspectives on Relational Leadership

CHAPTER 1

Biblical Foundation on Relational Leadership

The Bible is the major reference of Christianity which provides role models and basic principles of leadership. The strengths and weaknesses of the kings and prophets in the Old Testament are obviously the most referred-to examples of leaders and leadership. Their personal qualities, spirituality and leadership skills can be deducted from different Old Testament passages. In the New Testament, the teachings of Paul are the basic principles applied in church leadership today. The Chinese churches in general accept that the best example and illustration of God's principles of leaders and leadership are the life and teachings of Jesus of Nazareth. The ways that Jesus of Nazareth related to his disciples was similar to the ways Confucius related to his disciples in ancient China. They lived and worked together with the followers and made best use of different situations as teaching resources. More importantly, personality development is their common and major concern instead of knowledge and skills. A biblical understanding of the ways Jesus related to his disciples in order to develop them as future leaders set the framework of discussion before studying the Chinese cultural perspective.

One of the most popular understandings of the role of Jesus in relation to his disciples is that he was a great teacher. The purpose of Jesus' teaching is to transform the lives of his followers. Pheme Perkins (1990; Whitacre 1999, 100-114), Roy B. Zuck (1995) and Kendrick Strong (1978) discuss the fact that the teaching methods and philosophy of Jesus are significant means by which he developed the lives and ministry skills of his disciples.

Seung Hwan Shim (2007) even compares Jesus with Confucius in terms of their teachings and roles as master. Obviously, a great teacher is not limited to the transfer of knowledge but also to equip the disciples to become leaders of the next generations. Jesus had specific purposes in teaching and training his disciples. Therefore, Christian scholars are tempted to read the relationship between Jesus and his disciples functionally—Jesus selected the disciples according to their talents and designed a hidden curriculum for them. In *The Master Plan of Evangelism*, Robert E. Coleman (1993)[1] has listed the qualifications for being a disciple of Jesus and the different methods Jesus used to train his disciples to become church leaders.

The other popular understanding on the role of Jesus with his disciples is that he was a leadership trainer. Under this understanding, the role of Jesus is refined to organizational leadership. The term "leader" is rarely used in the New Testament. Jesus did not hold any office or position and he was misunderstood as king in leading the Israelites to revolt against the Roman government. None of his disciples were popular and influential when they were chosen be one of the Twelve. Misunderstanding Jesus as his contemporaries did—as an organizational leader role model—is another temptation. Jesus was not a person who holds influential political or social position. He did not teach his disciples how to run and manage a church or a movement with a leadership and management handbook.

Many publications in the past decades had reflected the trend of understanding Jesus as a trainer or organizational leader. *Jesus, CEO* (Jones 1995) and *Lead Like Jesus* (Blanchard and Hodges 2005), for example, are among the most popular titles. The purpose of relating Jesus of Nazareth to contemporary organizations—both Christian churches and secular institutions—is to improve organizational effectiveness through learning from the personality and moral values of Jesus. This is a direct application of the observable lifestyles and teachings from the Gospels to meeting the management needs of today.

Unlike other approaches, this chapter begins the discussion of Christian leadership from Jesus' historical and social contexts. The understanding and expectations to leaders vary in different cultures. Some common features

---

1. Originally published in 1963.

are assumed to be found in Jesus' time as well as today. The effectiveness of leadership behaviors depends largely on the historical and social contexts. The similarities between the historical context of Jesus and contemporary world are crucial in deciding the level of application of the leadership behaviors of Jesus.

Biblical models are helpful as references in understanding biblical foundations of leadership. J. Robert Clinton points out that five major leadership models were found in the Bible: the steward, servant, intercessor, harvester and shepherd models (1993b, 70). Spiritual leadership (J. O. Sanders 1994; Blackaby and Blackaby 2001) and servant leadership (Granberg-Michaelson 1982; Neuschel 1998; Wilkes 1998) are the two most well-known leadership styles of Jesus. These classifications come from the results of studying the teachings and lifestyles of Jesus. Practitioners in leadership can model themselves after the leadership styles and develop principles.

Jesus of Nazareth did not equip his disciples to achieve his own purpose without being concerned with their personal growth. Instead of developing the disciples functionally to become skillful leaders, Jesus adopted varieties of approaches so as to develop them as well-rounded influential persons. Beginning with the understandings and expectations of leaders in first century Palestine, three areas will be discussed: the accounts of leaders and leadership in the Gospels, the approaches of Jesus of Nazareth in developing followers, and the characteristics of relational leadership reflected in the Gospels.

Biblical Accounts of Leaders and Followers in the Gospels

The contemporary perspectives on leaders and followers are different when compared with the understandings in the first century Palestine and contemporary world. When we need to learn from Jesus' performance as an influential leader, it is necessary to find what kind of expectations were dominant for leaders in his time. As reflected in the Gospels in the historical and social contexts of first century Palestine, Jesus had obviously developed his disciples through intimate relationships and adopted varieties of approaches.

Leaders and Followers in the Graeco-Roman World

In Graeco-Roman society in first century Palestine, a leader was expected to have political influence. A more general description of a leader in the Graeco-Roman world is a person who could attract a critical audience in their public speeches (Clarke 2000, 17-18). In this respect, Jesus of Nazareth was a person who attracted many followers through his life and teachings. No wonder he was crucified under the excuse of being a "king" of the Jews: many Israelites expected him to be the messianic king after listening to his teachings. The Roman authorities believed he was a potential threat to the Roman rule.

From the Jewish perspective, the messianic expectation had shaped the leadership expectations of the general public. The messianic expectation was not purely a religious sentiment but also political agenda. The Jewish religious community expected a messianic king coming from descendent of David. He was expected to come and expel the Romans from Palestine. A new kingdom under the rule of the Messiah through military revolt against the Romans was the expectation of the militant sects in the Jewish society. The followers of Jesus with messianic expectation were those who believed strongly in the glorious past of the Israelite kingdom and were hoping to restore it (Malina 1996, 133). Hence, expecting a leader as the Messiah was political in essence. As noted by Richard A. Horsley, the messianic movement was popular in rural areas and directly related to the Jewish wars in the first and second century (2003, 49-52). When Jesus sat on a donkey and entered Jerusalem a week before his crucifixion (Mt. 21:1-11), the crowds were expecting him as the political messianic king.

Stability was one of the major concerns in the ruling class of the Roman Empire. In order to maintain political and social stability in this vast empire with varieties of cultures, an indirect rule approach was adopted. Many local agents had been appointed as governors—most of them are local kings and high priests—to govern over their own tribes (Horsley 2003, 31-34). In the study of Carolyn Osiek, three percent of the total population is the urban elites in Palestine, for example, the Herodians and Sadducees, who have actual authority and responsibility to maintain the social stability (1992, 41-42). A person like Jesus who attracts a significant number of followers is surely a challenge to the authorities. When Jesus was accused by the high priest, Pontius Pilate changed his attitude and decided to crucify Jesus after the Jews queried his loyalty to Caesar (Jn. 19:12). Pilate did not want to risk his political life by releasing Jesus if the action brought social instability.

Another aspect of the perception of leaders and followers in Roman society was the image and role of a father in a household. As religion was an inseparable part of social life, the role of a father was as the head of the household religion. Family was the basic unit of religions in the Roman society. The Imperial Cult—the worship of the Roman emperor—was conducted in a family (Fay 2008, 65). Therefore, the role of a father was also the role of a priest. Andrew D. Clarke comments,

> The home was an important locus of cultic ritual; and domestic religion provided a valuable link with the past and the family's ancestry. The household cult, however, was by no means as formalized as the public Roman religion with its officiating priests and civic magistrates (2000, 95-96).

The Roman government made best use of this tradition to extend its influence and control over every sector in its empire. As a result, the people in general would relate the image of a father in a household to the leader. A father therefore had extraordinary power over the family (Stambaugh and Balch 1986, 124). In addition to the authority of the image of a father, an intimate relationship between the leader and the followers is expected in the first century Palestine as well. Living and working together is not unfamiliar among the followers of Jesus. Even though the term "leaders" does not appear in the New Testament very frequently, the expectations to the leaders were commonly perceived in the society.

Rabbi and Leader

The term "leader" is rarely applied to the life of Jesus of Nazareth in the Bible. Only in Matthew 2:6 and Acts 5:31 have the Good News Bible translators used "leader" to describe the role of Jesus (Ellingworth 1998, 136). In terms of his relationship with his disciples, Jesus' roles as a teacher, rabbi or master are widely described in the Gospels. Jesus thus impacted his disciples' and others' lives through the teacher-student relationship. As F.F. Bruce confirms, "Jesus was popularly call 'rabbi' because he was recognized as a religious teacher, although he had never been a rabbinical disciple himself" (1986, 49). E.P. Sanders states that the role of leader was related to the responsibility in teaching the law in first century Palestine. "Since divine law covered all of life, one of the qualifications for being a leader was knowledge of the law" (1993, 139). Through teaching the law of Moses, a teacher influenced all aspects of the followers' daily lives.

In Palestine, religion influenced every aspect of daily life. Religious teachers were therefore attracting significant number of followers. Unlike other teachers of the law in his times, Jesus was not an officially recognized rabbi: people gave him this title out of respect. Therefore, Jesus' role as a rabbi was defined by the influence of his teachings instead of official position. In this rabbinic tradition, followers were not merely looking for knowledge but they were looking for wisdom of God (Hengel 1981, 31-33).[2] Obviously, being named as a rabbi in the Gospels showed that Jesus was an influential leader.

The Followers of Jesus

As for the followers of Jesus, they followed him primarily because of two reasons: they were either attracted by his teachings or were called by him to be his disciples. The strong and long-term influence of Jesus of Nazareth was reflected in his crucifixion. In that period of hardship, being a disciple of Jesus meant that he or she had to risk his or her life. One of his disciples, Judas Iscariot, betrayed Jesus for thirty pieces of silver (Mt. 26:14-16; Mk. 14:10-11; Lk. 22:3-6). Peter was not willing to risk his safety and denied his relationship with his master (Mt. 26:69-75; Mk. 14:66-72; Lk. 22:56-62; Jn. 18:15-18, 25-27). Some of the disciples were encouraged by the

---

2. The followers of the rabbi were not attracted by his title, personality, nor popularity but by the message of the Torah. Through studying the Torah, the followers were willing to sacrifice in order to become the disciples of the wisdom of God. When the people named Jesus as a rabbi, they recognized the message preached by Jesus as the wisdom of God.

fact that Jesus was raised from the dead. The followers remained as faithful disciples after Jesus' ascension. Many of them became the first generation church leaders. They were fishermen, tax collectors, women, and the socially oppressed and some "hidden" followers like the Pharisee Nicodemus (Jn. 7:50-52) and the council member Joseph (Lk. 23:50).

Instead of one-to-one discipleship training, a core team was selected. The twelve disciples were selected as the major core team; some scholars like Bruce and Sanders regard this number as the a symbolic representatives of the twelve tribes of Israel (Bruce 1930, 32; E. P. Sanders 1993, 122). A team approach was adopted, and the disciples were commissioned to make disciples of all the nations. The selection of disciples was not a single and individual event but aligned with God's salvation plan in which he had chosen Israel to be the "agent" for the salvation of all humankind. Jesus chose Peter, James and John among the twelve to be an inner circle to witness the transfiguration of the presence of God the Father (Mt. 17:1-13; Mk. 9:2-13; Lk. 9:28-36). One hundred and twenty followers were named as disciples and remained as Jesus' followers after his ascension (Acts 1:15). In the account of Paul, Jesus appeared after his resurrection in front of 500 witnesses (1 Cor. 15:6). All of them were followers, eyes witnesses and people impacted by Jesus' life and teachings.

These teams of followers were the potential leadership teams in the first century. According to the Bible translators, the term "leaders" is always used in plural form in the New Testament (Ellingworth 1998, 135). Jesus laid the foundation of team leadership during his time with the disciples. In the book of Acts, the frequent use of the plural form of "disciple" indicates that a team approach was a prevailing practice among the followers (Morris 1994, 115). Whether or not they followed Jesus voluntarily or called by him, Jesus commissioned them to spend their whole lives to make disciples. The early churches were founded through the process of making disciples. The first group of disciples took the major responsibility in laying the foundation of the future development of the churches. They were those who have leadership potential or transformed by the life and teachings of Jesus to become leaders.

The Selection of Potential Leaders

Among those followers of Jesus, the twelve disciples were obviously the major potential church leaders. Significantly, the Gospels lack evidence that Jesus chose his disciples according to their leadership capabilities or attitudes. Many scholars and practitioners of leadership development claim that Jesus had some criteria in choosing disciples. Jesus needed some capable leaders to help him realize the plan of God. He intended to educate those potential leaders to "bear witness to his life and carry on his work after he returned to the Father" (Coleman 1993, 27). According to this understanding, it was the strategy of Jesus to choose disciples who had some leadership competencies. In contrast, based on the narrations in the Gospels, they were only ordinary people coming from different social backgrounds. The disciples had only the "potential" and "possibility" to become future leaders. That was the reason why Jesus had to spend time with them and explained to them in detail about the truth of the kingdom of Heaven. The disciples are more the companions and colleagues of Jesus than merely his followers when they appeared in the Gospels (Marshall 1992, 125). Jesus was the one who gave instructions on how to manage and feed the five thousand followers orderly (Lk. 8:10-17). The story clearly shows that the disciples did not have any required ability or experience when they were called to be the followers of Jesus.

Jesus changed their characters and leadership skills in three years through living and working together with them. The disciples experienced life-changing lessons during those three years. Most of those selected were described as "ignorant," "narrow-minded," "imperceptible," and even "stupid" in the Gospels (Stanton 1989, 46; E. P. Sanders 1993, 123; Bruce 1930, 12-13). They were not fit enough to be leaders during the time when they met Jesus. Their attitude changed from close-minded to teachable, self-centered to obedient, self-distrustful to self-confident, fearful to trustful, skeptical to full of faith (Strong 1978, 15). The transformation of the life and behaviors are found among the followers of Jesus especially in the lives of Peter and Paul.

The messianic expectation is a common element that was shared by all the followers of Jesus. As mentioned, messianic expectation was common among the Israelites in the first century Palestine. As F.F. Bruce argues, the disciples were expecting the Messiah would come as a king like David to again rule over Israel and other nations. They carried their "militant enthusiasm" with them when following Jesus. After the series of lessons and activities, Jesus transformed their expectations by giving a new meaning to the role of Messiah as suffering God (F.F. Bruce 1979, 24-25).

Although some have commented negatively about the disciples being described as stupid, the disciples had some common qualities when they were called. First of all, they were obedient. They paid the price to follow Jesus because Jesus was not yet a famous religious leader when they began the journey with him. They took the risk of uprooting themselves from their hometown, broke their family ties, and lost their identities when decided to wander around with Jesus (Perkins 1990, 128-129). Obedience is the major observable quality from the account of the Gospels.

The second explicit criterion Jesus mentioned was the cost of discipleship (Mt. 10:37-38; Lk. 14:25-33). Literally, the criterion was to love God much more than the follower's life and family. God was the top priority in the life of a disciple. At the same time, this criterion can be interpreted as planning and preparation before the decision to become Jesus disciple (J. C. Maxwell 2007, 1282). Counting the cost was a commitment prior to taking the action of following Jesus Christ.

Jesus did a lot to transform the lives and expectations of the disciples. From the few criteria needed to become Jesus' disciples that were mentioned in the Gospels, the disciples did not have any distinctive talents or ability to become exemplary leaders. It is their mediocre quality as potential leaders that protruded the distinctive work of Jesus to transform their lives and leadership qualities. Jesus used multiple methods and approaches during his three years together with the disciples that made them to become different persons, leaders of a new expanding religion.

Approaches of Jesus Christ in Developing Followers

After understanding the concept of leaders and followers in the New Testament times, it is clear that Jesus of Nazareth is perceived as a leader under the influence of the messianic expectations of the Jews. He was a great teacher who had changed the lives of many followers. In this study, six approaches adopted by Jesus in developing disciples are identified in the Gospels.

Team Approach

The term "leaders" appeared in the New Testament in plural form only. It implies that Jesus treasured team leadership and used a team approach in developing leaders. Ajith Fernando concluded that "team ministry was the standard model of ministry in the New Testament" (Fernando 2002, 131-132). Jesus sent out seventy disciples two-by-two for mission, taught the twelve together, and brought three of them to the Transfiguration. Also, the ministry led by the apostles in the book of Acts often involved working together as team. The twelve are always mentioned as a group. Individual disciples were mentioned only occasionally (Wilkins 1992, 179). Obviously, the team approach was a common practice in Jesus' leadership of the disciples.

In Luke 8:1-3, we read the narrative of the first mission team. Jesus traveled with the twelve disciples and some women. This journey was a preparation for a later mission mentioned in Luke 9:1-6. Jesus included those who were healed by him to be witnesses of his work through giving testimonies. Some women came from rich families, which were major finance providers to the ministry (Morgan 1931, 160). While some biblical scholars focus on the purpose of this trip as evangelism and mission, a distinctive feature in the Lucan narrative, not many of them realize the importance of the composition of the mission team. The mission trip was a demonstration of team ministry, showing the disciples the importance of different elements of a mission team.[3]

Apart from the leadership team of the disciples, Jesus himself demonstrated a good team relationship through his intimate relationship with God the Father and the Holy Spirit. Throughout the Gospels and Acts, several teams are working together: first the triune God, second Jesus and his disciples, and third the different generations of disciples in the church.

---

3. It is important to note that Luke 9:6 mentioned evangelism, which had not appeared in the other Synoptic Gospels (Evans 2003, 210). See also Michael Wilcock (1979, 106), F. Scott Spencer (2008, 140) and Leon Morris (2008).

The Gospel of John recorded a number of passages that showed how Jesus related himself to God the Father and the disciples as a team (Jn. 5:19-47; 6:41-47; 8:38, 54-55; 12:44-45, 49-50). Jesus also used the parable of the vine and branches to explain the ideal relationships among God the Father, Jesus and the disciples (Jn. 15:1-10). No matter that the request of a fruitful life in this parable means fulfilling God's mission (Lindars 1981, 490) or personal character building (Wilkinson and Kopp 2001, 21), a fruitful life should begin with close relationship with the Father and the Son. According to Brian Edgar,

> To understand the mission of Jesus one has to comprehend the Trinitarian nature of God. . . . We see Jesus working in the power of the Spirit to fulfill the mission given to him by his Father, and in it we see actions of great spiritual power associated with humility, patience, and gentleness (2004, 156).

The relationship in the Trinity is not just intimacy but a relationship with the purpose of fulfilling God's mission together as a team.[4]

In addition to working team, the group of disciples was also a learning community. They lived and worked together for three years. They learned together as well. As Judith Lingenfelter comments,

> Jesus rarely addressed individuals when teaching; his stories and questions were almost always addressed to the crowd, to smaller social gatherings such as people sharing a meal, or to the twelve disciples (2003, 55).

Whether or not Jesus was intentionally teaching the disciples as a group, the pattern of a team approach in developing disciples is obviously seen. Through the team approach in his relationship with the disciples, Jesus

---

4. The works of the triune God can also be understood as a demonstration of the united community in love (Olson and Hall 2002, 63). This community is an extension and evidence of the presence of God, especially the works of the Holy Spirit that gives human beings the ability to work in unity. In the meantime, the continuation of the divine work of creation is indicated by the work of providence from God and the redemptive action of Christ (Gunton 1998, 10).

emphasized the importance of working together through a demonstration of the relationship between himself and God the Father. He worked together with the disciples and urged them to work together all the time. Team leadership in the early church was therefore the result because the experience of working together had already been their major ministry practice when working with Jesus.

Lifelong Approach

The second approach was a lifelong approach. Even though Jesus lived only three years with the disciples, his guidance did not stop after his death and resurrection. The teamwork expanded after Jesus left the disciples. Jesus promised to send the Holy Spirit to come and work with them (Jn. 16:5-15). The work of Christ was continued and manifested through the work of the Holy Spirit. In the beginning of Acts 2, Jesus' promise was realized when the Holy Spirit descended and led more than three thousand people to become Christians. Pentecost was the beginning of the work of the Holy Spirit within the Christian community. That the Holy Spirit guides and nurtures church leaders throughout their lifetime are one of the core beliefs in the Christian church. Spiritual growth is a lifelong process; therefore, the nurturing of a spiritual leader is a lifelong process as well.

In addition, through his prayer and the work of Holy Spirit, Jesus' concern for teamwork had extended beyond the twelve and the first century Palestine's community. God has worked with all generations of church leaders. Jesus' prayer in John 17 is known as the "prayer of the great high priest" which is concerned with his "inner circle" of disciples (Tasker 2000, 188-191; Edwards 2004, 158-162; Sun 2007, 230-238). He prayed for the disciples' faith and ministry (Jn. 17:6-19), unity and strength, and especially the church they would establish (Jn. 17:20-26).

In addition, through miracles, the working relationship between Jesus and his followers continues. As F.F. Bruce writes, "The miracles were so well known that the disciples could point to them as evidence of the continuing presence and power of Jesus. It was not simply the fact that they were miracles that was important: it was their nature" (1979, 48). F.F. Bruce points out correctly the importance of miracles in showing the relationship of Jesus and his disciples. Even after Jesus' ascension, as long as miracles appear, people assume the work of Christ together with them.

Inner Life Approach

Jesus' third approach to develop disciples was an inner life approach. Inner life refers to the maturity in spiritual life and morality of an individual. In the Christian faith, moral character is based entirely on the teachings of the Bible. A church leader is expected to have a good moral character that is consistent with the standards and requirements of the Bible. Among the biblical virtues, honesty and integrity are clearly noted as significant moral character. When talking to a woman of Samaria, Jesus taught that the most important element in worshipping God is not location, but "spirit and truth" (Jn. 4:23-24). The essence of true worship is not a question of when and where, but is a matter of the heart and spirit (Köstenberger 2004, 156-157). True worship is the participation into the "divine reality" (Borchert 1996, 208) which God requires of a true worshipper. The worship styles and the technical arrangement are less important than honesty and reality of the participant's attitudes in worship (Morgan 1933, 176). Furthermore, in confronting the Pharisees, Jesus severely denounced their hypocrisy (Mt. 23:1-36; Mk. 12:38-40; Lk. 20:45-47) which was the opposite of honesty. In Acts, only the sin of "lying to the Holy Spirit" is unforgivable. Ananias and Sapphira died because of the dishonesty (Acts 5:1-11). These passages showed the honesty and integrity are among the top of the list of leadership virtues.

Another precious collection from Jesus' teaching on moral characters is the Sermon on the Mount (Mt. 5:1-7:29). Targeting the disciples, Jesus taught about the "kingdom ethics" to shape the attitudes of the disciples in the beginning of his ministry together. The Sermon on the Mount covers almost all aspects of a Christian life. The central idea is that to live a life where God is the center and fulfill God's moral expectations is the priority in the disciples' daily life. Esther Ng, a Chinese scholar, agrees that Jesus gives higher moral expectations to the disciples than to his other followers (1996, 166). Michael Green describes the Sermon of the Mount as "the supreme jewel in the crown of Jesus' teaching" (2003, 88-89). Behavior is therefore one of the major concerns of Jesus in developing his disciples.

Other Biblical moral virtues like humble service (Mt. 18:1-14; Mk. 9:33-37; Lk. 9:46-48), forgiveness (Mt. 18:21-35), servanthood (Jn. 13:1-11) and prayer life (Mt. 6:5-13, 7:1-11; Lk. 9:1-13, 18:15) are important lessons of Jesus which were targeted at developing the inner life of his followers. These were the lessons that Jesus taught specifically to the disciples. Jesus decided to impact the lives of the disciples in three years so as to build a solid moral foundation to help them face the challenges after he left. Equipping a spiritual leader begins with the transformation of the inner life qualities of a person. Behavioral changes come from the changes in one's moral character which is the primary task of leadership development.

From these inner life qualities, some scholars have formulated different leadership styles of Jesus based either on morality or spirituality. To those scholars who focus on the virtue of servanthood, for example, servant leadership is emphasized. For others who want to highlight the importance of the relationship with God, leadership attributes and moral virtues are all included as characteristics of spiritual leadership.

Scripture-Saturation Approach

The fourth approach is Scripture-saturation. The term *Scripture*-saturation is borrowed from J. Robert Clinton (1997, 2003) and Ajith Fernando (2002). A Christian leader should be a person familiar with the word of God. Saturation by the word of God means valuing the importance and centrality of the Scriptures in the life and ministry of a Christian leader. A church leader is also expected to be a person of the word. He or she is familiar with all the books in the Bible. This familiarity to the word is not limited to knowledge; a church leader should also "shaped personally" by the word. Clinton termed this kind of Christian leader the "Bible Centered Leader." A Bible centered leader should apply the Scriptures into daily life in good quantity and quality. "Saturated" by the word of God is the basis of developing Biblical moral character in a leader. Fernando agrees: "Getting people into the word is the primary means of bringing them along the path to holiness" (2002, 158).

As a teacher, Jesus himself lived and taught the Bible very frequently. His disciples were impacted by Jesus' way of using the Scripture and modeled themselves after him. The frequent use of the Old Testament in the disciples' ministry therefore became a normal practice in ministry. Fernando found ninety references of the Old Testament quoted in the Gospels. By adding all the duplications, the total number of references is 160. In the book of Acts, 200 references were found (2002, 89). The Scripture-saturation approach is the very foundational approach in cultivating Christian values and inner life qualities of a leader.

Experiential Learning Approach

The fifth approach is experiential learning. The focus of experiential learning is on the quality of learning rather than the content of the curriculum. Moral character cannot be learned just by listening to lectures on moral theories but by modeling and practice. The quality of learning was surely one of the major concerns of Jesus in developing followers. Through experiential learning, the teacher does not emphasize how many lessons the students should attend, but how much they can actually use and apply in their future service. The disciples learned effectively through modeling themselves after Jesus. Demonstration and practice together with students are two main tools used in experiential learning. On many occasions, Jesus demonstrated how he put theory into practice. The disciples had deep impressions of what their master told and showed them. As F.F. Bruce suggests, "The Gospels bear witness to the fact that Jesus' own life was the practical manifestation of his teaching" (1986, 75). The life of Jesus was itself a training curriculum to transform the lives of the disciples.

Jesus demonstrated that his intimate relationship with God the Father was the source of his strength in ministry. Very often Jesus withdrew from the crowd or retreated to the wilderness (Mt. 14:13) or mountain (Mt. 14:23) to pray alone. Sometimes he invited Peter, James, and John to come with him. A typical example was his prayer in Gethsemane that demonstrated a total reliance on God the Father (Mt. 26:36-46; Mk. 14:27-31; Lk. 22:39-46). When he was busy, in times of grief, sorrow, and sadness, the very first thing his disciples saw Jesus do was to retreat and pray. In the conflicts and debates with the Jews and Pharisees, Jesus always focused on his relation with the one who sent him—God the Father—as his source of authority (e.g. Jn. 12:44-50).

Jesus was vulnerable because he had to bear the cross for the salvation of all humankind. Before he was arrested, his vulnerability was shown in his prayer (Mt. 26:30-46; Mk. 14:26-42; Lk. 22:39-46). Jesus demonstrated the vulnerability of a leader. The vulnerability of Jesus Christ was the sign of God's love (Nouwen 1996, 17). Jesus offered his life to demonstrate the openness and vulnerable nature of a leader to those he had chosen. Unlike other political and social leaders, a Christian leader accepts vulnerability as strength instead of weakness. Vulnerability is the strength of a leader because it reflects the humility of a leader and at the same time the power and glory of God.

Jesus also demonstrated servanthood as a major moral element in his life and ministry. He said, "Son of man came not to be served but to serve, and to give his ransom for many" (Mt. 20:28 NRSV). Through washing the disciples' feet (Jn. 13:1-20), Jesus demonstrated the real meaning of servanthood. This is the most obvious example of servant leadership. Jesus then asked his disciples to follow his example as a servant leader (Jn. 13:14-15).

In contemporary discussions on Christian leadership, "visionary" is a popular description for those leaders who focus on fulfilling the purpose and vision God gave them in their leadership. Jesus himself demonstrated a life with clear and focused purpose: the salvation of sinners. This is what Clinton called a "focused live," a life "dedicated to exclusively carrying out God's unique purposes" (1995, 2). In John 6:22-71 when Jesus faced a crowd of unbelievers and even challengers, he insisted on explaining clearly his mission no matter how difficult the situation was. He still insisted on his mission even though "many of his disciples turned away and deserted him" (Jn. 6:66). In facing the conspiracy to arrest him, he did not waste his time in debates, but focused on his mission: to free the woman who was captured in adultery from her bondage of sin (Jn. 8:1-11). He focused on his mission whatever situation he faced. The disciples learned to live a focused life from him.

Mission was surely one of the main subjects the disciples experienced and learned from the life of Jesus. He demonstrated methods of organizing mission among the Israelites and the Samaritans. The first demonstration of cross-cultural mission is found in John 4:1-42 when Jesus met the Samaritan woman and demonstrated how to begin a conversation with a foreigner. The disciples witnessed how Jesus changed a city (Sychar) through connecting with a despised woman from a despised race (J. C. Maxwell 2007, 1308). Through the transformation of an individual, the whole city changed and came to believe in Jesus as the Messiah (Jn. 4:39-42). Philip followed Jesus' pattern and became the first cross-cultural evangelist among the Samarians (Acts 8:4-8).

In addition, Jesus also demonstrated "mass evangelism" in front of the disciples (Mt. 4:23-25; Mk. 8:1-3; Lk. 6:17-19). Jesus sent out the seventy disciples for field education (Lk. 10:1-20) and this mission experience served as encouragement for them to carry out the Great Commission (Mt. 28:18-20). In their studies of the Great Commission, scholars such as Mortimer Arias and Alan Johnson (1992) and R. Geoffrey Harris (2004) state that Matthew's emphasis is on making disciples. Making disciples helped build a stronger foundation of the church because their faith was based on the teachings of Jesus. Harris writes, "This declaration precedes the sending or commissioning of the twelve, and Matthew evidently wishes to show that mission is an integral part of discipleship. The disciples are to be formed in imitation of their master" (2004, 47). In this respect, the disciples learned to make disciples by following the pattern they witnessed from their relationship with Jesus.

Jesus' way of developing disciples as leaders through demonstration and practice with them is shown in these highlights from the Scriptures. He did not teach what he would not believe or something he was unable to practice. He invited them to participate in the teaching-learning process so that they were not merely learning the theory from school but something really practical.

Empowerment and Delegation Approach

The sixth approach was empowerment and delegation. Through giving responsibility to the followers, Jesus gave authority to them in order to carry out the mission more effectively. The origin of empowerment came from God the Father. Two times God the Father spoke directly in public in the record of the Gospels. During Jesus' baptism (Mt. 3:17; Mk. 1:11; Lk. 3:22) and transfiguration (Mt. 17:5; Mk. 9:7; Lk. 9:35), God said, "This is my Son, the Beloved" to disclose and announce the intimate relationship of Father and Son. In Roman society, a father was the image of the leader, the Father-Son relationship was therefore understood also as empowerment and delegation. God the Father empowered his Son to represent him on earth, and authorized him to judge sinners. At the same time, this Father-Son relationship also showed the mutual respect between them (Clarke 2000, 86-92). In his interpretation of the transitional chapter in the gospel of Luke, Joel Green declares that the appointment of the twelve was a preparation for them to become future leaders. The delegation of responsibility on this mission trip described in Luke 9:1-17 was a way of nurturing their leadership qualities; which "will be actualized more fully in Acts" (J. Green 1997, 356).

Jesus gave the disciples the same empowerment and authority: "Whatever you bind on earth will be bound in Heaven, and whatever you loose on earth will be loosed in Heaven" (Mt. 18:18). Empowerment is not simply giving responsibility without providing further support and resources. In addition to the authority given by Jesus, the promise of continuous presence was a unique characteristic of Jesus' empowerment. In the Great Commission (Mt. 28:20), his continuous spiritual presence was not limited by physical distance and time. It would last until the end of the mission (Morris 1992, 749; Kenner 1997, 402; Harris 2004, 64). Jesus did not call his disciples based on their functions or what they could contribute in mission. Doing is not as important as 'being' in Jesus' way of developing disciples. He shared his ministry with them (F.F. Bruce 1979, 44) instead of using them in ministry. He understood what potential qualities they already had. Through living and working together with them, Jesus intended to develop their potentials into mature qualities and transform themselves from potential leaders into effective leaders.

Through these six approaches, Jesus developed the inner qualities of the disciples which were necessary for a leader to face challenges ahead. He demonstrated his teachings by working together with the disciples and provided a model of intimacy with God the Father so that the followers knew how to model after their master in practice. As a great and influential teacher, Jesus adopted different approaches to develop his followers. These approaches were not a static curriculum but were dynamic and flexible. The styles and methods of teachings were changed according to the situation. Jesus did not develop his disciples in a classroom setting, but in a real life situation.

The Characteristics of Relational Leadership in the Gospels

The Biblical foundations of leadership development are clearly found in the Gospels. The term "relational leadership" is the best description of the styles and methods of Jesus of Nazareth in developing followers. Relational leadership refers to the leadership styles that the leader uses to engage, mobilize and develop the followers through relating him or herself with them. Relationship precedes all other elements in leadership characteristics. Throughout his life and teachings, Jesus invested most of his time in training the twelve. Although one eventually betrayed him, the eleven turned the world upside down with the good news. As Lingenfelter and Lingenfelter affirm, building a close relationship with the students is an essential element of effective teaching which is the model Jesus demonstrated in developing his disciples (2003, 42). Behavioral changes happen as a result of relationship. Jesus' model of relational leadership has seven characteristics.

God-with-us Relationship

The first characteristic is related to the nature of a relational God. He is an incarnation God who loves us and became human to live with us. This is a "God-with-us" relationship. Different from other relationships, the "God-with-us" relationship begins as a one-sided relationship. Jesus gives everything and human beings need not to give anything in this relationship. His life was a practical manifestation of his teaching. As Perkins comments: "The lives of famous teachers were expected to reflect their doctrines. Combining episodes from a teacher's life with samples of teaching provided an effective way of passing on the views of a particular group" (1990, 62). Jesus indeed provided everything for human beings. All people need to do is to accept and learn from him.

God's continuous presence is a sign of this "God-with-us" relationship. Jesus spent three years with the disciples before his crucifixion. After his ascension, he sent the Holy Spirit as an extension of his presence with his disciples and later followers. In leadership development programs, the method is called mentoring. As Walter C. Wright defines, mentoring is "an intentional, exclusive, intensive, voluntary relationship between the leader and the follower. Mentoring is a relational experience in which one person empowers another by sharing him- or herself and his or her resources" (2009, 66). It is believed that human nature is relational. The best way to teach and learn is to have good and close relationship between the leader and the followers. The most reliable relationship is based on God's love and directed toward God's purpose.

Situational in Nature

Relational leadership is informal as well as being situational in nature—the second characteristic. Jesus taught his disciples not in a classroom and formal settings, but in any situation: on the hill slope or seashore, in the storm or crisis, and even in times of grieving or happiness. Clinton comments this kind of informal training "will make the most difference in a life" (Clinton and Clinton 1991, 1-7) because it happens throughout the lifespan of a person. Different situations provide different opportunities to teach and learn different skills. In a classroom setting, one can only learn knowledge about leadership. In a real situation, a person learns actual skills and attitudes, especially how to deal with crises, interpersonal relationships, and leadership values. Only through long-term relationships can leaders understand which situation is the best teaching opportunity.

Lifelong Process

The third characteristic of relational leadership is the lifelong process. Jesus spent three years living and working together with the disciples, but the teaching and learning process did not stop when he ascended to heaven. His relationship with the disciples continued through the work of the Holy Spirit. In his *Leadership Emergence Theory* (1988), Clinton emphasizes the lifelong process in developing a leader. It takes many years to witness the growth of an individual to become a leader. God chooses a potential leader in his or her early age—even he or she has not yet aware of the calling from God. A potential leader is nurtured, affected and shaped by different events by different persons throughout his or her lifetime. That is how Jesus impacts us continuously today, through godly mentors and the presence of the Holy Spirit.

Mutual Dependence

Relationship requires the willingness of at least two parties to be interconnected. The forth characteristic is therefore the mutual dependence of the leaders and followers. The mutual dependency and influence between God the Father and his Son, between Jesus and his disciples, and among the disciples are the models of relational leadership from the Bible. Jesus demonstrated a total dependency on God the Father alone. He also diverted the disciples' dependency on him to God the Father in his prayer for them (Jn. 17). He taught the disciples using a team approach in order to help them establish mutual relationships among themselves. After Jesus' ascension, the disciples became peer mentors and mutually depended on one another. In the book of Acts, the first generation church leaders worked, helped, and depended on one another. In addition to the team approach, Jesus created mutual dependence among the disciples. Jesus' relationship with his disciples demonstrated a model of team leadership with intimacy among the leaders. Even though one or two members may become a brilliant leader who overshadows others in the future, he or she is encouraged to rely on the others so as to perform the leadership role effectively.

Vision Driven

A relational leadership is also vision-driven—the fifth characteristic. Jesus gave the Great Commission to the disciples, which became the vision of all generations of church leadership. One of the major responsibilities of the church leaders is to transfer the vision to new leaders in different manifestations in different ages and cultures. "Leadership is about vision. It is about tomorrow, about hope, about mission," says Wright (2009, 23). This statement truly reflects an essential requirement for a Christian leader to lead the church or the ministry into a hopeful future. Jesus demonstrated this model. He encouraged the disciples by giving them the kingdom vision and led them to look for the glory of God instead of human success. The vision itself is a direct revelation from God, not the human-made dream

(Blackaby and Blackaby 2001, 69-74). Only a God-related leader can provide a God-given vision to the followers. Organizational and personal success is less important or even unimportant when compared with the value of the vision from God.

Inner Life Development

In relation to the inner life approach adopted by Jesus, the focus on inner life development of the followers is the sixth characteristics of relational leadership. In the Christian tradition, inner life development is more important than leadership skills development. The nurturing of one's inner life is believed to be achievable by modeling after the mentor and in a more long term commitment with the mentor or the teacher. Only through a long term relationship between leader and followers, can morality and spirituality be effectively developed. Relational leadership is therefore a long process of developing the moral character of the followers. The godly character of a Christian leader should be based upon the word of God. As discussed earlier, being Bible-centered should be the characteristic of mentoring in Christian community. A person saturated with the word of God will bear fruit in terms of behavioral changes.

Empowerment

Lastly, the relational leadership process is empowerment driven. Jesus promised to be with those taking part in the Great Commission. God can achieve salvation for all humankind alone without inviting Christians to work together with him. In contrast, because of God's love, he empowers humans to take part in the Great Commission. Through delegating to his followers, God nurtures the disciples, developing spiritual mutuality through actual working experiences with God and with other God-chosen people. This is an example of empowerment and delegation. Jesus is with us through his empowerment and invites all generations into a working relationship with him throughout the ages. The Christian mentor is supposed to follow this model in order to enable the mentee to have changes in abilities, attitudes, and characters (Clinton and Clinton 1991, 2-19). In relational leadership, empowerment is therefore a necessary characteristic for developing followers.

This relational leadership development model was not intentionally designed by Jesus when he nurtured his disciples. Instead, he became incarnate in the human world as well as in the human heart in order to help people to resume the relationship with God the Creator. Jesus himself is a relational God. After studying the process of how Jesus related to his disciples and how he developed them as first generation church leaders, relational leadership is the most obvious biblical model. Use of the term *model* here does not mean that one should follow exactly the patterns and methods used by Jesus; rather, it is a reference to the principles, directions, and essential elements mentioned above.

Summary

Relational leadership is not the only biblical model or leadership style performed by Jesus of Nazareth. Instead, it is one of the models demonstrated by Jesus in developing his followers as future church leaders. After a survey of the historical and social perspectives in the first century Palestine, this study discovers that Jesus fulfilled the messianic expectations of the Jewish people. In relating himself intimately with his followers, he nurtured them and developed their leadership potentials not by teaching them only the knowledge about leadership but by experiencing real life situations with them. It is therefore appropriate to conclude that relational leadership is the major pattern demonstrated by Jesus to develop his followers. The discussions in the following chapters will provide evidence and justifications to support the argument that relational leadership can also be applied to contemporary Asian culture.

CHAPTER 2

Theoretical Foundation of Relational Leadership

Relational leadership is biblically grounded because its major characteristics were demonstrated in the life and teachings of Jesus of Nazareth. Beginning with the intimate relationship with God the Father, the approaches of Jesus in developing followers emphasize teamwork and lifelong development; inner life and Scripture-saturation; experiential learning; empowerment; and delegation. The bridge between the first century Palestine Jewish-Christian community and the contemporary urban environment has been built by the Christian churches over many generations. Leadership research has been flourished in the political and business sectors in the past century. Most studies had been conducted among organizations in the USA. It is fair to comment that most leadership studies are culturally biased with strong American influences. Whether or not these research findings can be applied into non-political and non-business sectors, as well as non-Western cultures, they needed to be re-examined.

This theoretical development has emerged from studies of leadership attributes to the mutual interactions among the leader, followers, and situations. These interactions are based on the dynamic inter-personal relationships and the reactions of the leader and followers toward changes which are the significant cultural characteristics of Chinese churches. Leadership attributions, to certain extent, are reflected in the Confucian emphasis on the development of the human moral self. This chapter will study the characteristics of relational leadership from the Western theories which believe to have the intrinsic connections with the leadership expectation in the

Chinese culture. As this study is Chinese culture-oriented, the primary purpose of this chapter is to develop a leadership theory applicable to Chinese culture, building on the theoretical foundations established in the West. It is assumed that some common human behaviors are multi-cultural and that some research findings from Western culture can be borrowed and applied to other cultures. Some adjustments and modifications are necessary in due course.

The impacts of globalization on organizations and local communities are obvious. When compared to his early work before 1990, Gary A. Yukl's *Leadership in Organizations* (1989, 2010) gives more attention to the influences of multiple cultures on organizational leadership. One major impact is the increase of complexities in the situational variables in the leadership process brought about by different cultures. Yukl concludes that the cultural values are the internalized moral norms which affect leadership behaviors (2010, 437). Human behaviors can be divided into mono-cultural and multi-cultural in nature (K. S. Yang 2000). In recent years, some attempts have been made to study leadership theory and application from cross-cultural perspectives (Fuchs 2007; Kezar and Carducci 2009). It is important to note that different cultures have different emphases on human behaviors and interpersonal relationships. More research studies are needed in order to build up the broader applicability of leadership theories across the globe.

Leader and followers are two major elements in relational leadership. The systematic study of the personal qualities of a leader is known as leadership traits theory. The leadership attributes of a leader are the essential elements of leadership in all cultures, including both Eastern and Western cultures. A good and effective leader is believed to have some common and essential qualities. However, it is clear that personal quality cannot be the only contributing factor for good and effective leadership. No matter how capable the leader is, he or she needs followers. Without followers, neither leader nor leadership exist. The recent studies on followership give another foundation for developing relational leadership. To deal with leadership and followership at the same time is regarded as necessary and is a new paradigm in leadership studies (Stech 2008). Followers have great impact on the decision making process of a leader.

In between the leader and the followers is the situation they face. The other important foundation is therefore the impact of situations on leadership. The Western studies on situational theory have developed as a solid foundation, even though most studies are focused on internal organizational culture. Culture as an external situation exists in the forms of history, philosophy, and religion which deserve more attention, especially on their influences on the expectations of both the leaders and followers in the leadership process. The expectations of the followers are largely shaped by their culture; therefore, the external situation of an organization is treated as another contributing element in relational leadership. In Chinese culture, the expectation of the leader's morality and inter-personal relationships is high. The ways that the leadership behaviors affected by Confucian culture is yet to be discovered, however the impact of culture is especially obvious in East Asian collective culture. Relational leadership is the process of the interactive relationship among the leader, followers, and the situations, through which a leader fulfills the organizational and personal goals with the collaboration of the followers.

In this chapter, I will illustrate the relational leadership theory as a natural development of leadership theory which helps the organization or community to face the changes of the world today. Through the study of the leader-situations-followers paradigm, relational leadership is proved to be applicable to Chinese Christian church context.

Leadership Attributes and Leader-Centric Studies

Relational leadership begins with the value of leadership attributes. The beginning study of leadership as an independent discipline is no doubt focused on the personal abilities of a leader. A leader is believed to play a decisive role in the process of leadership. Many of the previous studies have even positioned leaders as the only important element in leadership; therefore, those studies were regarded as "leaders-centric" studies.

Traits, Great-man, and Leader-centric Studies

Most of the leadership studies in early twentieth century are focused on leadership traits. The focus of discussion is a person called a leader, hero, or great man. The history of leadership studies can be traced back 2,500 years (Kelley 1992, 17). The personal qualities of a leader, especially the abilities and skills in management, motivation, and dealing with adversity are the main areas of study. To some extent, different leadership study approaches or methods are only different types of leadership traits studies. Stogdill reviews and analyzes 289 studies about leadership traits from 1904 to 1970 which focused on the "leader as a person" (Bass and Stogdill 1981, 43-96). In addition, Stephen J. Zaccaro, Cary Kemp, and Paige Bader summarize other leader-trait research between 1990 and 2003, which specified the areas of cognitive abilities, personality, and motivation; social appraisal and interpersonal skills; and leader expertise and tacit knowledge (2004, 109-119). It is fair to comment that leadership traits studies have never been neglected. The personal quality of a leader has been well addressed in the Western organizational context.

Since the previous studies focus mainly on the personal qualities of a leader, people in general expect and believe a person with outstanding abilities and character can help to change adverse situations. Some followers expect contemporary organizational leaders lead like the kings and heroes in ancient times. Leadership traits studies in this context refer to leadership attributes, including ability, character, personality, and some psychological qualities. These attributes are consistently performed by the leader whether these qualities are natural-born talents or skills learned by education or technical training.

These leader-centric studies are important in the sense that they prioritize the necessities of some leadership skills in the leadership performance. The attributes facilitating a better result in managing an organization will attract more attention. This phenomenon reflects what Sergiovanni called result-oriented leadership culture (1986, 105-106).

Contributions and Application of Leadership Attributes

The major contribution of the studies on leadership attributes is to help researchers understand the relation between personal qualities and management performance. Some popular authors on organizational leadership—for example, Stephen R. Covey (1989), John C. Maxwell (1998), Peter F. Drucker (2005)—emphasize the value and importance of developing leadership attributes. Covey calls for a "paradigm shift" concerning the ways a leader perceives and understands the environment so that he or she can become effective (1989, 23-32). Likewise, Drucker talks about how to develop effectiveness as a habit in order to become a leader (2006, 23-24). According to Maxwell's definition, a leader is a person who has influence on others; therefore, to develop one's influence on others is an important attribute for a good leader (1998, 11-20). The common feature among these authors is the assertion on self-management. When facing a crisis, the inner qualities of an individual will make the difference between an effective leader and a less successful leader.

The other contribution is the discovery of certain attributes as essential elements to leadership effectiveness in some contexts. Different attributes may emerge as the most important leadership qualities in a specific situation. Some scholars highlight specific attributes as the main, if not the only attributes contributing to effective leadership. Jay A. Conger and Rabindra N. Kanungo (Conger and Kanungo 1987; Conger 1989) focus on charisma as the core element of a successful leader. Robert K. Greenleaf (2002, 1973, 1996a, 1996b) believes that servanthood is essential to successful leadership. Aubrey Malphurs (2004) teaches that core values or beliefs are essential to effective leadership. Burt Nanus (1992) adopts vision as the key in leadership. Sammuel A. Culbert (1996) finds that developing a leadership mind-set is the heart of leadership.

In other cases, scholars and practitioners prefer to employ multiple attributes in developing a successful leader. *The Leader of the Future* (Hesselbein, Goldsmith, and Beckhard 1996), a compilation of articles published for the purpose of studying the role of organizational leaders in the future, argues that qualities like ethical values, vision, and personality are all important attributes of future leaders. Peter Drucker clearly states in the foreword that leadership shall be understood as a process of fulfilling responsibility and achieving expected results. Leaders should become role models for followers (Hesselbein, Goldsmith, and Beckhard 1996, xii). The emphasis on multiple attributes in developing future leaders is in fact impacted by previous studies on individual leadership attributes. Further, popular leadership coaches and speakers like John C. Maxwell (1995, 1998, 2005; Maxwell and Doman 1997) and Ken Blanchard (Blanchard and McBride 2008; Blanchard and Hodges 2005) focus on developing leadership attributes by training different levels of leaders in an organization. They admit that an organization needs different levels of leaders with different abilities.

Since most of these studies are conducted by American scholars in the American context, they reflect the American expectations of a leader. This phenomenon is what Zaccaro calls the "functionalism" of American culture, which aims at finding the best qualities of an effective leader and maximizing the functional abilities of the leaders in organizations (Zaccaro, Kemp, and Bader 2004, 104). This view is under challenge because many recent studies have discovered the inadequacies of using leadership attributes alone in the whole process of leadership.

The Inadequacies of the Studies on Leadership Attributes

In the increasing interactions among different cultures in the world today, the traditional Western leadership theories focused on leadership attribution are not adequate to provide solutions for complicated issues. The theories need to be revisited in greater depth before being applied into the Chinese situations. The first inadequacy of the studies focusing on leadership attributes is that to consider only the personal qualities but neglect the situational factors. The situational influence and the interactions between the leader and the situations are as important as the personal qualities of a leader. A particular attribute can be a contributing element to effective leadership in one situation but may not necessary having the same effect in another situation.

The second inadequacy deals with the measurement of leadership attributes. The characteristics of leadership attributes are mostly defined according to personality, physical ability and intelligence and most of them are work-related abilities (Bass and Stogdill 1981, 73-89). All these characteristics provide only a general expectation of an effective leader but not essential elements of an effective leader. In fact, it is a common belief that there is no universal leadership attributes for all different situations (Zaccaro, Kemp, and Bader 2004, 104; Yukl 2010, 192-193). Common characteristics of the effective leader can be found in different studies, but they are not adequate to prove which characteristic is more essential than the other. These theories have no objective measurement of the leadership attributes and therefore cannot differentiate which quality fits a specific situation well.

Studying leadership attribution alone is inadequate for finding the key factor which decides the success or failure of a leader. Personal qualities cannot be the only factors leading to the success or failure of the leadership process. As Peter G. Northouse comments, leadership attributes are subjective and neglect the influence of situations in the leadership process (2007, 25). Bass and Stodgill describe these kinds of studies as dealing only with theoretical issues without adequate empirical evidentiary support (1981, 5-6). Even James MacGregor Burns comments, that these studies focus too much on the personality of the leader but too little on leadership (1979, 1). In contrast, the early development of leadership trait theories has their limitations. They serve as an important foundation for further research on different aspects of leadership study as well. Leadership traits are not the only element affecting the organizational effectiveness but also one of the contributing factors in the complicated leadership process. All theories of leadership cannot neglect how the personal attributes of the leader affect his or her judgment in making decisions, handling changes and crises, and developing followers.

The growing complexity of leadership studies increases the difficulty in finding a clear focus; however, this process has enriched the width and depth of the discipline. The complexity can be seen in at least two areas. The first area is the multi-disciplinary nature of leadership. Different fields of study are involved: psychology, political science, education, sociology, business management, and administration (Clinton 1992a, 9). The second area is the definitions. As Warren G. Bennis and Burt Nanus notes, more than 350 definitions of leadership have been listed, and many of these definitions are not agreed with one another (1985, 4-5). The issue is not a lack of research on leaders and leadership but a lack of "agreement on fundamentals" (Gini 1998, 5). To some extent, different definitions reflect the bias, not the consensus, of these scholars. As Bennis and Nanus rightly point out, "Leadership is the most studied and least understood topic" (1985, 20).

The study of leaders alone is inadequate to explain the complexity of the whole process of leadership in different cultures. It is especially true when applying these studies into the Chinese cultural context. The attributes leading to the success of organizational leadership in the West can hardly transplant into the Chinese context without adequate adjustment. Based on past studies on the leader's attributes, study of the interactions among the leader, followers, and situations becomes more possible.

The Impact of Culture: A Wider Scope of Situational Theory

The second important theoretical foundation developed in the West is the situational aspect of leadership. In response to the inadequacies in understanding leadership effectiveness, the environmental elements should be highlighted as they affect the performance of a leader. A leader has the good performance in one situation; however, he or she may become ineffective in another situation. The study about the impact of situations on leadership is called situational theory.

The Early Models of Situational Theory

Situations refer to the influence of the environment on the leader and followers. The consideration of situations as an influential factor in the leadership process began in the middle of twentieth century. As early as 1947, Cecil A. Gibb had already pointed out that leadership is not merely the quality of a person, but also his or her interaction with the situation:

> In fact, viewed in relation to the individual, leadership is not an attribute of the personality but a quality of his role within a particular and specified social system. Viewed in relation to the group, leadership is a quality of its structure (1947, 267).

Gibb is among the earliest scholars to point out the situational aspect of leadership. Leadership is a response to situation. An effective leader is supposed to have the qualities to deal with unexpected changes. The popularity of Mayor Giuliani reached its apex in 2001 because he successfully managed the crisis after the terrorists' attack in New York City. In contrast, his popularity and ability could not last for a long time, and he failed in his president nomination campaign in 2008.

Situational theory is a complicated approach in understanding leadership effectiveness. Too many variables can be included as situations, for example, stress, politics, economic, and other environmental factors. The measurement of the leadership performance is therefore almost impossible. Vroom-Yetton's Normative Model (1973) is an attempt to use a quantitative method to measure the effectiveness of the leadership decision-making process. The focus of the Normative Model is leadership behavior. As shown in Figure 1, both situational and personal variables are considered as major forces interacting with the leader's behavior. Furthermore, Vroom and Yetton state clearly that other than the leader, other situational variables can also determine organizational effectiveness. This model successfully narrows complicated organizational situations into a single element affecting organizational effectiveness: the leader's decision-making process.

The limitation of this Normative Model is also its "narrowness." Problem-solving as a single element influencing the decision-making process is too narrow. There are too many varieties of variables both inside and outside the organization that have impact on its effectiveness. External situations like political, social, and economic changes may lead to changes in the internal situation and in turn affect the decision-making process.

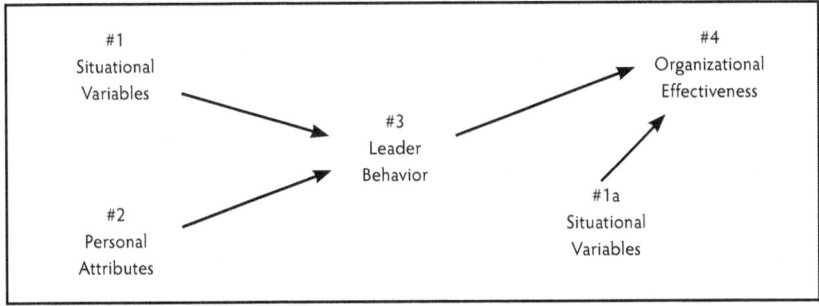

FIGURE 1: The Relationship of Variables Used in Leadership Research
(Vroom and Yetton 1973, 198)

Another limitation is to assume human behavior is something static and predictable. The human mind is dynamic and creative. Even in the same situation, the same person may make different decisions due to changes in the perceived information or in emotion. To a large extent, decision-making is affected by many variables. With only a few variables it is favorable only to the researchers to control the result but not necessary helpful to discover the whole picture of reality. The rationale is: if the environment is predictable, then the responses of the leaders are also measurable. A static environment is appropriate for comparing the result findings from limited set of variables but not actually for reflecting reality.

Fred E. Fiedler's study (1978) discloses a similar limitation. Even though Fiedler admits that situations are not static, he excludes all the variables except personal leadership styles. Among the leadership styles and attributes, he highlights the importance of inter-personal relationships. He calls situational theory a dynamic theory of leadership, however, he considers the interpersonal skills of the leader to be the dynamic force in handling the changes from the environment. A leader with good interpersonal skills can solve problems through motivating and changing the performance of the followers so as to improve organizational effectiveness. Interpersonal skills are one of the responses of the leader to the changes in situation and in response to the followers. The responses of the leader are the result of the interaction among the leader, followers, and situations. In order to investigate the thorough impact of situation on leadership, it is necessary to identify the factors affecting the interactions.

The Leader-Followers-Situation Interactions

The dynamic relationship among leader, followers, and situations is an important but complicated mixture of variables. The study of the interactions among leaders, followers, and situations reveals the fact that not a single factor can affect the leadership effectiveness. A leader-followers-situations paradigm is more complete and significant in explaining leadership effectiveness. The studies of leaders' behaviors are plentiful; more research studies need to be done on the other components—followers, situations, and their interactions.

Since the situation is composed of many variables, it is necessary to consider a more inclusive model in a situational theory of leadership. In addition to leader and situation, the followers' perspective is also essential in deciding leadership effectiveness. Richard L. Hughes, Robert C. Ginnett, and Gordon J. Curphy (2009) emphasize three areas necessary for understanding the whole picture of leadership: namely, the leader, followers, and situation. Figure 2 shows the relationship between the three dimensions; they are not three separate areas in leadership studies but an organic interactive process of leadership. In emphasizing leadership as an evolutionary process, Mark Van Vugt (2006, 2009; Van Vugt, Hogan, and Kaiser 2008) admits that leadership performance is the result of the interactions among leadership, followers, and situations.

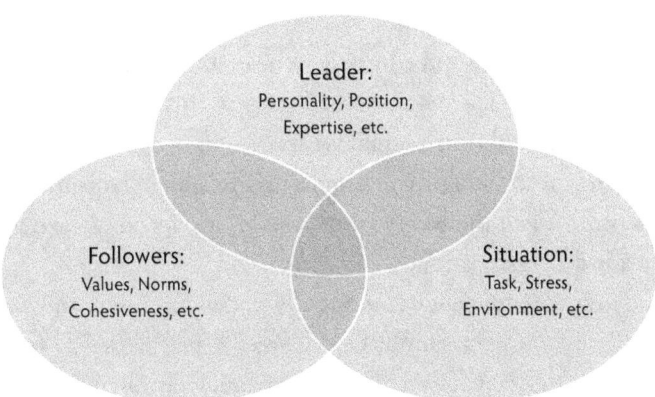

FIGURE 2: An Interactional Framework for Analyzing Leadership
(Hughes, Ginnett, and Curphy 2009, 26)

Leadership research is therefore not restricted to a leader but also includes the situations he or she faces and the followers he or she leads. The leader-followers-situations model is an inclusive paradigm that embraces almost all factors affecting the leadership process. A thorough analysis about different aspects of leadership is therefore possible.

Culture as an External Situation

Situations can be divided into internal and external situations; however, most models mentioned deal only with the internal situation of an organization. As a matter of fact, scholars have been aware of the differences between internal and external situations but do not take in-depth surveys about its significance. Stogdill (1950) has differentiated internal and external factors that affect the performance of a leader. A leader is not a free agent but has to work and live by many constraints. Bass and Stogdill have separated environmental theories from situational theories (1981, 27-30). They regard the studies of the situations outside the organization as the environment, and those studies are related to internal culture and structure as situations. For the sake of clarity, the terms *local culture* or *local situation* will be used to refer to the internal environment of an organization. Local culture refers to the organizational culture, internal structure, hierarchy, tradition, group dynamics, and working environment. The external culture, or macro-situation, refers to the environment outside the organization. The external culture is the social environment where the organization is located geographically and culturally. The contemporary social, political, religious, and economic environments belong to this category. Culture cannot be limited by political boundary; therefore, it can relate to religious and ideological traditions, for example, Christianity, Taoism, Islam, and Confucianism. When the term *culture* is used, it refers to the external situation outside an organization.

In studying the interactions among the leader, followers, and situations, the external environment cannot be neglected. The external or macro situations have greater impact on the leaders and followers when compared to the internal situation. Some studies have considered external or macro situations—such as political systems, social norms, religious traditions, and economic situations—as special situations. These situations are not regarded as the regular variables and major areas of concern in traditional leadership studies. Since most of the studies of leadership have been conducted in the USA, a relatively stable external situation gives the impression that the internal variables are more important.

The cultural phenomenon is more complicated in this age of globalization than in previous centuries. International organizations are everywhere today, and globalization is a challenge to traditional leadership studies. Hence, the study of culture is a necessary component that needs more in-depth studies. James Rosenau (2004) has rightly pointed out that leadership has been affected by internal processes and external pressures. Leadership is a process of fulfilling and handling expectations arising from both the internal and external situations.

The Limitations in the Study of Organizational Culture

Culture is a dominant force that shapes the values and behaviors of the leader, followers, and their organizational practices. Cultural factors are important elements that make differences in the responses of leaders to challenges. The inadequacies of the previous studies limit the cultural impact to some internal dynamics within an organization. The studies of organizational culture focus mainly on the events and phenomena inside an organization (Schein 2004, 37). The world we live in today is affected by different cultures at the same time. Even the internal situation becomes rather multi-cultural. Unless an organization is on a very local scale with very few staff persons, people may come to it from different cultural backgrounds and nationalities. The staff team of a computer programming company in California may include African Americans, Indians, Hispanics, Chinese from Hong Kong and Taiwan, etc. In order to understand the culture inside an organization, the leader can also learn the composition of cultures from different perspectives. Culture is believed to be a composition of different systems of beliefs which result from differences in human behavior. The moral norms and behaviors of the leaders and followers are affected by cultures and sub-cultures in the society in which they live and work (Sergiovanni 1986, 106-107; Kelley 2008, 10). In today's globalized era, it is not unusual to find an organization dealing with international business or having management teams from different countries.

Even within the Christian culture, the meaning of and expectations for leadership are different according to different Christian denominational backgrounds. Richard J. Mouw (2006, 119) defines Christian leadership as Christ's "three-fold office" of prophet, priest, and king while Cecil M. Robeck (2006, 141-143) claims that the power of the Holy Spirit provides the foundation for all Pentecostal leadership. Fredrica H. Thompsett (2006, 205) regards the Anglican understanding of leadership through what he calls "ordinary holiness," meaning to provide services and testimony both inside and outside of the church. Another Christian scholars, Richard J.

Wood (2006, 214) defines the leader as "consensus-seeker" and "consensus-builder" in the Quaker tradition. With all these differences regarding the understanding of leadership, the richness and complexity within a culture are easily shown. Given these differences, the traditional studies about how organizational culture affects leadership are inadequate to handle the complexities even within the American Christian culture.

The main concern of the international Christian ministry is the multicultural dimensions of the nature in leadership. How does a leader coming from one culture work effectively with the followers in a totally different culture? Without awareness of the differences in cultures, interpersonal conflict is the inevitable result. The need for cross-cultural leadership is the reality that ministry workers have to face today in a global community. People are living in an age in which almost everything became internationalized. International business, ministry, and research are commonly found in most major cities in the world. In these circumstances, the main leadership task is to deal with these changes. A leader makes decisions to deal with changes every day. Political or social movements happening today in the eastern hemisphere are affecting leadership decisions in the Western hemisphere. The global financial crisis which began in the autumn of 2008 in the USA is no doubt another example of the global crisis beginning from a local incident. Leaders in different countries and levels of government, business entrepreneurs, and the leaders of NGOs are all facing changes. Dealing with change involves the interaction between the leader and these situations. Leadership development in this sense means learning to deal with changes.

Leadership in a Changing World

In the study of the relationship between leadership and culture, the priority focus is on how to bring change within an organization. Hughes, Ginnett, and Curphy (Hughes, Ginnett, and Curphy 2009, 611-612) have developed a rational approach to organizational change. The focus of their studies is on the leaders who have the capabilities, techniques, and necessary personality attributes to drive change within an organization. After understanding the internal and external situations, the leader develops the vision and goal for organizational change. The ideal process is to bring the followers to come and create the change together. Christian leadership theorists also advocate that the leader be a change agent. Doug Murren (1997, 199-212) believes that change is necessary because new problems arise every day. Whenever problems arise, a new solution will be the result after a shift in the old paradigm—and that shift brings about change.

Burns points out that social transformation is important to the relationship between leadership and cultural change. He argues that the impact of cultural change is not only limited within the organization, but it also has social impact. Burns gives the example of Mao Zedong as decision maker during the Cultural Revolution in China. Mao had the charisma and ability to lead the change (Burns 1979, 401-421). Mao's role in the decision-making process was crucial; he was the one who was interacting with the internal and external situations and this situation finally led to social and cultural changes in China in the mid-twentieth century. Burns (2003) wants to focus the attention on what he calls "transformational leadership"—the leader who guides and brings changes inside and outside of the organization.

Transformation results from the interaction between a leader and the situations he or she faces. Both the leader and the situation influence one another. If situations include both the internal and external environments, then the leader is in fact facing the challenges from both the within and outside of his or her own culture. External culture is the major reason that the leader has to deal with change. It is challenging because external culture is the area a leader is least aware of. As a leader feels comfortable in the familiar culture, he or she may not be aware that the perceptions and expectations of the followers are already shaped by the culture. When facing a follower from another culture, the leader may find it difficult to understand the behavior and responses of this foreigner. For example, the perception of privacy between Chinese and American cultures is totally different. A Chinese staff member is willing to share personal information, such as age and salary income with other colleagues. However, in American culture such personal information is regarded as private and not disclosed easily. Transformation will only occur when the leader perceives the differences between two cultures and makes adjustments.

In addition to the complexity within a cultural system, the oversimplification of the researchers' understanding of situations is the other reason that the research on the relationship between leadership and culture is underdeveloped. The complexities of external cultural phenomena have been simplified into a few isolated and unrelated elements. Bass and Stogdill study leadership across different countries and concern multinational firms (1981, 539-549). They find great varieties of differences on leadership attributes and leadership style because of the cultural differences. Their findings show the problems of leadership in different external situations. Some contrasting views are found even on the same issue. Bass and Stogdill summarize three dimensions that help to understand the differences in these cultures: traditionalism versus modernity, particularism versus universalism, and pragmatism versus idealism (1981, 529-532). This generalization of complicated cultural phenomena helps the researchers to compare and contrast different cultural systems in a relatively simple way. However, the polarization of these different areas may hinder the understanding of the whole reality. For instance, in Chinese culture, both pragmatism and idealism are found at the same time. Chinese people have idealistic expectations of the leader who is called the "sage," assuming that a human can achieve moral perfection. A good leader is not just an effective manager but also a morally good person. At the same time, Deng Xiaoping, the former General Secretary of CPC exemplifies Chinese pragmatism when he said, "No matter whether it is white or black, a cat which catches rats is good." He judged a leader's effectiveness according to his or her ability and the results achieved.

The study of culture as an external situation is a necessary component of the interactions between the leader, followers, and situations. Interactions are both the responses to actions between the leader and followers, and their responses to the situations. Culture defines and sets the boundaries of these interactions. Relational leadership in this respect emphasizes the interactions among the different components of the leader-followers-situations paradigm.

Culture and Followership

The leader alone can hardly deal with complicated situations today. The leader has to rely on the followers so as to achieve organizational transformation. The role of followers is therefore important in affecting the performance of the leader. In contemporary leadership studies, both inside and outside of the organization, the impact of followers cannot be underestimated. The third foundational element in relational leadership is therefore the impact of followers. However, one cannot understand the true picture of followership without knowing the influences from culture.

The Leader-centric Studies on Followership

The studies on the role of followers in leadership began very early; however, the focus was not followers as an independent and valuable entity. The role of the followers is only a contributing factor to organizational effectiveness. First of all, the importance of followers is to help the leader to achieve organizational goals. The prerequisite in leadership team development is the recognition that a single person can no longer achieve a great vision. The main responsibility of a leader is therefore to equip and motivate the followers to fulfill the organizational goals. Peter Block (1987, 69-70) argues that the leader of an organization is not necessarily the best person who can lead the business effectively and successfully. Through empowerment, the potential abilities of the followers can be released and thus contribute to a greater success of the organization. Empowerment is not only about job assignments and responsibility delegation but is also about turning the organization's power structure around. Block sees the value and contribution of the followers. The mutual relation between the leader and followers can be more active and productive through empowerment.

Overall, the previous studies of the relationship between the leader and followers were one-sided. The main focus is on "follower readiness" to achieve the organizational goal. The followers are passively influenced or even manipulated by the capable leader to accomplish his or her goal. Hughes, Ginnett, and Curphy have listed three major areas of concern in the situational model of leadership: task behaviors, relationship behaviors, and follower readiness (2009, 586-587). These three areas can be summarized as leadership behaviors to fulfill the two primary purposes of being a leader: to communicate the vision effectively and to mobilize the followers to accomplish tasks. In these studies, followers are obviously only part of the management tools, but they have no independent identity, apart from their functions in the organization.

The other major theory that focuses on the relationship with the followers is Burns' transforming leadership theory (2003, 1979). Burns emphasizes the mutual relationship between the leader and followers. He distinguishes two major kinds of leadership process: transforming and transactional leaderships (Burns 1979, 4). The transforming and transactional leaders look to the needs and interests of the followers differently. The transactional leader fulfills the followers' needs through the exchange of interests. The transactional leader provides benefits to the followers in exchange of their loyalty and capabilities to the organization. In contrast, the transforming leader recognizes the needs of the followers and tries to satisfy their needs through elevating their potential. Both the transforming leader and the followers engage in raising each other to "higher levels of motivation and morality" (Burns 1979, 20). The leader and followers are not sharing equal responsibility or status: the former takes the initiative to motivate and change the latter. Followers are passive partners in leadership.

If the key term used to denote Burns' transforming leadership is elevation, motivation is another term that to distinguish Bass's similar concept of transformational leadership from other leadership styles in other studies (Bass and Riggio 2006; Bass 1985, 1990, 1997; Bass and Avolio 1994). Bass defines transformational and transactional leadership more widely. While Burns suggests that moral leadership is the ideal destination of leadership development, Bass expects the transformational leader to be a role model for the followers. In this sense, Burns indicates the relational nature of transformational leadership—the leader-followers' dynamic relationship will bring differences to organizational effectiveness. In addition, the transformational leader can be a charismatic leader, coach, or mentor. The primary goal of a transformational leader is to inspire the followers and challenge them to live and work to reach their potential. The transactional leader rewards or disciplines the followers according to their performance (Avolio 1999, 34-40; Bass and Riggio 2006, 5-9). The major difference in Bass's theory is the complementarities of transformational and transactional leadership. Transformational and transactional leadership are not two unrelated characteristics of leader but can be performed by a leader in different situations.

This transformational leadership, proposed by Burns and Bass is a step forward in understanding the leader-followers relationship. The followers are no longer merely an object passively manipulated by the leader but having great value in achieving organizational goals. Sharon M. Latour and Vicki J. Rast point out "without followership a leader at any level will fail to produce effective institution" (2004, 103). On the one hand, the transformational leader has the responsibility to elevate the followers; on the other hand the followers have the responsibility to increase their competence. A dynamic transformational leader can make the best use of his or her leadership skills to work with the followers, who are not objects being used but people who can be elevated or mobilized to reach their full potentials.

Other studies were conducted in order to research the applicability of the transformational and transactional leadership. Bennis and Nanus (1985) have conducted a five year study with ninety leaders and conclude with four strategies for developing effective leaders. Through vision, communication, positioning, and innovative learning, leaders develop themselves in order to guide others effectively. Even though these studies began to pay more attention to the followers, they are inadequate in describing how the followers shape leadership behavior. These theories are leader-centric because even the transformational leadership is focused on the role of the leader. The development of the followers' potential is the result of the requirement of the leader (Kuhnert and Lewis 1987, 687). In addition to the work of the leader, the followers contribute to the outcomes in organizational effectiveness. External culture is also neglected in these leader-centric studies; the forces impacting the expectations of the followers are therefore neglected as well.

Culture and Followers' Expectations

Contrary to the findings of the leader-centric studies on leadership and followership, the role of followers is decisive on leadership effectiveness. As Max De Pree states, the art of leadership is about "liberating people to do what is required of them in the most effective and humane way possible" (2004, 1). Without followers, leadership is nothing. To some extent, the success of a leader depends on the responses from his or her followers (De Pree 1992, 23; Wright 2004, 5; Beckhard 1996, 125). Many studies in the last two decades had begun to emphasize the importance of the functions of the followers.

As mentioned in the beginning of this chapter, most studies focused on business sectors and were characterized by the individualistic culture. Attention was focused on the individual versatility, achievement, responsibility integrity and self-employment attitudes of the followers (Lundin and Lancaster 1990). Individualism and functionalism are characteristics of American culture. Followers' expectations are in fact shaped by the culture they live. The first value of studying the relationship between culture and followers is to distinguish cultural bias in leadership studies. As Kellerman points out, sometimes followers follow the leader even though they believe that he or she is not good because this leader-followers relationship is based on self interest (2008, 49). Both the leader and followers benefit from this relationship in one way or the other. Although the possibility of having a relationship of mutual trust between the leader and the followers cannot be omitted, an ideal relationship between the leader and followers without self-interest is rare.

Western democratic society provides legitimate channels for the followers to express their interests and concerns. The rights of the followers are respected; therefore, the power of the followers is strong and influential. The leader-followers relationship can therefore be very active. In a paternalistic culture, when the validity of an idea is based on who the speaker is and what position he or she holds, the result is totally different. A more senior member of the community has more authority in decision-making while a young or new member's opinion is neglected. Different cultures produce different followers.

Although the followers in an authoritarian culture are not highly respected, it does not mean that they do not have the power to impact the decisions of the leader. In Scripture, the decisions and behaviors of the leaders changed in response to the followers. Aaron made the golden calf as a god for the Israelites while waiting for Moses to return from the mountain.

Aaron worked under the pressure of the followers and became an example of a bad leader (Ex. 32:1-35). The other example is the great leader Moses. When Moses was angry with the followers and did not trust the Lord in Meribah, he was punished and not allowed to step into the land of Canaan (Nu. 20:1-13). Unlike Aaron, Moses did not follow the decision of the followers, but his decision was distorted by his emotions, which was a result of the attitudes of the followers. The followers are actually affecting the performance and decision-making of the leader in different cultures.

Another value in studying the relationship between cultures and followers is to distinguish that different kinds of followers have different cultures. Different kinds of followers bring different impacts on the leader. Robert E. Kelley (1988) identifies four kinds of followers based on their attitudes and participation in an organization: sheep, alienated followers, survivors, and effective followers. In addition to organization situation, Kellerman (2008) classifies four kinds of followers in the country according to their levels of activism: bystanders, participants, activists, and diehards. She declares that bystanders are bad followers: they are inactive and isolated from the society. The bystanders are morally bad because they allow the leader to do whatever he or she wants to do. Bystanders intend to do nothing to support good leader as well as to slow down the progress of emerging bad leader (Kellerman 2008, 230). Psychologically, all types of followers need achievement (Burke 1963, 84-86). In the case of Nazi Germany, they might find achievements like national pride, self-esteem, or the sense of security Hitler promised. Some of the bystanders found the value of a strong German government; some of them believed what Hitler promised them in the future. Kellerman does not point out significant interactions between the culture and role of different followers. Therefore, a further study on the cultural heritage of Germany at that time may help to understand more about the situation of the followers.

Different cultures have different dominant groups of followers. Specific cultural traditions shape the expectations of the followers. The dominant type of followers may therefore represent the characteristics of a specific culture. For example, in a democratic society, the responses of the followers may be comparatively easy to discover, since their choices and preferences are easily seen in public polls, surveys, and votes. Participants and activists will therefore be regarded as the dominant groups in a democratic society. In an authoritarian society, however, bystanders may dominate since the government structure and culture forbid the people to voice their opinions publicly, especially when they have different views than the authorities.

Apart from the dynamic relationship between culture and followers, the relationship between the leader and followers can also be understood in a more active and dynamic way. The third value in studying the relationship between cultures and followers is to discover varieties of dynamic relationships between leader, followers, and different cultures. Recent studies (Hollander 1992; Maroosis 2008; Hopper 2008) have shown changes in perceptions of the relationship between leader and followers. A change of attitudes may come from the recognition of the inadequacy of the previous studies on leadership. The relationship between leader and followers is perceived as a dynamic and educational relationship that will benefit both the leader and followers. The leader is expected to spend time informally to build relationships with the followers in order to increase his or her influence on the followers.

Followers are the irreplaceable partners in achieving organizational goals. They are not necessarily regarded as those who only follow the orders of the leaders but also who contribute actively to the organization (Potter III, Rosenbach, and Pittman 1998). The role of followers as partners in an organization is a contributing factor to change the leadership performance. Max De Pree goes further, asking the leader to "learn the perspective of followers" (1992, 198). The role of followers has changed from a passive one to a more active role in an organization. A leader establishes his or her image as a trustworthy person and at the same time establishes mutual trust with the followers. The leader not only expects cooperation from the followers but also the building of a two-way collaborative relationship with the followers (Kouzes and Posner 1995, 167).

The expectations of the followers can impact the performance of a leader both positively and negatively. Barbara Kellerman asks why most research studies assume all leaders are morally good. This assumption creates three major problems: it is confusing, it is misleading, and it does a disservice to the people who study leadership (2004, 12). She accurately points out that almost all the studies on leadership assume every candidate is developing toward becoming a good leader. Without noticing the dark side of human nature, it is not possible to be aware of the emergence of morally bad leaders. Jean Lipman-Blumen is also aware of bad leaders. She calls them toxic leaders. Although a toxic leader may not be a morally bad person by nature, he or she brings about harmful results. Lipman-Blumen warns of the danger of creating a god if the followers idealize the leader only because of their psychological needs when facing the uncertain situations in the outside world. In most cases, the followers are responsible for the emergence of a toxic leader because they were "pushing the good leader over the toxic line" (Lipman-Blumen 2005, ix, 139-160).

In the discussion of bad or toxic leaders, it discovers a culture of mistrust to the human nature. Western culture is characterized by a Christian religious worldview which agrees that the human nature is fallible. Even though most people are expecting moral leadership, perfect leadership is not a possible option in leadership expectations (Kelley 1992, 18). Contrary to this occidental view, the expectation of a perfect leader in Asian cultures is common.[1] Culture shapes the leadership expectations of the followers.

To some extent, the followers decide if the leader as good or bad. The reality is that a good person can be a bad leader and vice-versa. Adolf Hitler was an effective and charismatic leader who led the Nazi government of Germany to become strong in the 1930s; however, most people would agree that Hitler was morally bad because he started World War II and executed six million Jews (Kellerman 2004, 29).

The shift from the focus on leadership attributes to the expectations of followers in leadership studies reflects the attention to the leadership crisis of the last two decades. The center of the power has shifted from the hands of the leader to the followers. Kellerman says,

> As it becomes obvious that today's leaders have less power and influence, and that today's followers have more, the literature on leadership and management is becoming slightly more

---

[1]. In Confucianism, the human nature is assumed to be good. A perfect humanity is therefore achievable through developing a moral self. Detailed discussions is presented in chapter 3 (Confucian culture and Relational Leadership in China) of this dissertation.

expansive, to include a small body of work that focuses on subordinates, as opposed to superiors (2008, 45).

Citizens in Western democratic societies have the right to vote and chose their leaders. Compared with the Asian citizens, Westerners have more power to influence the leader. In the global financial crisis beginning in 2008, in countries like the USA and France, which are strongly influenced by public opinions and labor unions, economic reforms were more difficult to implement because of the objections from the labor unions as they believed that these reforms will reduce the benefits of the workers. These cases demonstrated that the decision of the followers does impact the effectiveness of the leader in these cases.

Ira Chaleff's study (1995) moves away from the studies purely focused on expecting the leader toward the powerful impact of the followers on the leader. Although the main focus is still on how the followers support the leader, Chaleff shifts gear to encourage the followers to fulfill their responsibilities and challenge authority appropriately and creatively (Chaleff 1995, 87-90). Chaleff assumes that a good leader is willing to share leadership authority with the followers. Both the leader and followers are mutually responsible for their personal and professional growth. With a good leader and loyal followers, the leader-follower dynamic is a constructive force by which they can help each other achieve the organization goals and develop the followers' potential. As a result, the active participation of the followers in management becomes possible (Chaleff 1995, 11-32). The expectations of the followers to participate in the decision making process in democratic society come into effect with the change of leadership attitudes toward a more relational partnership with them.

In today's changing culture, the expectations of followers can help shape the character and style of their leaders. The charismatic leader has a close and interactive relationship with the followers. Today, followers usually expect the leader to bring changes to the organization or even to the society. The latest example is the election of Barack Obama as the president of the United States in 2008. As a charismatic leader, when Barack Obama was elected as the first African-American president, majority of Americans were expecting that he would bring changes to the whole nation, even the whole world. Charisma as a leadership attribute is closely related to the culture advocating changes today. In the meantime, the leader should find consensus with the followers in the process of change (Conger 1989, 17; Hollander 1992, 73; Kouzes and Posner 1993, 27). Rosenau (2004) shares the view that leader-followers relationship is an interactive process. Followers' expectations of the leader are closely connected with the charisma of the leader. The more charismatic the leader, the closer the tie with the followers will be.

The origin of the word *charisma* is found in the Bible, meaning a gift to leaders. In general today, having charisma means to have behavioral attractiveness for others to admire (Lipman-Blumen 1996, 30). Charisma is more preferable to be interpreted as an attribution of the leader perceived by the followers. As long as the followers observe and feel the charismatic attractiveness of the leader, they will perceive him or her as a charismatic leader (Conger and Kanungo 1987, 639-640). In this respect, the charismatic leader is defined by the followers according to what they perceive. Whether or not a person is accepted as a charismatic leader, his or her charisma is a combination of leadership attributes and followers' acceptance.

The interactions between the leader and followers contribute to a clear identification of their roles. The role of the leader and followers varies in different cultures. William L. Gardner and Bruce J. Avolio (1998) have studied the role of followers in constructing charismatic leadership through dramaturgical perspective. Gardner and Avolio use role play in a drama to illustrate the different character of the leader and followers. The core of their research is a search for and construction of the identities of both the leader and followers in the dramaturgical process. They call the process of leadership and followership development "leader identification" and "follower identification." In other words, both the leader and followers identify their roles from their interactions. After that they play their roles according to what they have constructed during the process of leader-followers interactions. The attributes of the leader are no longer the single factor in developing into a charismatic leader. This study recognizes the interdependence of the leader and his or her followers. The whole picture of leadership development is no longer limited by "leader-centric" studies (J. M. Howell and Shamir 2005, 96). If the followers' expectations are shaped by the culture, culture is therefore decisive in leadership functioning and organizational effectiveness.

Paternalistic Culture and Leadership

Followers behave differently in different cultures. Since relationship is a distinctive characteristic in Asian cultures, followers in these cultures can therefore be characterized as relational followers. If the personality of the leader weighted high value in leadership performance in the West, the personality of the Chinese leader is more decisive in Asian paternalistic culture.

In Asian culture, inter-personal relationships have a greater importance in the success or failure of an organization. To complete a task objective is as important as keeping good relationships with fellow coworkers. The impact of the followers on leadership in both Western and Eastern cultural contexts show some commonalities; however, the levels or extent of the influences are different. Hollander (1992) points out the leader-followers relationship cannot be understood in terms of a parent-child relationship. In reality, paternalistic culture is a dominant feature in the Asian world. Michael Maccoby (2008) recognizes the psychological and emotion needs of the followers who expect the leader to provide security and personal development through a mentoring relationship. A paternalistic relationship is therefore identified.

Studies on leadership in Chinese cultural contexts began earlier this century. Farth Jing-lih and Cheng Bor-shiuan (2000) have studied the cultural influence on business leaders in Taiwanese enterprises. They discovered that business leaders did not treat all their followers equally in terms of friendliness. The Chinese business leaders determined the extent of closeness according to the loyalty of the followers and social ties, for example, whether the subordinates were relatives, had the same family names, or lived in the same home town. The leaders' decision about how to relate themselves with their followers was not based on the performance and abilities of the followers but on their relationship to the leaders.

Behaving like the parent of a family is the major characteristic of paternalistic leadership. The relationship between the leader and followers is based on personal relationship and ethical values. Paternalistic leadership is one of the clear features of collective cultures which are commonly found in

China, Japan, and Korea. Society is perceived as the extension of a family. The positive side of paternalism in collective cultures is universal brotherhood. The leader and followers expect one another to live and work as if brothers and sisters in a family. An informal relationship similar to kinship is expected among the leaders and followers. Since the supervisor carries the image of a parent, coworkers naming one another as brothers and sisters are not uncommon in Asian organizations. As Lucian Pye comments,

> The amazing strength of those relationships can be seen not only in the intense feelings of obligation and indebtedness which they evoke, but also in their tendency to endure even when they cause annoyance and trouble—as when subordinates manipulate superiors (1985, 326).

An individual is asked to sacrifice for the benefit of the community. This characteristic is true in the family, organization, and society in Asian cultures.

Cheng has also studied paternalistic leadership in the enterprises in mainland China. To a large extent, the Chinese culture in Taiwan, Hong Kong and mainland China is similar (Cheng et al. 2003). Cheng points out some characteristics of paternalistic leadership: individualized consideration, high performance standards, and modeling. The authority of the leaders is similar to the parents of a family—the expectation of high performance of their children. Parents expect the children to have high academic achievement in Chinese society. Individualized consideration expects because of a close relationship between the superior and the subordinate. The parents are expected to have personal concern on their children. The children expect their parents to guide and protect them. A similar expectation also appears within a Chinese organization. The leader is expected to give personal attention to the followers. In many occasions, the followers bring their personal and family issues to their workplace to ask for help.

A parent is expected to be the role model of a family. A leader is expected to be a role model of competence at work and moral goodness in personal behavior. The meaning of modeling is obvious: the parents are being expected to perform as role models. The followers expect the leader to have a good reputation so that they can be proud of their superior as well as the organization. Loyalty is based on the perception of the moral image of the leader in addition to self interest. The expectations of the followers to the paternalistic leader are not simply about fulfilling the objective of the task or their self-interest but to contribute also for the benefit of the whole community. Paternalistic leadership is a form of relational leadership since they share a common feature: the irreplaceable role of relationship in a community.

Some common features of leadership expectations can be found between paternalistic leadership and other theories of leadership. In a growing trend, Western scholars now value the significance of a relational aspect of leadership-followership. Both the leader and followers need a close relationship. The leader needs to improve organizational performance, while the followers have paternalistic expectations.

Another common feature is the expectation of moral leadership. Personal attributes are an indispensable part of leadership studies. Everyone is looking for the best leader according to his or her own expectations. No one wants to see an ineffective, morally bad leader in his or her organization. In this respect, morality is a common expectation in all cultures. As Burns remarks,

> Consider our common usage. We don't call for good leadership—we expect, or at least hope, that it will be good. "Bad" leadership implies no leadership. I contend that there is nothing neutral about leadership; it is valued as a moral necessity (2003, 2).

People in all cultures expect morally good leaders based on personality, moral character, attitudes, and abilities. Personal attributes are the major criteria. In Asian culture, the expectations of the leader as a role model, parent, teacher, or mentor are closely related to their moral image and behavior. Even though paternalistic culture is distinctive in Asian society, some of its features are commonly found in both the East and the West.

Toward a Relational Leadership Model

After studying the leader-situations-followers paradigm in previous sections, the interactive relationship among the three elements determines the effectiveness of the leadership process. The leadership theories themselves reflect the responses of scholars to their particular situations. Both Western and Chinese scholars find common characteristics of relational leadership. In recent decades, some studies about relational leadership have been conducted. In contemporary society, leaders face the diversified needs. As mentioned in the beginning of this chapter, not a single person in this generation can respond to all the different expectations from the followers by his or her efforts without the support from others. In this changing social environment, the contribution of the followers is necessary for leadership success. Relational leadership is therefore a model which developed naturally in response to the changing situations of the world.

The insights into relational leadership began around three decades ago. The leader-member exchange theory and the path-goal theory were attempts to value the importance of followers in a relation-oriented leadership style (Dansereau and Graen 1975, 46-78; Graen and Cashman 1975, 146-147; Hughes, Ginnett, and Curphy 2009, 586-601; Yukl 2010, 122). Differentiating between task behavior and relational behavior is helpful in handling the expectations of the followers as well as achieving organizational goals. The role of relationship is a means to equip and motivate the followers.

The common features of different models of relational leadership can be summarized as the need for collaboration in this diversified world. The situation of the twenty-first century is diverse because of the trend of globalization. When people from different cultures work and live together, their needs should be rated higher than organizational needs. For example, Susan R. Komives, Nance Lucas, and Timothy R. McMahon (1998) emphasize inclusiveness, empowerment, purpose, ethics, and process as the major components of relational leadership. In facing the diversity of cultures in contemporary society, equal importance is given to achieve personal goals.

Through the collaboration and team efforts of the leader and followers, a "win-win" situation of both the leader and followers will be achieved.[2]

The other model of relational leadership developed by Adrian Kezar and Rozana Carducci (2009) emphasizes some similar components of relational leadership. Promoting learning process, embracing complexity, collaborating team leadership, embracing cultural context, and upholding ethical and spiritual leadership are the five main components of relational leadership. Kezar and Carducci admit the complexity of the reality and that the only way to achieve leadership success is by collaboration.

These newly developed models of relational leadership reinforce the trend of honoring the collaborative efforts of the leader and followers to improve organizational effectiveness. In addition, some components of relational leadership are consistent with biblical teachings on relational leadership. Ethical or moral leadership is essential in the Christian leadership context. Team leadership is another common characteristic in different relational leadership models as it is agreed that no single leader can face the challenges in this world alone. As the world becomes more complex, the value of followers returns. Leadership attribute is the essential element to develop moral leadership as well as successful team leadership. These Western theories are applicable to the Chinese cultural context as both the West and the East share some common beliefs.

Summary

Leadership attribute is an important foundation for investigating a deeper understanding on the performance of a leader. An effective leader is important to the overall performance of an organization; however, the personal qualities of a leader cannot dictate the organizational effectiveness. Consideration of the roles of situations and followers is inevitable. After

---

2. The assumption in this model is the recognition of multiple truths and realities. (Komives, Lucas, and McMahon 1998, 61). Relativism is the characteristic as this model denies the existence of universal truth. Moral relativism is a fair comment. Even though moral relativism is not accepted in our Christian churches, it is true to admit that the leader does not monopolize the truth. The interpretation of the truth can also be the right of the followers in the church.

studying the theories of leadership attribute for over a century, Western scholars have returned to morality as the basic expectation of leader. It is not ability alone that can achieve success but the inner life qualities, including integrity and other ethical values, of both the leader and followers. The leader needs to become a role model for the followers, and therefore the inner life qualities are an essential binding force to develop a leadership team.

Situational theory was well illustrated and discussed in the past century. Only half of the necessary elements of variables in affecting leadership performance have been thoroughly studied: internal situation or internal organizational culture. My proposal is that the impact of culture in shaping the values of leaders and followers is significant in organizational effectiveness. Two factors are important. First, this is an age of globalization. Organizations are mostly multi-cultural. Second, the awareness of cultural bias of the researchers has shown that a careful study of the worldviews of the other culture is required, which may shed new light on the old issues. The trend among Western scholars is toward a relational perspective in leadership theories.

Culture is closely connected with the expectations of the followers. Recent studies of leadership are concerned with the role of followers in affecting the organizational effectiveness. In dealing with the followers' issues, a relational approach is necessary. Followers are no longer merely servants who contribute wholeheartedly to the success of the leaders. The influence of the followers is decisive, and therefore the development of followers should be regarded as a top priority in leadership. In the specific situation of Asian cultures, the leader-followers relationship is different because of paternalistic culture. The emphasis on relationship and morality are important features in paternalistic leadership.

In the development of followership, identifying the physical, psychological, and social needs of the followers is important. Identifying the needs of the followers is in fact part of a process of establishing a healthy relational self-concept (Lord and Brown 2004; Howell and Mendez 2008). A healthy relationship begins with a true picture of the self. Then, the development of the self is an essential part of the process of followership development. Developing leadership attributes shows some common features of developing the moral self in Confucian culture. Self-cultivation is an important element of human nature development in Chinese Confucianism. Similar patterns of relational leadership in different culture are found. It is clear that relational leadership is one of the bridges between the West and the East. A culturally adaptable leadership theory is going to become obvious after the study from a Confucian perspective in the next chapter.

CHAPTER 3

Confucian Culture and Relational Leadership in China

Based on what has been discussed in last chapter, culture as an external situation brings different mindsets and practices of leadership. No systematic leadership theory has been developed so far in relation to Chinese culture. This chapter argues that relational leadership is compatible with Confucianism. Chinese Christian churches find relational leadership a culturally adaptable and practical leadership style. The main thesis of Confucian leadership development is that leadership development is a process of personal growth which develops the human nature into its fullest potential. The relationship between the self and heaven is the key element affecting human relationships in Confucian China. The understanding of human nature, the idealistic conception of a sage, and self-cultivation as a method of leadership development are the three major aspects of Confucian leadership development.

In contrast with the American individualistic culture, collectivism is one of the major characteristics of the Asian culture. East Asian countries like Japan, Singapore, and Korea are highly affected by Chinese Confucian culture; therefore it is appropriate to begin the exploration of the impact of culture on leadership with Confucianism.

Culture can be defined as "the attitudes and behavior that are characteristic of a particular social group or organization" (Miller 2006). It is a common understanding that the "attitudes and behavior" of the Chinese people are influenced by Confucianism. Among Chinese Christians, the ways of thinking, perceiving, and interpreting Christian faith are largely impacted by Confucianism. Chinese pastors, however, have little awareness of the cultural influences of Confucianism. The terminologies used in preaching and daily conversations in Christian ministry reflects the Confucian worldview. It is necessary to explore why and how the Chinese pastors are affected by Confucianism. Before the discussion of Chinese leadership development, a cultural foundation of the Chinese churches should be analyzed.

Confucianism, Wang Yangming, and Leadership Development

Before the three aspects of Confucian leadership development are being studied, a brief background of Confucianism in relation to leadership development is given below. Founded by Confucius (551-479 B.C.) more than 2500 years ago, Confucianism is indisputably the dominate philosophy influencing Chinese culture. As summarized by Liu Shuxian, Confucianism is a morally, socially, and this-world conscious tradition (1998, 7). Confucianism is generally characterized as a humanistic culture. The primary concern is how a person can become truly human, that is, how people can live harmoniously with one another under the Mandate of Heaven (*tian ming* 天命) (Tu 2008, 3). The ideal destination of personal growth is to achieve the embodiment of true humanity, known as *sheng ren* (聖人). The term *sheng ren* literally means a holy person or a sage. As a *sheng ren*, one is expected to live according to the Mandate of Heaven and to express the moral ideal through his or her moral life. A sage is expected to govern according to the principles of Heaven (*tian li* 天理) in promoting and safeguarding harmonious relations between people in the society. With this ontological and social aspect of personal growth, the expectations of leader are therefore different from the models in American based leadership studies.

Before knowing how to be a leader, one should know how to be a good man or woman. The term *leader* is rarely used in Confucian tradition. The term *junzi* (君子), which means a profound person, can be borrowed to denote a person of good quality who lives according to innate knowledge. A sage, who developed from a *junzi*, is regarded as the ideal of a perfect leader.

Not characterized as having good management skills as in the Western concept of a leader, a sage rather lives a model life for others to follow.

Although there is no distinctive leadership development theory in Chinese tradition, the goal and methods in education to develop followers are well defined. The goal of Confucianism in developing followers is to make them sages. A sage is a morally perfect human. "Moral education was the backbone of his educational program; he [Confucius] also taught his disciples how to serve as officials on all levels in the government" (Liu 1998, 15).

Similar to Jesus of Nazareth, Confucius was the greatest educator in Chinese history, but he had no successful practical experience in governmental or organizational leadership. After Confucius, several Confucian scholars were actively involved in government administration, for example Dong Zhongshu (董仲舒 179-104 B.C.) in the Han dynasty (202 B.C.-A.D. 220) and Han Yu (韓愈 A.D. 768-824) in the Tang dynasty (A.D. 618-907). They made some modifications and developments in consolidating Confucianism as the foundation of Chinese culture. It was not until the Song (A.D. 960-1279) and Ming dynasties (A.D. 1368-1644) that Confucianism came to another zenith since Confucius. This stage is usually called Neo-Confucianism to distinguish it from the classical Confucianism represented by Confucius and Mencius (371-298 B.C.). The Confucian understanding of human nature has been enriched by Confucian scholars in different ages. Among the Neo-Confucians, Zhu Xi (朱熹 A.D. 1130-1200) helped to incorporate Confucian teachings into the curriculum of the civil examinations and Wang Yangming (王陽明 A.D. 1472-1529) helped to consolidate and further expand the influence of Confucianism. Wang Yangming is the major consolidator who expanded the concept of innate knowledge of the good; which is called *liang zhi* (良知). The concept of *liang zhi* then became the major component of human nature in the Confucian tradition. To be a sage, one has to have the extension of the innate knowledge of the good (*zhi liang zhi* 致良知) in his or her human nature. The innate knowledge of the good successfully connects the Confucian understanding of human nature with social participation. Further, Yangming was the one who taught the concept of universal sagehood (眾人皆可成

聖), which shared some similarities with the Christian understanding of sanctification (J. Yeung 1996, 93-98).

To understand the Chinese conception of leadership development, the first step is to understand the Confucian concept of human nature. The expectations of a leader are largely shaped by the understanding of and assumptions about human nature. Wang Yangming's understanding of human nature provides the direction of Confucian leadership development. Western studies of Wang Yangming began in the 1960s when his works were translated by Frederick G. Henke (1964) and Chan Wingtsit (1963b). Julia Ching (1972, 1973, 1976) and Tu Weiming (1976b) translated and interpreted the works of Wang Yangming, but they indeed developed their understanding of Neo-Confucianism from Yangming's philosophy. Tu Weiming (1979, 1985) has introduced and developed the Confucian understanding of the "self" based on Wang Yangming's understanding of human nature.[1]

In fact, Wang Yangming's philosophy is not unfamiliar among Christian scholars. It is interesting to find that Wang Yangming can be compared to Martin Luther in the West in terms of their roles on reforming their respective traditions (S. Zhao 1993, 206-207). Some comparative studies on Wang Yangming and Western philosophy have been done in the 1990s. For example, Jason Yeung (1996) has compared the philosophy of Wang Yangming with Martin Luther and Søren Kierkegaard respectively and Heup Young Kim (1996) has compared Yangming with Karl Barth. Although there are some other studies about interfaith dialogues between Confucianism and Christianity, most of them have remained in the metaphysical level and do not directly benefit the development of the Christian church (Leung 2003b, x-xi). Therefore, my argument is not about metaphysical interfaith dialogues between Christianity and Confucianism but is an attempt to study their compatibility in the context of leadership development.

The personal quest in truth reflected in the life story of Wang Yangming is an illustration of the path of Confucian leadership development. After

---

1. Apart from the above mentioned scholars, the information used in this dissertation based mainly on the *Complete Works of Wang Yangming* (1992)

a life which was a mixture of hardships and political success, he finally achieved peace of mind and was satisfied with what he experienced. Even though no one named Yangming as a sage; he was a good role model as a leader in his times.

Wang Yangming, also named Wang Shouren (王守仁), was born in Yu Yao (餘姚) in Zhejiang. Wang Yangming was born in a family of the government official. He was educated under a traditional education system where he learned Confucianism. The curriculum for the civil examinations was designed by the great Confucian thinker Zhu Xi in the Song dynasty. In the civil examinations of the Song dynasty, students had to read the original texts of the *Four Books* (四書): *Lun Yu* (Analects 論語), *Meng Zi* (Mencius 孟子), *Da Xue* (The Great Learning 大學), *Zhong Yong* (The Doctrine of the Mean 中庸), and commentaries by Zhu Xi.

The civil examinations in the Ming dynasty adopted the same Song dynasty curriculum. Becoming a civil servant was the dream of most people who studied hard. The only way to get admitted to government positions was to pass the civil examination through studying hard the Zhu Xi's commentaries on the *Four Books*. The influences of Zhu Xi on both culture and politics remained strong in the Ming dynasty. In this background, Yangming had no choice but to begin his quest for knowledge from the works of Zhu Xi (Y. Wang 1992, 33.1223). Zhu understood that *li* (理), the principles of the universe, existed in the physical world. Through investigating things by observation and meditation (*ge wu* 格物), one can attain these principles. Yangming tried hard to learn from Zhu's doctrine but without success. Yangming had once practiced this investigation through meditating on bamboos. If Zhu Xi's doctrine of investigation of things was practical, he should have found the principles after spending days and nights in front of the bamboos. However, Yangming described the result:

> [I was] working day and night without reaching the principle, until I also fell ill through mental exhaustion on the seventh day. So, we lamented together that sagehood is unattainable (Chan 1963b, 249; Ching 1976, 29; Y. Wang 1992, 3.120).

Instead of encouraging Yangming to acquire knowledge, the practice of Zhu's investigation of things indeed defeated him. Yangming then turned to find a solution to his quest for truth from other directions.

It was not uncommon for a scholar in traditional China to open himself for experiencing different religious practices. At the early age of eleven, Yangming met a Taoist priest in Bejiing. The Taoist priest gave him a poem written with a typical sense of Taoist fortunetelling (Y. Wang 1992, 33.1221). Later, after the disappointing of his quest from Zhu's investigation of things, Yangming returned to his hometown Yu Yao and founded "Yangming Grotto" in a cave to take up the Taoist practice for pursuing longevity (Tu 1976b, 58; Huang 1987, 104; Y. Wang 1992, 33.1225). As Julia Ching points out, one of the major reasons why Yangming accepted Taoist religious practices was because of his poor health. Nevertheless, Taoist practices could not satisfy Yangming's quest for principles.

In addition to Taoist practices, Yangming related himself with Buddhist monks at the same time. Based on the study of Kusumoto Fumio, Ching points out again that Yangming travelled extensively and visited many Buddhist temples throughout his lifetime. His experiences with the Buddhist monks strongly indicated that Yangming had a keen interest in Buddhism (Ching 1976, 39-41). Yangming had practiced Zen Buddhism himself for some years. From his poems and the dialogues with his students, it is clear that Yangming brought with him the concepts, terminologies, and practices of Zen Buddhism into Neo-Confucianism (Tu 1976b, 66). Even though he had never identified himself as Buddhist, he was misunderstood as a Zen Buddhist and accused of being heretic in bringing Buddhism into Confucianism (Ching 1987, 169).

The path of Yangming's political life was never easy. The adversities in his early years brought him deep reflections on the meaning of life and truth. He was also disappointed in his political career in the beginning. For the intellectuals living in the mid-Ming dynasty should feel upset if they were honest to themselves and wanted to contribute their own intelligence to the nation. Eunuchs dominated the government key positions. They persecuted their opponents as they wished. Wang Yangming fought against the eunuch Liu Jin (劉瑾) and was persecuted and banished to serve in Long Chang (龍場), a poor and remote town in Guizhou in southwestern China

(Huang 1987, 103). In fact, after his frustration and feeling of depression from the political reality, Yangming experienced enlightenment spiritually and intellectually in Long Chang. In his later letter to Wang Chunfu (王純甫), Yangming said,

> It was only with my three-year exile in Kweichow [Guizhou], where I suffered every possible difficulty, that I received some insight, and began to believe that the words of Mencius about "being born in sorrow and calamity" are no deception (Y. Wang 1992, 4.154).[2]

Unlike his predecessors who did not experience political success with their Confucian political beliefs, Wang Yangming received initial success in politics after his exile in Guizhou. When Liu Jin died in 1510, Wang had been appointed to major posts like the vice-minister of the court of imperial stud, the chief minister of the court of state ceremonial in Nanjing, the left assistant censor-in-chief, and the governor of southern Jiangxi between the years 1510 and 1519. After he pacified the bandits in Fujian and Jiangxi areas and defeated the rebellion in southern Anhui, he was promoted to become the provincial governor of Jiangxi in 1519. In 1521, the emperor made him minister of war in Nanjing (Huang 1987, 103-104). Yangming's father died in 1522. He took leave for three years to mourn for his father according to the Confucian tradition. Because some senior government officials were jealous of the military success of Wang Yangming, they prevented him from resuming his post after the three year mourning period.

One of the excuses in forbidding Yangming to resume his duty was that he had formulated the doctrine of "extending the innate knowledge of the good," known as *zhi liang zhi*. Yangming was accused of giving "heterodox teaching" because his way of acquiring principles was different from the orthodox teaching of Zhu Xi's investigation of things (Ching 1976, 33). The reason behind this accusation is the different perspective of his version of Confucianism with Zhu's. This accusation of teaching heretical doctrines lasted even after Yangming's death (Chan 1963b, xxix).

---

2. This translation of Wang Yangming's letter is quoted in Ching (1972, 18).

Later in 1527, Yangming again defeated the rebels in Jiangxi and Guangxi when he resumed his duty in Nanjing. He died in the age of fifty-seven in 1529 from serious illness. Before Wang died, his disciple Zhou Ji (周積) asked him if he had any last words. Yangming replied, "My mind is bright and clear. What more is there to say?" (Y. Wang 1992, 35.1324). Yangming's response reflected his satisfaction in acquiring knowledge and wisdom throughout his life.

Wang Yangming's disciples systematically collected his letters and recorded his conversations with the students into a book called *Instructions for Practical Living*. Yangming did not intentionally develop his philosophy, but diversified schools of thoughts developed after his death.

In addition, the formulation and development of Wang Yangming's philosophy are closely related to his life experiences. His learning experiences of Taoism and Buddhism helped him to incorporate some practices of other aspects of Chinese tradition into Confucian self-cultivation. His negative experience with Zhu Xi's investigation of things forced him to carefully study Mencius' school of classical Confucianism. Yangming followed and further developed the School of Mind beginning from Lu Xiangshan (陸象山 A.D. 1139-1193), the contemporary Confucian philosopher of Zhu Xi. Furthermore, Yangming's experiences in government administration and military office led him to become a master in practicing what he taught. Because of his position and influence, Yangming's school of Confucianism had a lasting effect on political and cultural development in the late Ming and Qing dynasties (A.D. 1636-1912).

The Beginning of Leadership Development: Human Nature

Neo-Confucianism developed in Song and Ming dynasties which was the second golden age after classical Confucianism. Wang Yangming is regarded as the follower of Mencius (372-289 B.C.), a major philosopher in classical Confucianism. Different from the Christian tradition, in which human nature is perceived as fallible, the most distinctive characteristic of Mencius' philosophy is the understanding of human nature as intrinsically good. The concept of *liang zhi* was developed by Wang Yangming, following and expanding on the Mencian understanding of human nature. According to Confucianism, human nature is the source of every possibility of personal growth.

Jen and *Liang Zhi* in Human Nature

Except for the philosophy of Xun Zi (荀子 298-238 B.C.), human nature is generally accepted to be good in the entire tradition of Confucianism. Only Xun Zi proposed an opposite belief that human nature is evil and that education is the way to get rid of evil. Since Xun Zi was not as influential as Mencius, the assumption of human nature as good has been the unchallengeable doctrine of Confucianism since the third century B.C. The most important responsibility the Confucian scholars faced in different generations was how to differentiate and cultivate the good nature of humanity. The term to describe the good essence of human nature is *jen*, which can be translated as benevolence, kindness, or even love (De Bary, Chan, and Watson 1960, 26; Liu 1998, 18). Even though Wang Yangming did not mention *jen* quite often as philosophers mentioned it in classical Confucianism, *jen* is the basic and the most important assumption behind his understanding of human nature.

Jen is assumed to be the very nature of human existence. Confucius never responded directly to questions about the nature and origin of *jen*. Confucius said, "Is benevolence really far away? No sooner do I desire it than it is here" (*Analects* 7.30).[3] *Jen* exists right here and now, the difference is whether he or she wishes to practice *jen*. Confucius' disciple Zi Gong (子貢) said, "One can get to hear about the Master's accomplishments, but one cannot get to hear his views on human nature and the Way of Heaven" (*Analects* 5.13).

Confucius kept silent on human nature and the Mandate of Heaven not because of their unknowability but because Confucius rather emphasized how to live a life of *jen* according to the Mandate of Heaven. "Although Confucius himself never said that human nature is good, he is convinced

---

3. Unless specified, all the translation of *Analects* in English is selected from D.C. Lau (2002).

that there is great potentiality in man" (Liu 1998, 19). Confucius believed *jen* is in our human nature, and everyone should have the potential to live life with *jen*. Confucius therefore focused on advocating the daily practices of *jen*. Actual realization of *jen* is more important than its theoretical assumption.

Mencius was the first Confucian philosopher who directly pointed out human nature is good. According to Mencius, *jen* is inborn in human beings (Liu 1998, 34). Good deeds are the natural outflow of a person's being, and there no need for any extra effort or manipulation of human nature by any form of external force. Mencius gave an example, saying that if anyone comes across a child about to fall into a well, a natural action is to help the child immediately. The action behind is a natural compassion coming from the human nature (*Mencius* 2A.6). In addition, Mencius said, "When left to follow its natural feelings, human nature will do good. This is why I say it is good. If it becomes evil, it is not the fault of man's original capability" (*Mencius* 6A.6).[4] *Jen* is naturally revealed in the form of compassion when people face the suffering of others. Further, evil comes from the environment but not from human nature (Liu 1998, 38). Therefore, education is valuable because it helps cultivate and expand the original nature of the good.

The knowledge of the good in human nature is understood as *liang zhi* in Wang Yangming's terminology. This Chinese term *liang zhi* is difficult to translate into English directly. These Chinese words literally mean "good knowledge," and they usually refer to a person's awareness of the virtue within him- or herself; therefore, they are usually translated as "the innate knowledge of the good." Mencius said, "The ability possessed by men without their having acquired it by learning is innate ability, and the knowledge possessed by them without deliberation is innate knowledge" (*Mencius* 7A.15).[5] Innate knowledge of the good means that there is no need to go through the cognitive process of differentiating between what is good and what is evil. Even a child can behave well without thinking. Education is

---

4. This translation of *Mencius* is selected from Chan Wingtsit's version (De Bary, Chan, and Watson 1960, 90).

5. Translation from Chan Wingtsit (De Bary, Chan, and Watson 1960, 80).

ineffective in leading someone to become a good person if goodness does not exist originally in human nature. Yangming agreed with Mencius that *liang zhi* was inborn in human nature. He pointed out, "There is no human nature that is not good. Therefore there is no innate knowledge that is not good" (Chan 1963a, 683; Y. Wang 1992, 2.62-63). Since Yangming followed the Mencius tradition, the understanding of human nature as a moral self became the dominant presupposition of his philosophy.

Jen exists in a unity with Heaven (*tian* 天). The human practice of *jen* can be understood as the extension of the Mandate of Heaven in human society. Heaven is not a place or a thing, but the origin of everything (Liu 1998, 66). The source and origin of morality therefore comes from Heaven, and it is called the principle of Heaven. Confucius said, "When you have offended against Heaven, there is nowhere you can turn to in your prayers" (*Analects* 3.13). Heaven does not just produce moral standards for humanity, but also cares and is responsive to the human situation. Confucius is so clear in his quest for the truth, whereas perfection is a lonely journey. He said, "If I am understood at all, it is, perhaps, by Heaven" (*Analects* 14.35).

Tang Junyi (唐君毅) has pointed out that in the relationship between Heaven and human society, the highest morality comes from Heaven; therefore Heaven is the ultimate reference of morality (J. Tang 1977, 833-837). The active this-worldly participation advocated by Confucian tradition is due to the belief that Heaven participates in human affairs.

Heaven is the model of a good emperor: "It is Heaven that is great and it was Yao[6] who modeled himself upon it" (*Analects* 8.19). The model of a good leader, including emperor and government officials, is a person with good morality according to Confucianism. Moral perfection is the life goal of every individual; the emperor especially is considered "Heaven's son," a representative of Heaven.

In Wang Yangming's terminology, *liang zhi* refers to Heaven and vice versa (Chan 1983, 340; Y. Wang 1992, 3.111). Yangming identified the innate knowledge of the good as the same substance as Heaven. The

---

6. Emperor Yao (堯) was a model of ideal leadership in ancient China. Traditionally, three kings and five emperors have been regarded as models of ideal leadership. All of them were pre-historic figures.

actualization of the Mandate of Heaven through human moral behavior is a joint action of human beings and Heaven.

Principle and Truth in Human Nature

The origin of human nature is good because human nature is the extension of the ultimate truth in the universe. In Confucian terms, truth is the principle of Heaven. Together with the principle of Heaven, *liang zhi* is assumed to be part of human nature. Principle originated from Heaven; therefore, it also called the principle of Heaven, *tian li* (天理). Developed by the Song dynasty, Neo-Confucianists Cheng Yi (A.D. 1033-1107 程頤) and Zhu Xi, principle is the essence of everything and the truth that exists metaphysically. In Confucian terms, principle is the moral essence of all things (Ching 1976, 57). Principle is therefore the universal truth of morality which exists in the world. The difference between Wang Yangming's and Zhu Xi's philosophies lies in the locus of the universal principle and the means whereby people can find it. Zhu Xi's teaching on the investigation of things believed that principle lies in the physical nature. In contrast, Yangming taught that "mind is principle" (*xin ji li* 心即理). The principle exists in the mind of human nature. Therefore, the quest for principle outside the mind is a movement in the wrong direction.

Wang Yangming's use of the term *mind* included both mind (*xin* 心) and nature (*xing* 性). In Neo-Confucian terms, *mind* and *nature* are usually used together. The Chinese concept of *xin* is not just referring to the heart in the physical body but also to the spiritual consciousness. The translation of *xin* in philosophical terms is usually "mind-heart" or simply "mind." In other respects, *xing* usually refers to the essence, substance, or nature of a person. Thus, *xin* refers to the spiritual dimension while *xing* refers to the physical dimension. Both *xin* and *xing* are inseparable.

However, Yangming followed Mencius' teaching that mind and nature are one. Mencius said, "A person, in giving full realization to his mind-and-heart, knows his nature; and knowing his nature, he knows Heaven" (*Mencius* 7A.1).[7] The mutual relationship between the human mind, nature, and Heaven are so tight that they cannot exist without one another.

---

7. This translation is selected from Daniel K. Gardner (2007, 95).

This oneness can be understood in Yangming's illustration: "Even Heaven and Earth cannot exist without the innate knowledge that is inherent in man. For at bottom Heaven, Earth, the myriad things, and man form one body" (Chan 1963a, 685; Y. Wang 1992, 3.107). The humankind and Heaven exist together and become the organic universe. The unity between the human and the Heaven is the reason why the innate knowledge of the good can be at the same time in the human mind as well as in Heaven. Human beings are able to perform the Mandate of Heaven because they are originally coming from the same source.

To Yangming, principles and mind are a unity. One cannot seek for principles outside his or her mind: "For the principles of things are not external to the mind. If one seeks the principles of things outside the mind, there will not be any to be found" (Chan 1963a, 681; Y. Wang 1992, 2.46). Apart from his personal experience, Wang Yangming illustrated this concept by the example of practicing filial piety. If investigation of things means to find the principle from the thing that contacts with an individual, the principle of filial piety should therefore exist in the parents but not the son or daughter (Chan 1963a, 682; Y. Wang 1992, 2.45). No one can practice filial piety without prior knowledge in his or her mind. According to the assumption that human nature is good, the innate knowledge already indicates what filial piety is. The principle of filial piety therefore should exist prior to the observable action of respecting and honoring the parents.

The decision to be a good person is made by each individual. Hence, the doctrine that "mind is principle" is consistent with Mencius' assumption that human nature is good. When a person naturally follows the guidance of his or her mind, he or she will behave in a morally good way and in turn live a life according to the principles of Heaven (J. Yeung 1996, 57). Moreover, if the mind and human nature are good, where does evil come from? Yangming described evil as something that comes out of human selfishness: "The mind is principle. To have no selfish mind is to be in accord with principle, and not to be in accord with principle is to have a selfish mind. I am afraid it is not good to speak of the mind and principle as separated" (Chan 1963a, p. 677; Y. Wang 1992, 1.26).

Principle is the absolute good. If the mind is separated from principle, selfishness comes into existence, because the mind is at a distance from the absolute good. Human beings cannot control the principle of Heaven but only their mind. The mind is therefore the only possible area that permits the existence of evil. Deviation from principle causes a selfish mind to exist and become evil. Fung Yulan explains selfishness as a human being's personal likes and dislikes, a subjective emotional preference to be good or evil (1983, 618). Fung has changed a moral decision to an emotional decision. Instead, Yangming regarded selfishness as a desire rather than the emotion of human nature.

Yangming understood the evil coming out of the deprivation of the good: "The highest good is the original substance of the mind. When one deviates a little from this original substance, there is evil. It is not that there is a good and there is also an evil to oppose it. Therefore good and evil are one thing" (Chan 1963a, 684; Y. Wang 1992, 2.62-63). Yangming's understanding of the existence of evil carries a sense of the Greek philosopher Plotinus' view of the emanation of the good (Gerson 2008). Plotinus described the process of emanation of the ultimate good that produces evil while Yangming argued the separation from the highest good, evil then comes into exist due to the deviation from the original good. Yangming believed in the co-existence of good and evil. However, the process of developing innate knowledge of the good would rid a person's life of evil.

Wang Yangming was described as an "idealist of the monistic type," because he believed that the mind covers everything of human existence (Henke 1964, xiii). He tried to explain how every aspect of human existence is related to the mind, including the differentiation between good and evil. However, the origin of evil then becomes problematic. If the evil comes from the selfishness of human mind, one cannot put the blame on the environment as a cause of evil. The origin of evil is one of the major disagreements between Christianity and Confucianism concerning human nature. Christianity emphasizes the sinfulness of human nature while Confucianism believes human nature is good. If one follows Wang Yangming's notion of selfishness as the cause of evil, the relation between evil and human nature is connected to some extent. The question is the role of human responsibility in the existence of evil. What Yangming argues for the existence of selfishness is just the human responses to the environment. The practice of controlling or disciplining the mind is a way to get rid of the temptation to selfishness. The development of human nature is directed toward its original status to recover the unity between the mind and the principle of Heaven. The ultimate goal of the journey of human development is to become a sage.

Through knowing that the ultimate source of goodness comes from Heaven and that human nature is closely connected with Heaven, one can achieve moral perfection, at least theoretically. Human nature is not a static substance that exists alone but has a dynamic relationship with the ultimate reality. In terms of leadership development, the human nature of the leader and followers comes from the same source. They interact with the situations where the ultimate reality exists. To become a good leader is therefore possible only through interaction with the situations together with the followers. The interactions are the channels of reestablishing relationship with the source of the good. Through the relationship with Heaven, human beings can achieve unity with Heaven and become morally perfect. This is why the Chinese people believe that moral perfection is possible.

The Goal of Leadership Development: The Sage

The ideal destination of personal growth is to become a sage. A sage is a morally perfect person who can live according to the Mandate of Heaven. A *jun zi* is only a profound person, or a good person with proper behavior. A sage is a person with perfect morality (Tang and Zhang 1999, 109). The Chinese characters for the word *sage* (聖人) literally mean a holy person—a person without any defect. Becoming a sage is therefore the process of full realization of oneself as a human being (Tu 1979, 17). In the eyes of Confucius and Mencius, the possibility of becoming a sage is highly practical. As Mencius said, everyone can be Emperors Yao and Shun (舜) (*Mencius* 7B.2). Yao and Shun are the ancient models representing the three kings and five emperors. Everyone on earth can model him- or herself after Yao and Shun and learn from them how to be a sage.

The characteristics of a sage are clear. When Confucius and Mencius declared the three kings and five emperors as the models of perfect sages, the Confucians implied the expectation of political contributions. In

Confucian understanding, morality has social and political dimensions. The pursuit of personal holiness is only a beginning. *The Great Learning* had already taught the path of a sage: cultivating the self (修身), regulating the family (齊家), administering the state (治國), and pacifying the world (平天下). A sage begins with cultivation of the self and aims toward the target of maintaining the peace of the world. The *Doctrine of the Mean* gives some other indicators of a sage, for example, a model of practicing filial piety to the parents (chapter 17), a religious representative of the people to embrace all the rules of ceremonies and conducts (chapter 27), and a man or woman full of intelligence, insight and wisdom (chapter 30) (Chan 1963a, 102-112). These characteristics show an image of a perfect person with good morality and excellent ability.

Confucianism seems to idealize the image of a leader which is unattainable by ordinary people. In fact, Tu Weiming comments, a sage is "primarily an ethico-religious ideal" but is not unattainable because it is a "standard of inspiration" (Tu 1976b, xii). In other words, the expectation of a sage gives motivation to those who would like to make progress toward personal growth. The possibility of being a sage gives hope to an individual to live as best as he or she can. The process is more important than the result.

Whether or not a leader is a sage is decided by the followers. Ironically, once a person is recognized as a sage, he or she will be protected by the followers from being imperfect. No one is allowed to denounce a sage. For example, a recent Chinese movie *Confucius* has aroused some discussions whether or not the film maker should add the love story between Confucius and Nanzi for the sake of merely increasing the entertainment value (McLeod 2010; Unknown 2010). The majority of the critics feel uncomfortable because they think that the film maker did not respect a sage by adding the element of love story which is not recorded in history. It is also true in Chinese churches that once a pastor becomes a role model, no one can release any information which hurts his or her reputation of him. In another example, when Leung Kalun (2003a) found evidence supporting the Chinese government's accusations of adultery against Watchman Nee (1903-1972), Leung was overwhelmingly criticized after his book was published.[8] Watchman Nee is a model of perfection in contemporary Chinese churches because of his theology and his willingness to suffer. Once a person is regarded as a sage, he or she can no longer be an imperfect person. The impact of followers is clearly evident in this respect.

Wang Yangming gave further justification of Mencius' belief that everyone on earth can become a sage. He taught that the innate knowledge of the good is an attribute naturally born in everyone, implying that everyone can be a morally good person. Responding to a student who asked for the most primitive realization of the innate knowledge of the good, Yangming agreed with Mencius that the sagehood of emperors Yao and Shun began from loving their parents and their brothers and sisters (Chan 1983, 190.271; Y. Wang 1992, 2.85). As the *Great Learning* said, the path of becoming a sage begins with cultivating oneself and maintaining a good relationship with one's family. Family is the very basic form of human relationship and the most obvious realization of the innate knowledge of the good. Wang Yangming believed that practicing filial piety is a necessary beginning in the process of becoming a sage. The ancient sages had already demonstrated the process as role models, therefore, becoming a sage is possible in theory.

Yangming taught that becoming a sage is not about learning some knowledge or skills from the physical world but rather involves looking inwardly to develop the potential sagehood that everyone has. It is the decision of a person whether to be a sage or not. If he or she is willing to become a sage, he or she should begin with inner transformation of his or her own self toward the models presented by the ancient sages (Tu 1976b, 88-89). A person's human nature already contains all the necessary qualities to become a sage. There is no need for the divine or some other external force to help him or her develop the sagehood within. The most crucial question is how to develop *liang zhi* in order to develop into a sage.

---

8. Watchman Nee was the founder of the Little Flock, a contextualized and influential Protestant denomination in China. Nee was attacked by the Chinese government in the 1950s for his religious beliefs and economic situation and was accused of adultery. He died in jail in 1972.

The Process of Leadership Development: Self-Cultivation

Liang zhi as an essential component of human nature makes the cultivation of a sage possible. Leadership development in this sense is equivalent to the development of *liang zhi*. Wang Yangming called the process an extension or full realization of the innate knowledge of the good. As Confucianism is a practical philosophy which ideally applies all theories into practices for the sake of personal and social improvement through moral transformation (C. Y. Cheng 1979, 37), the way to develop a person's *liang zhi* is the "foundation stone" of Yangming's philosophy (Chan 1963b, xxx).

Following the concept of the "investigation of things and extension of knowledge" (*ge wu zhi zhi* 格物致知) in *Great Learning,* the acquisition of the principle is the very first step before the extension of the innate knowledge of the good. In other words, the very first step to develop a sage is to know where the principle is. After knowing the principle, one has to find ways to acquire the principle. It is also important to note that Confucianism believing in self effort to attain sagehood, the nurturing or cultivation of the self is a personal effort only. Confucianism leaves no room for divine intervention in human self development. The divine intervention Christianity believes in is not necessary in Confucianism.

Acquisition of Principle

Both the School of the Mind and the School of Principle agreed on the acquisition of principle as a way to become a sage. The difference between Zhu Xi and Wang Yangming lies in the question of where and how to acquire principle. From Yangming's point of view, Zhu's teaching was purely intellectual and external, which is unrealistic. Yangming held an opposite view that principle is totally moral and internal (Chan 1963a, 655). Furthermore, the followers of Yangming like Huang Zongxi (黃宗羲) (1601-1695), the Confucian scholar in the late Ming and early Qing period, even commented that Zhu's way of acquiring knowledge was superficial, only an abstract quest without substance coming from the power of imagination (Huang 1987, 101). There are debates over Zhu's and Wang's doctrines on investigation of the things. Yangming insisted that principle exists in human nature; therefore the quest for principle outside of human existence is not possible. In the *Inquiry on the Great Learning*, Yangming mentioned that since the highest good is in the mind, to investigate is to rectify the mind (Chan 1963a, 665-667; Y. Wang 1992, 26.971). As the core of Yangming's philosophy, "mind" carries three different meanings: an original good and pure mind, a mind polluted by the selfishness of human, and a restored real mind of a sage (Ching 1976, 57). It is necessary to rectify the polluted mind in order to clear the obstacles to find the principle and become a sage. The restoration of the real mind is therefore the primary target for those who want to be a sage. In contrast to Zhu's external acquisition, Yangming assumed that since the mind and things are one and principles internally resided in the human mind (Chan 1963a, 655-656), the inward quest of principles is therefore the only way of self development.

As a matter of fact, Yangming was closer to Mencius' teachings as they both assumed principle is part of human nature. As Mencius said, "True goodness, righteousness, propriety, and wisdom are not welded on to us from without. We possess them from the very beginning, but we just do not think about it" (*Mencius* 6A.6).[9] When Yangming assumed that principle can be found inwardly in human heart and mind, he followed Mencius' teaching on mind and heart as a place to accommodate the principle from Heaven. The strength of the Yangming School was to keep the spirit on the quest for principles no matter how bad the external situation. Even though one may face a harsh and upsetting political environment as Yangming himself did in his career, nothing can stop one's quest for sagehood because it is entirely an internal activity of the mind. External situations cannot interrupt the quest for truth (Tu 1976b, 121). The process of realization of one's mind and nature can be understood as a process of seeking the heavenly principles. The result of nurturing of the mind is discovering the principles of Heaven in human nature (Chan 1963a, 681; Y. Wang 1992, 2.46).

The philosophy of Yangming has been criticized as too subjective. If one's own mind is being polluted by one's selfishness, how can one rectify one's own mind without external help? How can a polluted mind be restored to the original real mind of a sage? Chan Wingtsit criticizes Yangming's

---

9. This translation of *Mencius* is selected from Daniel K. Gardner (2007, 88).

theory as "entirely subjective and confuses reality with value" (1963a, 655). Chan correctly points out that the mind is a different subject for investigation than things are. If the principles lie in the mind, it is not necessary to be investigated as the principles are already there. Therefore the notion of investigation of things cannot be applied. These comments have left some room for the Christian belief in the necessity of divine intervention in the form of salvation to transform human nature.

The Unity of Knowing and Acting (*Zhi Xing He Yi* 知行合一)

Besides knowing where and how to acquire principle, the other way of developing sagehood is combining knowledge and action. In fact, Yangming termed this concept the unity of knowing and acting. As Confucianism is a culture characterized as pragmatic, the emphasis on the equal importance of knowledge and action is not a surprise. Having ancient wisdom is not enough. Only those who act on it accordingly can make a difference in helping to improve the situation of humanity. For example, as Confucius said, a person who knows 300 poems in the *Odes* but is incapable of performing his or her role as administrator is useless (*Analects* 13.5). Zhu Xi also recognized the "mutual dependence of knowledge and action" (Chan 1963b, xxxiv).

In the terminology of the Neo-Confucians, knowledge refers to moral value. Epistemology was not the concern of Wang Yangming; the concepts of the mind (*xin*), the innate knowledge of the good (*liang zhi*), and action (*xing*) are all related to moral value and its manifestation (J. Yeung 1996, 57). In other words, *knowledge* is nothing cognitive, but is the awareness of inner feeling and spiritual status (Tu 1985, 19). The origin of moral value is the Mandate of Heaven. *Action* refers to the moral action consistent with the moral value. The difference between Wang Yangming and his predecessors is his identification of knowledge and action as one: "My idea that true knowledge is what constitutes action and that unless it is acted on it cannot be called knowledge can be seen in such ideas as those expressed in your letter that one knows the food before he eats it, and so forth" (Chan 1963a, 681; Wang 1992, 2.42).

Yangming taught that true knowledge must come along with true action. It does not mean that knowledge is prior to action, but wherever there is knowledge, there is action. Even though the observable action comes late after the formulation of the idea of good deeds, having the idea is equivalent to the beginning of the action.

The discovery of *liang zhi* reveals only part of the reality of the true knowledge of the good. True knowledge assumes true action. Action and knowledge cannot be separated. According to Liu Zongzhou (劉宗周 A.D. 1578-1645), knowledge is the action which can be realized by extending or manifesting *liang zhi* (Huang 1987, 58). A further explanation was given by Liu's disciple, Huang Zongxi, who mentioned that action is the way to learn to become a sage according to Wang Yangming's teaching methods. In facing his disciples, whether to teach them through careful questioning, cautious reflections, or clear discernment, Yangming's approach is to teach and learn through actions (Huang 1987, 100). A delay of action simply gives a chance for the deviation of true knowledge; therefore the teaching of Yangming requires no defer of practicing what the students had just learned (Tu 1976b, 151).

Although the equal importance of knowledge and action is well noted in Confucianism, Wang Yangming was the first one who identified knowledge and action as one (Chan 1963a, 655). More than simply being identical, knowledge and action can also be regarded as two sides of a single process in acquiring principles (Nivison 1953, 120). In Wang's reply to his disciple Xu Ai (徐愛 A.D. 1487-1518) concerning the unity of knowledge and action, he said,

> Those who are supposed to know but do not act simply do not yet know. When sages and worthies taught people about knowledge and action, it was precisely because they wanted them to restore the original substance, and not simply to do this or that and be satisfied (Chan 1963a, p.669; Y. Wang 1992, 1.2).

The purpose of practicing and realizing what the student has just learned is to restore the original mind. In this respect, a sage is the one who successfully masters his moral knowledge through his or her behavior. Knowledge and action as a unity is not simply a way of acquiring knowledge but a path for individual to become a sage.

The other aspect of the unity of knowing and acting is the Heaven-human unity. A human being is the agent which realizes the Mandate of Heaven. When knowledge refers to the moral value of Heaven, action is therefore its realization in human society. The unity of Heaven and everything else is an important component of Yangming's philosophy (L. Chen 1991, 259-260). The identification of the Heaven and everything in human society is to identify the adversities in the human society (Y. Wang 1992, 2.79). A sage can response to the needs of the society immediately without delay. The expectation of a leader is therefore consistency in his or her knowledge and action. Consistency and honesty are some of the attributes of moral leadership.

Self-Cultivation

Developing *liang zhi* begins with self cultivation. In Confucianism, self is understood as a moral subject. When the Mandate of Heaven is attainable in human nature, the cultivation of the self is the first step in the journey of developing sagehood. Chinese culture is a culture of relationship; however, before building the relationships with others, one has to cultivate his or her moral self individually. Ideally, *jen* and other moral virtues have to be developed individually before one can have the social and political impact on others (Liu 1998, 19). This is the path laid down by the teachings in the *Great Learning*: from self-cultivation to pacification of the world. Self is always the center of relationship in Confucianism (Tu 1985, 53). Through knowing and developing one's true self, one has the ability to impact the community with one's virtues; therefore, realization of one's inner morality is a priority over all social participation (Tu 1976a, 72).

Self-cultivation is by nature a process of self-realization. According to Yangming, the mind is polluted by selfishness. Rediscovering the real self is what everyone needs to do in order to become a sage. The process need not involve a lecturer and a curriculum, because the principle is already there in human nature. It is a process of "objectless awareness" until the rediscovery of a real mind (Tu 1985, 20). Life is a process of rediscovery of one's own real mind. The final destination of the quest of rediscovery is to become truly human.

Furthermore, self cultivation is bound by traditional Confucian ethical values. Difference with Taoism and Buddhism, Wang Yangming insisted there is no need to sacrifice the physical body in self-cultivation. Even though he once practiced Taoist and Buddhist meditation; he knew well self-denial is one way to achieve self-cultivation. Rather, he chose to follow the traditional Confucian virtue on filial piety: because the human body belongs to a person's parents, no one has any reason to sacrifice his or her body for any other cause (Ching 1976, 224). Since self-cultivation is an "ethical and intellectual activity" (Tu 1976b, 114), Confucian values should clearly dominate the process, even though it has no stated curriculum

In fact, whether Confucianism is an organized religion or not, the norms and values work like religious boundaries that limit the perception and activity of daily practices.[10] Ethical values of Confucianism are not simply part of the humanistic culture but also the religiosity of Confucian culture. The rediscovery of the true self in relation to the Mandate of Heaven is transcendent by nature (J. Tang 1988, 335-339; 365-374). The ultimate purpose of self-cultivation is to connect the human self with the transcendent self of Heaven. The manifestation of the result will be the virtues revealed through the sages.

The fundamentally different understanding of human nature between Christianity and Confucian does not restrict the method of cultivation of the human *liang zhi*. Whether becoming a sage is the final destination of personality development or not, a direction is needed for self-cultivation. To some extent, self-cultivation is the same by nature, whether dealing with human sinfulness or selfishness. The major difference between Confucianism and Christianity is the agent of change of self-cultivation. The Christians believe that it is the work of God while the Confucians regard it as merely human effort. However, the basic method is similar: to begin with the discipline of the self.

---

10. A similar situation appears in Western leadership studies in Christian culture. For example, the servant leadership is based on the role model of Jesus of Nazareth, which has been applied to the business sector and has become one of the most popular leadership models even in the non-Christian sectors in Western society.

In short, Confucian leadership begins from self-cultivation—an inward process of seeking the innate knowledge of the good. Through connecting one's moral self with the Mandate of Heaven, one can fully realize the human ideal—sagehood. Everyone is assumed to have leadership potential. A traditional Chinese saying is "in learning there is no first or last, but whoever is enlightened is the champion." The process of leadership development is therefore a process of self-actualization.

A Review of the Characteristics of Confucian Leadership

Seven characteristics of leadership are present in the Confucian theory of human nature represented by Wang Yangming's school of the mind. These characteristics can be applied to the leadership of the contemporary Chinese government and the churches as well.

An Idealized Human Being

Followers in Confucian China expected their leader to be an idealized human being. Such an expectation was not considered unrealistic. As the Mandate of Heaven and the *liang zhi* are one originally, the cultivation and extension of *liang zhi* is the way leading to human perfection. Human behavior can be idealized as human nature gives the possibility of achieving moral perfection. The expectation of a perfect leader seems to contradict the doctrine of fallibility of human nature in Christian tradition. One has to be aware that moral perfection is the human ideal in Confucianism which based on the assumption of human nature. Moral perfection is the ultimate goal and human beings have the potential or possibility of achieving this goal.

The doctrine of "creation in the image of God" is a good complimentary concept to the potential of becoming an idealized leader. Human beings are created in the image of God which gives them the potential to follow and imitate God. If humans did not have such potential, the expectation that they could make progress in improving morality would be unrealistic and unimaginable. The image of God gives the possibility that human beings can be like God. In the Confucian tradition, the Mandate of Heaven gives the possibility of moral perfection as well. If the discussion on Chinese leadership is restricted to the possibility of becoming a morally perfect leader, the Christian-Confucian dialogues about leadership will be more fruitful. A further investigation of leadership potential will be decisive in finding leadership attributes that are mutually agreeable in both Christianity and Chinese cultures.

Moral Leadership

The Confucian expectations for a perfect leader lie in morality. Perfect should not be understood in terms of ability and leadership skills but in terms of the morality of a person. As noted clearly in Confucianism, the focus of discussion is morality. The image of the ancient sages is moral leadership. Behavior and relationships with others are all counted as characteristics of moral leadership. Heaven is regarded as the ultimate standard and reference of morality. A sage is expected to live according to the Heavenly principle, which is morality. Followers can tolerate the leader who is not capable enough but not one who is morally bad. The phenomenon is also very common in Chinese churches: the congregation can accept the church leader with poor management skills but not one with bad behavior. Moral standards are therefore the core value in leadership expectation in Chinese culture.

Modeling

A sage is the example for the followers to imitate. The ancient three kings and five emperors were not only references for the idealized leaders, but were also the role models for the leaders in all generations to follow. A sage is an idealized image of leader. An idealized leader in the Chinese sense is not without defects or weaknesses, but is morally persuasive so that he or she can be a role model for followers to imitate. The existence of an exemplary leader is a way of learning through modeling. Modeling is therefore the most popular method for developing leaders in Chinese culture. Followers expect a person who is better in morality performance than other leadership attributes because they perceive a leader as their role model. As a consequence, followers may have a projection of an idealized leader, though not necessary one who is literally perfect without weaknesses.

Extension of a Family

The beginning stage of becoming a sage takes place in a family. The Mandate of Heaven had revealed to the kings and emperors, therefore, they were the Heaven's sons. The kings and emperors were the fathers of the nation. The nation is an extension of a family. A similar concept can be found in Israelite history: the image of Abraham is at the same time that of a family father and a leader of the whole nation. A sage performs the role of the father to care for and develop the subject people as younger family members. A church or an organization is an extension of a family. The power structure and the relationships follow the patterns in a family as well. When the Christian community promotes brotherly love among one another, family relationships are obviously the most familiar analogy in human experience. A leader is therefore required to have excellent inter-personal skills in order to maintain harmonious relationships and motivate the congregation.

Paternalistic Leadership

Paternalistic leadership is a logical consequence when the leader of an organization carries an image as a parent in a family. A leader who practices paternalistic leadership gives personal care and concern to the followers and identifies their relationship according to their family and social backgrounds. The followers give total loyalty and obedience to their leader as if he or she were their parent. A mature leader with good reputation is expected to be the "parent" of this community. The traditional concept of "Heaven's son" may not exist literally, but the expectation that the church leader has better knowledge about God than the congregation prevails in the Chinese churches. A church leader is expected to know more about God and have a closer relationship with God than the followers do. God thus replaces Heaven. On some occasions, the church members may replace God with their leader who has the image of the parent.

Inner Life Quality

In relation to leadership expectations and moral leadership, the focus of leadership development is to develop one's inner life. Inner life includes at least the morality and spirituality of a person. The goal is to seek for maturity in moral and spiritual life. The human self is assumed to have the quality of the Mandate of Heaven. Morality is a revelation of the Mandate of Heaven. The purpose of the cultivation of the self is therefore to expand and develop the qualities already existing in human inner life. As a result, inner life development does not expect something foreign to enter into the self but recovers the true and original unpolluted self. Hence, leadership development should be an education which cultivates the moral self instead of giving only knowledge and skills about management.

Pragmatic Culture

The emphasis on the unity on knowing and acting denotes pragmatism as a main feature of Wang Yangming's philosophy. Obviously, as the pragmatism found in politics and society in China today shows, Chinese culture is influenced by Wang Yangming. "Now having listened to a man's words I go on to observe his deeds" (*The Analects* 5.10) is a saying of Confucius which tells of the consistency of works and deeds in actual life. A similar situation is found in the Chinese churches. A church leader is expected to be consistent in what he or she has said and lived. Theory is not unimportant, but a practical theory is much more valuable than merely doctrines.

A Summary

After this review of the characteristics of Confucian leadership, it is clear that many of these characteristics can also be found in the relational leadership models in biblical and contemporary Western theoretical perspectives. The expectations of the leader and the methods of leadership development are highly relationship-oriented instead of task-oriented in Chinese culture.

The God-human relationship is the beginning of Christian relational leadership. The inner life qualities are more important than the leadership skills as the spirituality and morality of a leader determine his or her leadership effectiveness. In Confucianism, The source of inner life qualities is Heaven. Even though the Confucian believes that the innate knowledge of the good resides in the human mind-heart, the connection with something external to the human self also exists. In this respect, Christianity and Confucianism share something in common in the development of a leader through the cultivation of the moral self.

Beginning with the moral expectation of the leader, both the Christian and Confucian cultures emphasize modeling as an effective way to develop followers. Jesus of Nazareth demonstrated the role model method himself and asked his followers to imitate him. In Confucian China, people looked for some models like the three kings and five emperors. People expected the leaders to behave like the sages in the past. Thus, similar leadership expectations exist in both traditions.

Some other elements in the Western relational leadership models may not present as obvious as the morality, modeling, and inner life qualities. As long as they do not contradict one another, those characteristics can be regarded as distinctive features of relational leadership in different cultures. It is important to note that this dissertation is not searching for an identical theory of leadership in Christianity and Confucianism, but rather borrows some applicable components from the West and at the same time discovering some compatible elements in the east. The purpose is to develop an indigenous Chinese approach in developing leaders.

Part II: Chinese Theological Roots of Relational Leadership

CHAPTER 4

Situational Factors Influencing the Understandings and Expectations of Leaders and Leadership in China

In part I of this dissertation I have reviewed the understanding and expectations of leader in three different perspectives, namely biblical, Western, and Confucian traditions. The perceptions and values of relationship are different indifferent cultures, however some common elements of relational leadership are found in different cultural perspectives. When one puts Chinese culture under a magnifying glass, one can see some historical and cultural factors that have shaped the distinctive characteristics of traditional leadership development. In the twentieth century, China was characterized by political, economic, and social chaos. The Christian church, however, became significantly transformed during this century into an indigenous church. Chinese theology and church leaders were developed. How these significant historical situations shaped the theology and practices of leadership development in China is an important theme of leadership studies. The external situation was complicated in early twentieth century China. How did the external situations—the Chinese culture, political, and social environment—affect the development of the first generation of indigenous church leaders? A study of the historical background in China may help to answer this question.

Situational theory is a thoroughly discussed topic in Western leadership theory. No study has been done on the situational impact on Chinese church leaders in the past. Lee Maucheng (1989) is the only scholar attempting to apply J. Robert Clinton's *Leadership Emergence Theory* (LET)

(1989) on the study of the development of the Chinese church leaders. Clinton points out that a spiritual leader is equipped by the situation in which he is engaged, including the interactions with the people, historical and current events, and the opportunities in his or her life journey. Situations surrounding the leader are not coincidental but occur within the will of God. Clinton lists six important stages for personal growth of a leader, namely: sovereign foundation, inner-life growth, ministry maturity, life maturing, convergence, and afterglow (1989, 314-317). Through these stages, one can understand the work of God in the life of a leader.

Lee Maucheng, a student of Clinton, has studied the life histories of John Song[1] (宋尚節, 1901-1944), Yang Shaotang (楊紹唐, 1898-1966), Watchman Nee (倪柝聲, 1903-1972), and Wang Mingdao (王明道, 1900-1991) and has compared them according to the stages developed by Clinton. Lee tries to make use of Clinton's LET to help understand the leadership development patterns in early twentieth century; however, Lee fails to see that the interpreter's own situation also limits the analysis of leadership development. Lee has changed the last stage of LET from "afterglow" to "disappearing" in the discussion of Yang Shaotang's later years (Lee 1989, 111).

Like many of the overseas Chinese Christians in the 1980s, Lee believes that Yang's participation in TSPM in his later years was a failure. Since "afterglow" usually refers to a positive ending of a person's life, Lee prefers to say Yang's ministry was "disappearing" because of Lee's negative sentiment toward TSPM in the 1980s. In light of the current adoption of Yang's teachings in both TSPM and house churches in mainland China, it is clear that Yang's afterglow began after his death. Because of the complexity of the religious and socio-political situations in between 1900 and 1960, a simple description of stages may not be clear enough to express the situational impacts upon the leaders. This chapter is an attempt to analyze the events and their impacts on the church leaders in China from 1900 to 1960.

Five significant situational impacts shaped the theology and practices of the contemporary Chinese church leaders. They are the Western missions

---

1. The name "John Song" is also known as "John Sung" in the Wade-Giles romanization.

and revival movements, fundamentalism, the anti-Christian movement, the indigenization movement, and the Three-Self Patriotic Movement.

Impacts of Western Missions and Revival Movements

The first half of the twentieth century can be characterized as a period which saw a transition in Chinese church leadership from the Western missionaries to the local Chinese church leaders. At the Centenary Missionary Conference in 1907, the only ones in attendance were Westerners. Even after 100 years of Protestantism in China, no Chinese representatives were present (The Special Committee on Survey and Occupation China Continuation Committee 2007, 128). The local Chinese church workers were regarded as merely the assistants to missionaries (Q. Tang 2001, 657). Tang Qing even criticizes the slow church growth as a product of the Western style of Christianity. As a result, Christianity was labeled as foreign religion in the eyes of the Chinese because the church was financially controlled by Western missions and the organizational structure was foreign to the Chinese people. In the beginning of twentieth century, Chinese Christians were being criticized as "fed by the foreign religion." Chinese pastors were the "lackeys" of foreigners. Leadership was still in the hands of the Western missionaries. It was hard to find the signs of an indigenized, self-governing, or self-sustaining church (Q. Tang 2001, 644-646, 657-660).

As the twentieth century dawned, both the independence and indigenization of the Chinese church had progressed significantly. Some Chinese pastors became influential leaders. Even though they were being trained by Western missionaries, they were able to influence the decision-making of the mission.

One such pastor was Jia Yuming (賈玉銘, 1880-1964), who was born in Shandong in 1880. After becoming a Christian, he enrolled into Tengchow College (文會館), founded by Presbyterian missionary Calvin W. Mateer (1836-1908). Together with his good friend Ding Limei (丁立美, 1871-1936), a well known evangelist, Jia dedicated his life to serving God. Jia continued his theological education in the equivalent of a contemporary

Master of Divinity program in the Reformed tradition. Jia became a church pastor at the age of twenty four in Shandong (Cliff 1998, 63; Xie 2008, 45-48; Yu 2006, 378-380). Unlike Jia Yuming, Yang Shaotang was born into a Christian family in Shanxi. His family was one of the earliest Christian families after his parents converted to Christianity through the work of the CIM missionaries. Influenced by his father, a humble servant, Yang committed himself to serving God as a full-time volunteer without salary (Yang 1941, 141-142). Yang met his other mentor when he attended the high school founded by CIM missionaries in Hong Tong, Shanxi. The principal, Rowland Hogben, disciplined his students to follow the footsteps of Christ, teaching Yang proper attitudes in learning, personal growth, and behavior (Lee 1989, 113). Upon determining to become a full-time minister, Yang decided to attend the Presbyterian North China Theological Seminary in Shandong. By that time, Jia Yuming was teaching in this seminary (Yu 2006, 121-122).

Both Jia and Yang benefited from the help of Western missionaries. They did not choose to refuse to work together with the missionaries as Wang Mingdao did. Jia Yuming had been working together with the Western missionaries as a seminary teacher; for example, he had been the professor and principal of Jining Women's Theological Seminary in Nanjing, as well as vice-principal of North China Theological Seminary in Shandong. Yang Shaotang cooperated with CIM missionary Elizabeth Fischbacher in Shanxi after graduating from seminary. After he established the Spiritual Action Team—an organization that encouraged the church workers to live, learn, and work together—Yang accepted the request of David Adeney from CIM to work together with him in youth ministry (Lyall 2003, 88).

To Western missionaries, working together with the local Chinese pastors was a more effective strategy for serving China than simply working alone by the Westerners. On the one hand, it was safer to face the increasing national sentiment against foreigners when working along with local people. On the other hand, as Kenneth S. Latourette points out, the missionaries believed that the turn of the century was a good chance for evangelizing China. They believed that Confucianism and Buddhism were fading away from the religious beliefs of the Chinese people. The beginning of the twentieth century was the time for Christianity to fill the religious vacuum even though the door of China was being forced to open by the West (Latourette 1969, 377).

The general attitude of most Chinese people toward the Western missionaries was not friendly in the 1920s. The Westerners were regarded as imperialists. Some of the seminaries run by the Western missions were labeled as bringing liberal traditions to Chinese churches. Not many pastors received Western theological education that was accepted by the fundamentalists. Jia Yuming and Yang Shaotang were the exceptions. Yang's close relationship with CIM did not affect his prestige among his Chinese coworkers. Both Jia and Yang could assimilate what they learned from the West and apply it to the Chinese context.

The transition of power and leadership from the Western missionaries to the local Chinese pastors made an impressive impact. On one hand, the missionaries were willing to give up their administrative power; at the same time, the Chinese pastors were ready to become the leaders. In the 1920s, revival movements swept across China. These waves of revival carried some similar features to the Pentecost events described in the book of Acts. Many people became Christians and many pastors and missionaries repented in the revival meetings. Many young men and women dedicated themselves to serve the Lord. Among these revival movements, the Shangdong Revival (1927-1937) is the most important (Culpepper 1968; Leung 1999a, 5-7). The work of Holy Spirit is one of the clear signs of these revival movements; thus, some missionaries and pastors like Wang Mingdao began to emphasize teachings on the Holy Spirit. Jia and Yang visited Shangdong to investigate the charismatic characteristics of the revival movements. They responded by increasing the emphasis on prayer and the indwelling of the Holy Spirit in their training of church workers. The emphasis on spirituality can be regarded as a significant impact of the Shangdong Revival in their ministry (Yu 2006, 123).

Many local church leaders emerged during these waves of revival in China. Before the twentieth century, no church leader was well known throughout China. After the 1920s, a number of pastors were named as "revival evangelists," namely, Ding Limei, Yu Cidu (余慈度), Jia Yuming, Chen Chonggui (陳崇桂), Zhu Guishen (竺規身), Yang Shaotang, Wang Zai (王載), John Song, Ji Zhiwen (計志文), Zhao Junying (趙君影),

Zhao Shiguang (趙世光), Zhang Xuegong (張學恭), Shei Xinwo (石新我), Li Jian (李既岸), Jian Weizhen (焦唯真), Lin Jingkang (林景康), Nie Ziying (聶子英), Zhou Zhiyu (周志禹), and Cheng Jigui (成寄歸) (Leung 1999a, 11-12; Yu 2006, 251-355).

Most of these individuals were under forty years old and without formal theological education. They did not belong to any denomination or foreign mission organization. They travelled to different provinces, preaching in revival meetings. As Daniel H. Bays points out, the Chinese churches had a certain degree of strength and resources to face the challenges brought by these waves of spiritual revival (1993, 164). Many of these young male and female evangelists were the products of the revival meetings and in turn became the preachers in the next wave of revival movements. Their messages were mostly about repentance. Some of them replaced the leadership of the foreign missionaries because of their increasing influence. Furthermore, except for John Song, most of the young evangelists had a high school education. Although most of them were educated in Christian schools and were born into pastors' families, they denied the value of formal learning and instead upheld the direct teaching from the Holy Spirit (Leung 1999a, 17-18; J. Zhao 1981, 7-8).

Jia and Yang became popular preachers during these revival movements. They were the first generation of revival evangelists in China. Unlike other revival evangelists, they received formal theological education, emphasizing more of the biblical truth instead of simply proclaiming the messages of repentance. They stressed the importance of redemption and life change. Inner life reconstruction was a common focus within their theologies in relation to leadership development.

Impacts of Fundamentalism

If determined by the number of followers, fundamentalism should be considered the dominant theological point of view in the church in China. Biblical inerrancy, salvation through Jesus Christ alone, and evangelism as the only major ministry of the church are all the characteristics of fundamentalism in China. The term "fundamentalist" was not commonly used in China in the early twentieth century. Usually, the terms "spiritualists" or "conservatives" were used to represent fundamentalists in contrast to the "modernists" or "non-believers" (Bays 1995, 127; Ying 2001, 31-33). The fundamentalist church leaders believed that the nurturing of the inner life was the most important ministry. This so-called inner life was the foundation for spiritual growth, which defined the maturity of a Christian. In contrast, the "modernists" were labeled as unfaithful to the biblical truth. The "modernists" gave up their principles in order to compromise with the political authorities. The split between the two camps became obvious in the early twentieth century.

In addition to the differences in some theological and political issues, the methods of developing leaders were distinctly different. As Ying Fuktsang points out,

> In general, the seminaries run by Christian universities were all affected by open, tolerant, liberal and critical spirits of the institutions. The universities emphasized the direction of academic research. These practices challenged the traditional doctrines of the church and were difficult to meet the needs of pastoral training (Ying 2001, 29).

Confronted by this situation, both the Chinese and some Western church leaders from the fundamentalist background preferred to leave those Christian universities and run an independent seminary. The American Presbyterian missionaries disagreed with the direction of the seminary inside Qilu University. They then decided to start the new North China Seminary (Ying 2001, 29). For a similar reason, Jia Yuming started the Spiritual Institute and Yang Shaotang started the Spiritual Action Team. Jia and Yang preferred to train church workers by themselves instead of relying on a seminary. Others like Wang Mingdao, Watchman Nee, and John Song shared a similar attitude and criticized the modernists through preaching and publications.

In Jia Yuming's Spiritual Institute for example, living the life of faith was one of the fundamental beliefs in developing church leaders. Jia welcomed all those who decided to become full-time ministers and those who were already working in the church as pastors to enroll as students (Cha 1983, 114-115). Instead of theological knowledge, spiritual life was the most important element in this institution. Although the Spiritual Institute did not emphasize characteristics of the charismatic movement like speaking in tongues, an anti-intellectual tendency was quite evident (Ying 2001, 30). Yang Shaotang based his model of the church on the description in the book of Acts. Yang believed that anything not mentioned in the Bible should be abandoned. He objected to the employment procedure for a pastor in the church simply because the Bible did not mention this procedure (Yang 1939, 79-80). In short, the fundamentalist doctrines affected the expectations and the ways of developing church leaders.

Impacts of the Anti-Christian Movement

The anti-Christian movement in the 1920s was one of the most influential events that changed the development of Christianity in China. In the same decade as the revival movements, students and intellectuals outside the Christian community launched fierce attacks on Christianity as a representation of the penetration of Western culture. The emerging church leaders had to answer the question: in what ways can Chinese Christians transform a Western religion into a Chinese religion?

The anti-Christian movement did not simply have a religious focus but was also motivated by cultural and political agendas. The signpost was the establishment of the Anti-Christian Student Federation (ACSF) in response to the meeting of the World Student Christian Federation in Qing Hua University in Beijing in 1922. ACSF claimed themselves to be the successors of the May Fourth Spirit, calling for scientific, rational analysis and rejecting irrational superstitious beliefs. As part of the rising nationalism, the ACSF targeted the missionary activities connected to the Western powers. Apart from superstitious belief, the ACSF opposed Christianity as a tool of imperialism. The motivation behind the mission work was to invade China politically, culturally, and economically through religion. In addition, the ACSF accused Christianity of controlling and manipulating the Chinese educational system as there were many Christian-run universities and different kinds of schools throughout China (Y. Leung 2006, 228). Between 1922 and 1928, anti-Christian sentiments had spread through the major cities in China. By this time, the ACSF had successfully attracted support from different sectors of society. According to a document released by the Communist Party of China (CPC), the CPC and the Nationalist Party were helping to mobilize and promote the ACSF (The Party History Research Centre of Beijing 1989, 26; Tao 2006, 88-90; Yeh 1987, 46). As a result, more than 5,000 Western missionaries left China in the 1920s. In July 1927, of the 3,000 Western missionaries who stayed behind in China, only 500 were still working in the inland areas. All other missionaries had escaped to the major cities and lived under the protection of their home countries (Latourette 1973, 820).

The church was no doubt affected by such a widespread and influential social movement. Church leaders from liberal traditions involved themselves in the discussions on cultural indigenization of Christianity. Fundamentalist church leaders worked wholeheartedly on developing Chinese-style church structures and ministry. The emerging young church leaders in the 1920s were inevitably affected by the concerns about indigenization in the Christian churches.

Many reasons behind the far-reaching anti-Christian movement were observed. On the one hand, Christianity was believed to be a tool of Western political and cultural invasion. Some Western missionaries worked closely with their governments and wanted to "Westernize" China. In the eyes of the Chinese intellectuals, Christian evangelism was only an excuse for cultural and economic invasion. Education controlled by the Christian churches was clear evidence of cultural invasion. After 1949, the Communist government adopted this viewpoint in its religious policy against Western missionary activity in the PRC (Cohen 1965, 40).

On the other hand, conflicts between Christianity and Chinese cultures were evident. Jessie G. Lutz traces back the missionary movement in the nineteenth and twentieth century and concludes missionaries as a cultural product from the West (1965, vii-viii). When the Western missionaries came to China, they brought their cultural practices along with the gospel. Institutionalized religion was one of the major components of the culture of their home countries. Some clashes between the two cultures were therefore understandable. Missionary activities did not aim only to convert people's religious beliefs but also to persuade the converts to accept Western culture. In the eyes of many Chinese people, Christianity and imperialism are inseparable.[2] The indigenization of Christianity in China was consequently the same issue as bringing conformity to Christianity and Chinese culture. The major issue was how to live and present Christianity in a Chinese style. As Wang Zhixin comments,

> In 170 years, [Christianity] has not planted its roots in Chinese culture. We are still using the legacies of the West—customs, culture, and ideology—and are even trying hard to cultivate them. As a result, we have no capacity for developing Chinese culture. Christianity and Chinese culture have therefore become an estranged couple (Z. Wang 1925, 12).

This statement by Wang represents the voices of many church leaders in the early twentieth century. Scholars like Cheng Jingyi (誠靜怡), Zhao Zichen (趙紫宸), Wu Leichuan (吳雷川), and Xie Fuya (謝扶雅) began to explore the issue of the indigenization of Christianity in China. They published books and led discussions of different models for integrating Christianity and Chinese culture (Yao and Luo 2000, 183). As Chao Tianen (趙天恩) (1988) comments, those models truly reflect the scholars' rich knowledge of Chinese culture, but they also show that the scholars did not really understand Christian theology. As a result, the models are not satisfactory. Moreover, these people were the first generation of Chinese Christian scholars to attempt to find a bridge between Christianity and Chinese culture. Their efforts were indeed the forerunners of the indigenization of Chinese churches.

Apart from the discussion about cultural theories, the most important part of the indigenization effort was the practical application in the

---

2. The connection between Christianity and imperialism is the foundational attitude of the Chinese government toward foreign Christian activities in China. The TSPM had accused the missionary activities as the tools of imperialism from the beginning of the PRC until the last decade. For details, refer to *Tien Feng* in the 1950s (Editor 1950, 2; 1950, 3) and Luo Guanzhon's *Learning from the History of the Past* (2003).

churches. In response to the need for independence from the Western missions, the slogan of "self-governance, self-propagation, and self-support" was very attractive. This "three-self" concept was an important step in beginning the process of indigenization. "Self-governance" and "self-propagation" were related to the development of local church leaders. Apart from inadequacies in the quantity and quality of local leaders, the problem of "self-support" was an even harder problem. In 1922, two-thirds of the church expenses were covered by the financial support of Western missionary organizations. These financial problems could not be overcome in a short period of time (Yip 1980, 18).

In the very same decade as the anti-Christian movement, a group of young church leaders emerged. Among them were Yang Shaotang (twenty-seven years old), Wang Mingdao (twenty-five years old), Watchman Nee (twenty-two years old), and John Song (twenty-five years old). According to Yu Leekung,[3] the mid-1920s was a dividing line for the emerging young leaders; those evangelists who were "young, able, and had the power from the Holy Spirit." The churches were revived under their ministries. With the increase in the number of Christians, income from donations increased at the same time to fulfill the need for "self-support" (Yu 2006, 124). Significantly, Yu does not mention any need of the missionary enterprises when he discusses the financial capabilities of the local church, including coverage for educational expenses and medical services. To some extent, providing salaries for local pastors and funding evangelistic activities can be considered as a late but good beginning for a church with a hundred-year history. With the rise of those young leaders, the future of the church was optimistic, even in the face of the challenges of the anti-Christian movement.

Thus, church leaders like Wang Mingdao, Jia Yuming, and Yang Shaotang were eager to develop indigenous churches without the help of Western missionaries. These leaders understood to teach and preach in a Chinese way were essential in developing an indigenous church. The metaphysical discussions about Christianity and Chinese culture were not their

---

3. Yu Leekung's (于力工, 1920-2010) family was the neighbor of Jia Yuming's family in Shandong for a few generations. Yu provides some valuable first-hand observations and analyses of the development of Christianity in China in the early twentieth century.

concerns. When the ACSF challenged Christianity as a form of foreign invasion, Jia was the vice-principal of a seminary while Yang had just graduated from seminary; both of them must have been aware of the need for an indigenous church. Later, they responded by leaving the missionary-run organization and founding their own training institute.

Impacts of the Indigenization Movement

The product of the anti-Christian movement was the speeding up of the indigenization of the Chinese churches. Indigenization refers not only to the inter-cultural dialogues between Christianity and Chinese philosophies, but also the transformation of church ministry from Western to Chinese styles. Jia Yuming and Yang Shaotang grew and worked in the early twentieth century. The establishment of the Spiritual Institute and the Spiritual Action Team can be regarded as a response to the challenge brought by the anti-Christian movement. With the increasing number of local young church leaders, more indigenous local churches were developed.

The number of baptized Christians doubled in thirty years, from 178,251 in 1906 to 567,390 in 1936 (Latourette 1969, 378-379; Q. Tang 2001, 646). Apart from the Western denominations and missions, the local churches were growing very fast. Some Chinese pastors, such as Jia and Yang, were willing to cooperate with the Western missionaries. Some others like the Jesus Family founded by Jing Dianying (敬奠瀛, 1890-1957), the Church Assembly Hall (CAH) or Little Flock founded by Watchman Nee, and the Christian Tabernacle founded by Wang Mingdao were more than willing to separate themselves from any connection with Western co-workers. These three groups were the most popular indigenous churches developed in the 1920s.

Jian Dianying founded the Jesus Family in Shangdong in 1921. As the Jesus Family was a charismatic religious sect, its members lived together and surrendered their property, modeling themselves after the description of the early church in the book of Acts. Everyone in the church lived as if belonging to the same family. The Jesus Family spread all around China and established 127 "families" before 1949 (Bays 1996, 312; Yao and Luo

2000, 195-197; Yu 2006, 386-391). Wang Mingdao's Christian Tabernacle was the most famous indigenous church in China. The church had no connection with any denomination or missionaries; however, Wang was willing to partner with other churches. He was invited to speak in different provinces in China. The CAH was deeply affected by the Plymouth Brethren.[4] Watchman Nee founded the CAH in 1922 in Fuzhou and expanded into the major cities in Eastern China. Impacted by the doctrines and practices of the Brethren, Nee rejected the existence of denominations (Yu 2006, 65-72).[5]

Until the 1940s, the membership of these newly developed local churches made up 20-25 percent of the entire Christian population in China. The growth rate of church members was much faster than in those churches with Western denominational backgrounds (Bays 1995, 126). The church administration was run by local church leaders without foreign financial support: the leaders realized the "three-self" principle in developing indigenous churches.

Local church leaders developed local church ministries. After the onset of the twentieth century, local Chinese churches began to support theological education and evangelistic events by themselves without needing support from the West. Jia Yuming was a seminary teacher under the support of the American Presbyterian Church for twelve years. Jia eventually became the vice-president of the North China Theological Seminary of the same denomination. He later left the North China Theological Seminary and became the president of Nanjing Women's Theological Seminary, which was a joint ministry of the American Presbyterian Church and Methodist Episcopal Church.

---

4. In his testimony, Watchman Nee, the founder of the CAH in 1936, declared that his theological formation was deeply influenced by Margret E. Barber (1866-1929), a British missionary who introduced Nee to the theology of the Plymouth Brethren (Weigh 1974, 9-10). The works of J.N. Darby (1800-1882) were especially important to the development of Nee's theology (Nee 1967, 59-61; Lam 2003, 21-23).

5. The structure and organization of the CAH are similar to the patterns of the Plymouth Brethren; for example, the church had no paid staff, no ordained clergy, and a weekly bread-breaking meeting. In addition, visiting Brethren from the UK to China in the 1930s had recognized the impact of Darby on Nee through the sermons and practices of the CAH (Kinnear 1973, 110-119).

The reason Jia left North China Theological Seminary, according to Daniel H. Bays, was that he wanted to have more freedom to develop his conservative theology through his publications (Bays 1996, 314-315). However, Yu Leekong points out that Jia had a conflict with the president of North China Theological Seminary, Watson M. Hayes, on the issue of millennium: Jia maintained a "premillennialist" point of view, while Hayes insisted on "amillennialism." They were not able to compromise with each other and finally decided not to work together (Yu 2006, 379). Such cases were rare in the first hundred years of Christianity in China when almost all the financial resources were managed by the Western missions. With the rise of more local Chinese church leaders, more independent churches and ministries were developed.

Another area of indigenous church development was leadership training and theological education. Between 1907 and 1920, the number of ordained Chinese pastors in all denominations had increased 200 percent (The Special Committee on Survey and Occupation China Continuation Committee 1985, 90). As a matter of fact, the people trained by the Western mission organizations did not necessarily benefit the Chinese churches directly. According to the survey of the China Continuation Committee in 1922, the number of Chinese church leaders increased sharply. No Chinese representative attended the China Centenary Missionary Conference in 1907, but the ratio of the representatives of the Western missionaries and Chinese delegates was the same in 1922. The Committee wanted to argue that indigenization was flourishing in the Chinese churches; nevertheless, the increased number of representatives consisted of mostly workers in Christian organizations but not church pastors. The huge Christian missionary enterprises in the areas of education and medical services required many local people to help keep the ministries running. Other reports show a growth rate of 492 percent in the number of local workers only in the medical services but not in church related ministries (The Special Committee on Survey and Occupation China Continuation Committee 2007, 128-130).

Based on information released in the 1920s, a group of emerging young church leaders appeared after the church revival movements. The missionary enterprises had also provided opportunities for lay Christians to take part in ministry. While the church leaders enjoyed and praised the revivals in the local churches, at the same time they failed to see the future needs of the church and prepare enough pastors through leadership development (J. Zhao 1981, 14-15). Worse still, the huge Christian enterprises absorbed the most talented Christians. One can imagine that the church leaders had to take care of the increasing numbers of organizations, including hospitals, clinics, schools, and publishing houses. The resource allocated to the development of the church leaders was therefore diverted. According to Latourette, the "influence of Christianity was proportionately much greater than its numerical strength" as the Christian population was less than 1 percent of the total Chinese population in early twentieth century China (1969, 410).[6] In this respect, the Western mission organizations were ineffective in developing local church leaders.

In the 1920s, some Chinese indigenous training institutes were established. The local church leaders discovered the importance of developing Chinese church leaders in a uniquely Chinese way. Watchman Nee was one of the local leaders that did not encourage his followers to receive theological education other than their own training centers. The CAH organized its own training program for church leaders. Jia Yuming's Spiritual Institute and Yang Shaotang's Spiritual Action Team were all aiming at equipping church leaders by their own methods. Different from those seminaries emphasizing academic research or knowledge-based learning, the Chinese institutes were focused on practical training. In addition to the institutions Nee, Jia, and Yang founded, the Jiandao Bible School and Hunan Bible School were all conservative Chinese church leaders which emphasized practical training instead of academic research (Ying 2001, 29). Many church leaders turned to focus on developing the inner spiritual life instead of cognitive knowledge of the Bible. The slogan "to rationalize the spirit, to spiritualize the rationality," which was used in Jia Yuming's Spiritual Institute, represents the distinctive characteristic of this school (Yu 2006, 348-385). According to

---

6. The editors of the survey commented that the numerical strength on the growing rate of Christian enterprises had exceeded the affordability of the Christian churches in terms of the low percentage of the Christians in the whole Chinese population. Local donations accounted for only 24 percent of the total budget of all Christian ministries (The Special Committee on Survey and Occupation China Continuation Committee 1985, 94-95).

one of Jia's students, the purpose of establishing the Spiritual Institute was to equip church workers with basic theological truths that did not belong to any denomination (Y. Chen 1989, 122). In contrast, Yang Shaotang emphasized working and learning at the same time. The choice of the name Spiritual Action Team already signified practical training as its major feature. During the Sino-Japanese War in the 1930s, Yang was invited to speak to university students in North China. Many young Christians dedicated themselves to become full-time ministers in the church (Yu 2006, 279). The influences of these local church leaders extended to different parts of China. With an increasing number of trained workers in the churches, the number of churches and Christians increased rapidly.

Impacts of the Three-Self Patriotic Movement

One of the great transitions periods of the Chinese churches in mainland China was the coming of the Communist government. The impact of the CPC did not begin in 1949, but two decades earlier in the anti-Christian movement. In the 1940s the CPC supported the founding of the Chinese Christian Three-Self Patriotic Movement and began to persuade church leaders to support Communist China. Whether or not to join the TSPM was a critical political and religious issue facing church leaders in the 1940s and 50s.

The factors the church leaders had to take into consideration were complicated. Even though the Communist government had guaranteed religious freedom, the church leaders were still hesitant to trust an atheistic government. In the eyes of some fundamentalist church leaders like Wang Mingdao, the Communist government and the TSPM had no relation to the church: the spiritual community belonged to God. The government officials were non-believers and therefore there was no need to connect with them structurally. In contrast, Jia Yuming and Yang Shaotang decided to join the TSPM, and they came to symbolize the recognition of the TSPM by the fundamentalists. House church leaders later commented that Jia and Yang were wrong in joining TSPM. The decision to join showed the weaknesses of Jia and Yang in compromising with the Communists (Zhuo 2008, 2008a).

Nonetheless, Jia and Yang brought along their own expectations when they joined the TSPM. According to the son of Yang Shaotang, the image of the CPC between 1948 and 1950 was comparatively better than the Chinese Nationalist Party. Yang even helped to take care of those in the Red Army wounded during the civil war. Some church leaders believed the promise of Zhou Enlai, later Prime Minister of PRC, about freedom of religion under the Communist government. Jia and Yang believed that the CPC would allow the church to continue its ministry freely. Yang did not expect that the CPC would bring any hardship to the churches. Jia Yuming wanted to continue his ministries of training workers with the Spiritual Institute and publishing his books after 1949 (Xie 2008, 64; Yang 2004).

While Wang Mingdao was indifferent to the new government, Jia was actively involved in the reestablishment of the Chinese churches. Jia had been actively promoting unity among churches since 1910 (Kwok 2002, 63-66). He led the founding of a united association of the Presbyterian churches and the China Christian Church (Jia 1914). It is understandable that he would join the TSPM under the premise of founding a united Chinese church under the new government. Jia was even appointed one of the vice-chairpersons of the Preparatory Committee for a new seminary in Nanjing (Wickeri 2007, 107-108). As national Christian leaders, Jia and Yang were honored in the beginning years of the PRC; Yang was appointed the vice-secretary of the national TSPM and Jia became one of six vice-chairpersons (Cha 1983, 118).

The situations changed rapidly in the 1950s. The Denunciation Movement in 1951 forced the church leaders to draw a clear line of demarcation between themselves and the missionaries, as the latter were accused by the government of being agents of Western imperialism. During the 1950s, both Jia and Yang retained their prestige in the church to some extent, because they refused to criticize other church leaders during the Denunciation Movement (J. Zhao 1981, 38). Yang also expressed his frustration to David Adeney about the pressure to criticize Christian brothers and sisters in the Denunciation Movement (Lyall 2003, 19). Beginning in 1957, many fundamentalist church leaders were persecuted in the anti-rightist movement in the 1950s. Ding Guangxun (K.H. Ting) played a leading role in criticizing conservative Christian leaders like Jia Yuming in the anti-rightist movement (Wickeri 2007, 150-151). During this time, the Spiritual Institute was forced to combine with Nanjing Union Theological Seminary. Yang was accused of "continuing to release toxins of imperialism" in his sermons. Later, at the onset of the Cultural Revolution, Yang was labeled "anti-revolutionary" and sentenced to clean farms.

The situation changed again in the 1990s. Jia's and Yang's books were still circulating in both the TSPM and house churches after they died in the 1960s. Even though many house church leaders regarded Jia and Yang's decision to join the TSPM as a stain on their characters, they respected the personalities and theological insights of Jia and Yang. In the 1990s, after a decade of the reform and openness policy of the Chinese government, Jia's and Yang's contributions on theological education were recognized. Their books were allowed to publish again in TSPM. Today, they are honored as role models for Chinese church leaders.

One should note that since 1949, the CCC seminaries and Bible schools have been the only officially recognized theological education institutions in China.[7] All seminaries were forced to close during the Cultural Revolution; however, the significant role of the seminaries in equipping church workers has remained the same after they were reopened in the 1980s.

Summary

This chapter has briefly analyzed the situations faced by Chinese pastors in the first half of the twentieth century. The social and political events in China have impacted the expectations of the church leaders. The call

---

7. Theological education in China is not academic research-oriented. Even though Bishop Ding Guangxun (丁光訓 1915-), the president of Nanjing Union Theological Seminary wrote many theological essays, especially about the relationship between church and state, the major concerns of the students are still evangelism and the daily operations of the church (Wickeri 2007, 247). One reason is the academic qualification of the majority of the students is only up to the secondary school level. No academic master's degree offered by these seminaries is accredited by the government or any international theological institution.

for indigenization of the Chinese churches ushered in the most significant change for that generation of leaders. Since the China Centenary Missionary Conference in 1907, both the Western missionaries and the Chinese church leaders expected to speed up the indigenization process. The rise of Chinese nationalism was one of the reasons for the anti-Christian movement, which became a catalyst to speed up the process.

The preliminary requirement for indigenization was the establishment of local leaders. The expectations that more local church leaders would take leading positions in missionary enterprises and church ministries increased during this period. In addition, the congregations in general expected a Chinese way of preaching, church administration, leadership training, and theological education. By the 1920s, many young church leaders had emerged before and after the revival movements. They responded differently to the social situation. Some of them, like Jia Yuming and Yang Shaotang, chose to keep a good relationship with the missionaries on the one hand and develop their own ideal church worker training institutes on the other hand. Their decision to join the TSPM after 1949 can also be traced back to their cooperative attitudes toward different organizations to achieve unity in the Christian body.

The importance of this development during the first half of the twentieth century should not be underestimated. Even though the social and political situations in China were not stable, the foundation of the Chinese churches had been laid. Bays accurately points out, the seeds of Chinese church revivals after the 1980s in the PRC were laid in the 1930s by young local church leaders (Bays 1996, 175). This fourth coming of Christianity to China is significantly different from the previous three times. The spiritual foundations had developed, and the impacts of these early twentieth century church leaders had grown over several generations.

China experienced political chaos in the twentieth century, including world wars and civil wars, cultural transformation, and Communist rule after 1949. However, the political movements from the 1950s to the 1970s were not able to destroy this solid spiritual foundation. The teachings and models of these early church leaders remain as laudable legacies for contemporary Chinese churches. This foundation became tradition embedded with Chinese as well as Christian values. Contemporary Chinese theology developed in response to the situations in early twentieth century China. Under those circumstances, the Chinese theologians have given their best efforts to incorporate the Christian values and Chinese cultural traditions. Leadership development is also a product of these historical and cultural situations. Both positive and negative effects of the adaptation of Confucian tradition into Chinese Christianity are found. A more detailed analysis of the Confucian influences on Christianity will be discussed in next chapter.

CHAPTER 5

Confucian Christian Theologians and Relational Leadership

In response to the historical and cultural situations in early twentieth century China, the Chinese Christians have developed indigenous church institutions and theology. The theory of leadership development has been neglected. However, the essential elements of relational leadership are found in the works of local pastors and theologians. This chapter is going to systematize the leadership theory embedded in the writings and sermons of some Chinese pastors and theologians. Only a few discussions on the patterns and methods of developing church leaders have taken place over the past 200 years of Chinese church history. The study of leadership can only be found as part of the subject on church administration in most major Chinese theological seminaries today. Unlike the situation in the West, Chinese Christians are a religious minority in almost all regions of Chinese society, including mainland China, Taiwan, Hong Kong, and even North America. The major concern of the churches is evangelism. As a result, the concern of evangelism triumphs over the study of Christian leadership theory and over the indigenization of Christianity in China.

During the Reform and Openness Policy of the Chinese government over the last three decades, the major challenge of the churches has been the lack of trained pastors to meet the needs of the Christian population, which has grown tremendously. In addition to evangelism, pastoral training becomes the most important ministry in China. In facing the ministry opportunities brought by the speedy economic development and globalization, the PRC churches have been challenged to take a more active role in the world mission. Many of the church workers' training programs that exist in China today are direct adaptations of Western models. Whether the Chinese can formulate their own effective model of leadership development has yet to be discovered.

After 200 years of Protestant Christianity in China, indigenous ways of developing church leaders should be listed at the top of the Chinese churches' agenda. As a matter of fact, the expectations of leaders in Chinese churches are not new. In Chinese culture, which is characterized by Confucianism, a general expectation of the leader can be summarized in the terms: *nei sheng wai wang* (內聖外王), translated as "inward sageliness and outward kingliness." *Nei sheng* is personal sageliness achieved by good morality. Good morality is a necessary quality of a leader. The success of a leader is therefore measured by his or her morality. Morality and leadership are always connected in Confucian tradition (Ying 1997, 407-409).

Nei sheng wai wang originally referred to expectations of political leaders, but the Chinese church has similar expectations of church leaders as well. A good church leader is defined by his or her morally good character. Measuring the actions and behaviors of a person has thus become the major criterion in defining a good leader in Chinese churches. For example, Wang Mingdao emphasized Christian behavior as evidence to prove whether someone is a true Christian or not. As corruption and human sinfulness begins from within, bad behavior results from inner corruption. Mingdao therefore taught that salvation of the inner life is the only way to bring about the transformation of a sinner (Wang 1984b, 5-10). Similar concepts can be found generally among Chinese church leaders today. Ying Fuktsang comments that *nei sheng wai wang* is one of the major characteristics of Chinese pastoral theology; however, the adaptation of *nei sheng wai wang* to leadership development has never received the attention it deserves (Ying 2008, 118-119). In this respect, *nei sheng wai wang* includes some of the characteristics of the Chinese relational leadership mentioned in chapter three, namely, idealized humanity, moral leadership, and inner life qualities.

The indigenization of the Chinese churches is not a major concern of the majority of the Chinese pastors. Instead of pastors, scholars are the main proponents of the study of indigenization. Both Christianity and Chinese culture have a long history and variety of subcultures, many areas and topics are worthy of discussion and dialogues. In the past decades, most of these discussions were focused on metaphysical concepts. As commented by Leung Kalun, these types of intercultural dialogues did not contribute directly to meet the need of the growing Chinese churches (Leung 2003b, x-xi). In the books written by Chinese pastors and the sermons they preach, terms like *tianli* (Heavenly principle), *liang zhi* (innate knowledge of the good), and *cibei* (慈悲 mercy), which are common to Chinese Buddhism, Taoism, and Confucianism, are often employed to illustrate Christian concepts. In addition, the characteristics of Chinese relational leadership can be found in the teachings and writings of the Chinese pastors.

On the other hand, the debates over the similarities and differences between the concepts of the Christian God and the Confucian *Heaven* have historically not made any impact on Chinese church pastors. Pastors use these two terms interchangeably. As a result, lay Christians adopt the Confucian and Buddhist terms to express their feelings and thinking about their Christian God in daily conversation. Studies and dialogues between Christianity and Chinese culture should include such practical aspects in the daily operation of churches. Leadership development is one of these aspects needed to be discussed in details.

A culturally applicable leadership theory cannot be developed without considering the specific historical and cultural contexts of the Chinese churches. The influence of Confucianism in China can be found almost everywhere. The ways to develop a moral self in the process of sanctification should be one of the major concerns of the Chinese churches. The Confucian school of the mind and the moral culture of China are two major cultural forces that shape the expectations of contemporary Chinese pastors. The process of human development in Confucianism can be understood as the Christian concept of sanctification. The development of a disciple is focused on developing his or her *liang zhi* so that he or she can finally become a leader with a noble personality. No one can neglect the importance of developing the moral self in studying the Chinese understanding of leadership development because this is one of the major characteristics of Confucian philosophy.

Three Chinese theologians and pastors illustrate the influence of Confucianism in leadership development of the Chinese churches: Wang Mingdao, Jia Yuming, and Yang Shaotang. The first reason these pastors were selected is that their influence has been long lasting and extensive. Wang Mingdao is one of Lyall's "three mighty men" in Chinese church history (Lyall 2000). He is well known for his attitude toward the TSPM churches. Since the 1940s he had refused to join the TSPM churches, and he paid the price by being sent to prison. Wang Mingdao's pastoral writings have been widely circulated and his fundamentalist theological perspective is the framework for pastoral training in the house churches. His works have been published and distributed throughout the Chinese-speaking world in seven volumes as the *Collected Writings of Wang Mingdao* (1983; 1977a, 1977b, 1978, 1984a, 1984b, 1984c). A brief chronological life story of Wang Mingdao is listed in appendix C.

Jia Yuming and Yang Shaotang both died in the 1960s, but their works have been widely circulated in both the TSPM and house churches. Jia Yuming wrote many theological textbooks between the 1920s and 1950s, including his *Systematic Theology* (1992a, 1992b, 1992c, 1992d),[1] *Pastoral Theology* (1926b, 1926c), and *The Essential Meaning of the Bible* (1959, 1981a, 1981b, 1981c, 1981d, 1988). Jia worked in leadership positions in several seminaries and institutions. In 1948 Jia was nominated as the vice chairman of the World Gospel Conference in Holland (Cha 1983, 116). He was recognized as one of the most influential Chinese church leaders in the first half of twentieth century. More detail on Jia's life can be found in appendix D.

Yang Shaotang spent most of his time working in the churches in Shanxi in central China and was widely welcomed by many different churches all over the country. The fundamentalist China Theological Seminary, for example, invited Yang to be the keynote speaker on their annual retreat camp in January 1941. Over 200 people attended. In addition to the teachers and students of the seminary, many pastors from Shanghai attended the camp and listened to Yang's sermons. Out of the seven speakers, only Yang's

---

1. Jia's *Systematic Theology* was originally published in 1921. The edition used in this dissertation was revised and republished in 1949, then reprinted in 1992.

speeches were recorded and published afterward. Yang's sermons comprised 75 percent of the whole collection (Yang 1941). Most of Yang's publications were related to the training of church workers: *The Church and the Worker* (1939),[2] *God's Workman* (1961), *Victory and Reward* (1998),[3] and *The Course of the Church and Church Growth* (2005a).[4] More details on Yang's life are listed in appendix E. Both the government-registered churches of the TSPM and the unregistered house churches in the PRC have been deeply influenced by the works of Jia Yuming and Yang Shaotang. Their books are widely circulated in different parts of China. In the past thirty years when the churches in the PRC did not have adequate resources for the pastors, most pastors equipped themselves by reading and applying Jia and Yang's writings in their ministries.

The second reason these pastors were selected is that all three of them were representative of fundamentalist theologians in China. Wang Mingdao was the pastor of the Christian Tabernacle, a small congregation in Beijing with only several hundred members, which he founded. He did not receive either formal theological education or belong to any denomination. He had never been affiliated with any foreign missionary organizations but was willing to partner with different churches and denominations. He spoke across the country in revival meetings and Bible study camps. In contrast, Jia and Yang were closely connected with foreign missions and received theological education in their seminaries. However, they did not limit themselves in their own denominations but were willing to serve the churches in other denominations. Jia Yuming came from an American Presbyterian Church background where he worked together with other Western missions and local pastors. Yang Shaotang was nurtured by the missionaries of China Inland Mission (CIM). He focused on ministries in Shanxi in his early years and worked with other denominations and missions to serve churches throughout the country. Unlike Watchman Nee, who limited himself to

---

2. *The Church and the Worker* was originally published in 1941. This is the collection of Yang's sermons at a summer retreat camp organized by pastors in Beijing.

3. *Victory and Reward* was originally published in 1948. The version used in this dissertation is a combined edition published by TSPM.

4. *The Course of the Church* was originally published in 1951 and *The Church Growth* published in 1958. The version used in this dissertation is a combined edition published in Hong Kong.

serving only the Church Assembly Hall, Jia and Yang had great impact throughout the whole of China (Lyall 2003, 88).

The third reason these three pastors were selected is that Chinese and English Christian scholars studying Chinese church development should know about them. Even though many Chinese scholars have collected and written about the life and works of Wang Mingdao, English-language studies are rare. Unlike Watchman Nee who was widely known in the West and his works, which are very popular among English- and even Spanish-language readers even now, Wang Mingdao is much less known, and only a few of his works have been introduced to the West. Wang Mingdao, Jia Yuming, and Yang Shaotang have similar importance in contemporary Chinese church history. Without understanding their theologies and works, the study on the Chinese church development is incomplete.

Jia and Yang worked in the same period and have similar impact on Chinese churches; however, none of their works has been translated into other languages. Apart from some testimonies and autobiographies, only a handful of studies have been done on the lives and work of Jia and Yang. In recent years, Kwok Wailuen (1997, 2001, 2002, 2003) from Hong Kong and Xie Longyi (1995, 2008) from Taiwan have studied the exegesis and theological perspective of Jia Yuming. No specific research has been done so far on Yang Shaotang. Lee Maocheng's doctoral thesis (1985) is a combined study of the lives of Yang Shaotang, John Song, Wang Mingdao, and Watchman Nee. Leslie T. Lyall's *Three of China's Mighty Men* introduces Yang Shaotang, Wang Mingdao, and Watchman Nee together, but he tells his readers that his selection of these three men was based on his personal relationships with them but not on their importance to the churches (Lyall 2003, 2). None of these publications has given adequate analysis on the status and influence of Yang Shaotang.

One important clarification must be made about the terms *leader* and *leadership* in the Chinese Christian context. In the early twentieth century, pastors in China seldom used the term *leader* or *leadership*. The more popular term they used to refer to leader is *church worker*. Church workers included pastors, deacons, elders, and other who had the responsibility and influence in the church. In the following sections I will use the terms *worker* and *leader* interchangeably.

In this chapter, evidence is provided from the lives and teachings of Wang Mingdao, Jia Yuming, and Yang Shaotang which shows the characteristics of the Chinese relational leadership discussed in chapter three. Mingdao, Jia, and Yang have some similarities in their leadership and at the same time have some different emphases. According to their different emphases, three major areas of the Chinese relational leadership in the Confucian context will be discussed. They are the emphasis on morality, idealized humanity, and pastoral mentoring relationship. An evaluation of the positive and negative impacts of Confucianism on the Chinese churches will also be discussed.

Wang Mingdao: A Confucian Pastor

As Confucianism is the dominant philosophy in Chinese culture, the attitude and behavior of all Chinese people are under its influence. The moral expectation of a leader is a high priority. The encounter of Christianity with Confucianism has aroused research interest in the past. Nonetheless, the ways in which the Chinese pastors are influenced by Confucianism have not been discussed adequately. Under the influence of Confucianism, leadership development can be understood as the process of personal growth. A similar concept in Christianity is called sanctification. In the study of human nature in Confucianism, personality development is also a major concern. The goal to become a sage through finding and developing the inner moral self is a way of developing one's personality. The focus of this section is to study the teachings of a Chinese pastor who emphasized the development of the Christian personality within a Chinese context. Under this circumstance, morality of the leader is one of the major emphases on the Chinese relational leadership. In this respect, some Chinese pastors have successfully integrated the Christian faith with the Chinese culture in the area of personality development.

The ministry and teachings of Wang Mingdao has been chosen to illustrate the influences of Confucianism on Chinese pastors. His popularity and significance in contemporary Chinese churches are well known. Wang Mingdao was born into a Christian family, but his father committed suicide due to his fear of possible torture from the Boxers in 1900 (Wang 2005, 2-3).[5] As an influential pastor in China throughout the twentieth century, Wang Mingdao was famous for his fundamentalist teachings on Christian ethics. He was only a senior pastor of a small congregation called the Christian Tabernacle in Beijing; however, his teachings were adopted by churches throughout China. Mingdao's popularity was proved by the invitations he received to lead evangelistic and revival meetings all over China, the subscriptions to his publications by most of the churches in the country, and the fact that other churches accepted his theological justifications in resisting the TSPM (Szeto 1980, 244-247; Leung 2001b, 56-57). The teachings of Wang Mingdao can represent the beliefs of the majority of Christians in China especially in the last century.

As a prisoner for over twenty two years, Wang Mingdao's firm resistance to join TSPM earned him designation of the symbol of the house church movement. He compared himself with the prophet Jeremiah, saying that his calling was to become "a fortified city, an iron pillar, and a bronze wall" (Jer 1:18 NRSV) against the world. He actually worked like a prophet to speak on the corruptions inside the church, which won him prestige as the conscience of the churches in China (Wang 2005, 73; Shi 2001, 35). According to David Aikman (2003, 56-57), the influence of Wang Mingdao has faded away after his twenty year imprisonment and only his refusal to join the TSPM has remained as an impact among the house churches. However, Aikman forgets the fact that the writings of Wang Mingdao have extended his influence over half a century. His popularity is partly due to his persecution by the Chinese government but also partly due to the wide acceptance of his fundamentalist theology and ethical teachings in nurturing young Christians.

Based on Wang Mingdao's autobiography (2005), diary (1997), and 516 articles collected in *The Collected Writings of Wang Mingdao* (1977a, 1977b,

---

5. The Boxer Uprising or Boxer Rebellion was a violent anti-foreign, anti-Christian movement supported by the Empress Dowager Ci Xi of the Qing dynasty in the years 1898-1901. Many foreigners, especially missionaries, were killed by the Boxers. The movement finally led to the formation of a military alliance of eight nations to attack Beijing.

1978, 1984a, 1984b, 1984c, 1984d),[6] some clear signs of Confucian tradition can be found in his sermons and articles. For example, morality and interpersonal relationships are his major concern in regard to Christian living. In addition, even though many Chinese writers have written about Wang's life and testimony, only a few of the books are scholarly works. For example, Leung Kalun (1997, 1999a, 2001b, 2003a) has given historical perspectives on the studies of Wang Mingdao's theological background and his relations with the government; and Lam Winghung (1982, 1990, 1998; 2001) has made in-depth studies on the theology of Wang Mingdao in relation to Chinese culture. As for the study of Mingdao's leadership pattern, only Lee Maocheng (1989) has written a descriptive study based on J. Robert Clinton's LET (1989, 1990). Unfortunately, Li's study does not discuss the implications of the teachings of Mingdao on developing leaders and followers.

Wang Mingdao did not receive any formal theological education, but he did receive formal Confucian education from the time he was nine, where he learned the Confucian classic *Four Books* (Wang 2005, 9). The Bible was first on his most-read book list, and the *Four Books* ranked second. He was very familiar with Chinese cultural traditions (Lam 2001, 27). Even though Leung Kalun comments that Wang Mingdao did not formulate significant and distinctive theological doctrines before the 1950s, Mingdao's fundamentalist theological thoughts are well developed in his publications (Leung 2001b, 56-57, 2003a, 4). He was influenced by the dominant missionary movement of his time—the fundamentalist theology brought to China by the conservative Protestant missionaries in the nineteenth and twentieth Century (Leung 1997, 297).

Personal Pursuit of Truth

Some common beliefs or practices concerning Confucianism and Christianity can be found in the pursuit of truth of a Chinese Christian. Wang Mingdao knew Confucianism well before he became a Christian, so

---

6. The *Collected Writings of Wang Mingdao*, a combined edition of all the articles written by Wang Mingdao, has divided all his works into seven volumes, and forty-two chapters have been divided.

he naturally interpreted his journey of faith in Confucian terms when he found some similarities between them.

The first sign of the Confucian impact on Mingdao was his decision to convert. He was encouraged by his classmate to become a Christian at the age of fourteen. As he was educated in the Confucian classics, he admitted that the strongest persuasion to him was the words of Confucius about planning for the future with a great will (Wang 2005, 23). The original saying of Confucius is in fact the best description of Mingdao's life and ministry: "I set my heart on the Way, base myself on virtue, lean upon benevolence for support and take my recreation in the arts" (*Analects* 7.6). Mingdao replaced the Confucian "Way" or "Dao" with the Christian concept of truth. In Mingdao's terminology, the "Way" is the way of God—the calling and mission from God. His teachings focused on developing virtues, and he emphasized treating others with benevolence.

After he became a Christian, Wang Mingdao dreamed of becoming a politician. He wanted to be "the Lincoln of China" when he was fourteen years old (Wang 2005, 24). Wang's dream of a future career followed the typical purpose of study for a man in traditional China: he should have some dream of making a contribution to the nation. Wang resisted the call to be a servant of God for three years. He studied hard and prepared for his future career and never planned to be a pastor during his teenage years (Lam 1982, 33). He was finally willing to become a pastor because he witnessed the behavior of the Christians he worked with while he was a teacher in a Christian school. He thought that those church attendees who claimed to be Christians were not really Christians according to the standard of the Bible. What Wang committed to do was to renew the Church of Christ spiritually. Church revival became his major concern in his early years as a pastor (Wang 2005, 37). He founded the Christian Tabernacle because he disagreed with other denominations. In his eyes there were seldom real Christians and real churches, and most existing "Christians" needed to repent and return to following the standard of God; to live their lives according to the Bible (Wang 2005, 128). In addition, he refused to ordain pastors simply because there was no direct reference from the Bible (Wang 2005, 137). It is obvious that Wang Mingdao began his quest for truth in a Confucian way. In his early years, he was more of a Confucian than a Christian.

Ethical Expectations

In the Confucian tradition, a leader is believed to be a *jun zi*, or even a potential sage; high ethical expectations are understandable. Wang Mingdao extended these expectations of good morality to all Christians. He admired the concept of being a good Christian since his conversion. The meaning of a good Christian was simply good moral behavior (Wang 2005, 15). A true Christian was the bearer of the cross of Christ and the witness of the love of God. Good morality was the best way to fulfill the life goal of glorifying God. Wang believed that the Christian had a higher standard of moral expectations than non-believers, and church leaders should be the role model. He taught that the white color of Heaven represented the expectation of God on the church concerning moral purity. He wrote:

> Without purity, no matter what else you embrace in your life, you can never satisfy the heart of God. In the church today there are those who emphasize the building of huge places of worship; there are those who emphasize doctrines; and there are those who emphasize the fulfillment of prophecy. But only rarely do you find those who emphasize purity of living (Wang 1983, 3).

The ethical model triumphed over all other areas of church ministry. Moral teaching was weighted even more than the authentic teaching of doctrines.

Wang Mingdao repeatedly disclosed his ethical expectations to all Christians. For the young Christians who wanted to marry, the first criterion was faithfulness to God and the second criterion was morality. According to Wang, education and ability should have lower priority than the first two criteria (Wang 2005, 188-189). He believed that only those Christians who lived an exemplary life could be qualified as church pastors (Wang 2005, 127).

Wang Mingdao required all followers of Christ to live a holy life, but the difference between his teachings and those of Confucian philosopher

Wang Yangming was the purpose of self-cultivation. For the former, the purpose self-cultivation was the glory of God, whereas for the latter it was personal goal of sagehood. In fact, Yangming's concept of "preserving the principles of Heaven and getting rid of human desires" can be applied to Mingdao's expectation of his church members through his teachings. If the "principles of Heaven" is replaced by the "will of God," the concept of and requirements concerning human action are similar.

Whenever Mingdao heard accusations regarding the misbehavior of other church leaders, he felt very upset. For example, in a study on the life of Watchman Nee, Leung Kalun finds from his copies of Wang Mingdao's diary that Mingdao was disappointed about Nee's sexual relationships with other women and stated that Nee should be expelled from the church. Mingdao felt very sad that the church tolerated the ethical sin of their leader (Leung 2003a, 87-91).[7] A church leader should be the model for others to follow. Wang Mingdao always reminded himself and others to be aware of the moral traps of money, fame, and sex. Young leaders were attracted to Wang Mingdao because of his image as a moral leader.

The other dimension of ethical expectations was reflected in social relationships. Wang Mingdao did not put emphasis on the Christian's social responsibility; instead, he focused on personal responsibility. Within the boundary of the "Five Relationships" (五倫) of traditional Confucian culture—master and servant, father and son, husband and wife, among brothers, and among friends—all must be maintained according to both Confucian tradition and biblical teachings. To Mingdao there was no contradiction between the Confucian "Five Relationships" and biblical truth. The ethical expectations were the same (Wang 1977a, 62-67).

---

7. In the diary of Wang Mingdao published in 1997, all of Wang Mingdao's comments on Watchman Nee that Leung identified in his study were omitted except one. The diary entry for July 14, 1946 was kept, but the comment in question was only a sentence indirectly indicating Wang's disappointment in Nee (Wang 1997, 283). If the reader did not have any background knowledge of what Nee had been doing, the reader would have no idea of what Mingdao wanted to say. This selective publication of Wang Mingdao's diary gives the impression that the editor or the publisher wanted to protect the moral image of a famous and influential church leader and thus omitted all the negative comments about Watchman Nee on purpose.

Direct Communication from God to the Human Conscience

The Chinese term *liang zhi* carries the meaning of conscience, which was believed to be an inborn human quality to know what is good or evil. The idea that the mind is the principle denotes the possibility of a human connection with heaven. Whether the human mind is the principle of having the quality to connect with the Heaven in order to know the principle, Christians usually identify Heaven as God. Wang Mingdao replaced the principle with the truth of God. *Liang zhi* is inspired by the Holy Spirit so that humans are able to know the truth of God.

Mingdao maintained that all Christians can be inspired by God so that they know what to do. Through reading the Scripture and prayer, Christians can make decisions according to the will of God. For instance, Mingdao did not allow the church to collect donations from Christians because a donation was the individual's willingness to respond to God (Wang 2005, 138). The willingness to give the donation signified a direct relationship between God and human beings. Even the church leader had no right to interfere with the individual personal relationship with God to ask for donation. The individual's relationship with God is established by reading the Scriptures and modeling the lives of other spiritually-mature Christians. According to Wang Mingdao, the will of God was easy enough to understand and practical enough to follow. God's revelations through the Scripture provided clear and direct instructions for Christians to follow (Wang 1977a, 39-45).

Pragmatism

Most of Wang Mingdao's teachings are highly practical. How to be a good Christian was the main concern before the 1950s which was reflected in most of his teachings and writings. This concern was also the reason that he focused much of his attention in his preaching and writing on how to be a witness of Christ. Of the 516 articles published in the seven volumes of the *Collected Writings of Wang Mingdao*, at least one-third (about 171 articles) deal directly with matters of Christian living. For example, thirteen articles are about how to talk appropriately, eight articles are about marriage, and thirty-nine articles are about Christian behaviors in daily lives. In fact, Wang Mingdao was a very detailed person and preferred to give step-by-step guidance to young Christians because he wanted everything he taught to be practical.

Wang Mingdao was not concerned about abstract and idealistic theory. The doctrines he wrote about dealt with practical issues that Christians have to face every day. Apart from Christian living, he wrote apologetics for both evangelism and defense against what he called the "liberal theology" of the TSPM pastors. He never wrote anything theoretically about the indigenization of the Chinese church, nor did he write anything about dialogues between Christianity and Confucianism (Lam 1990, 117). An indigenous church means a church familiar to the daily lives of ordinary people because it is more easily accepted by non-believers.

The Importance of Knowing and Acting

While Wang Yangming emphasized the unity of knowing and acting, Wang Mingdao taught that actions are reflected in the true knowledge. Mingdao mentioned the importance of biblical truth and teachings. Biblical knowledge is the truth inspired by God through Scripture; biblical teachings are the application of the former to daily living. Teaching the congregation about biblical truth without emphasizing its life changing practices is useless (Wang 2005, 141). Sanctification is a matter of practicing and living according to the moral standard of a Christian. Mingdao wrote,

> The people of the world did not pay attention to our practices of prayers and church attendance, but to our behavior. The most influential area of a Christian to other people is his behavior. The [noun] most closely related to God's glory is our behavior. . . . God looks into our hearts, but a human being looks at our behavior (Wang 1977a, 25-26).

Spiritual persons are not defined by their knowledge of the Bible or attendance at Sunday services but by how they live consistently with their faith. A life that bears the fruits of the Holy Spirit is really what they wish for. This concern can explain why over one-third of Mingdao's written articles deal with Christian living and behavior. His message, therefore, concerned the close connection between faith and daily life, biblical knowledge and actual practice (Lam 1982, 73). Behavior is the true reflection of one's beliefs. The book of James in the New Testament was thus one of Mingdao's most favorite books. He expected the behavior of Christians to be the result of life transformation and true reflection of their faith.

Self-Reflection and Cultivation

The beginning of the development to become a sage, according to the Confucian classic *The Great Learning*, is self-cultivation. Likewise, becoming a leader does not begin with learning management skills but with the cultivation of the moral self. Wang Mingdao had a strong sense of self-reflection, which is the first step of self-cultivation. The purpose of everyday reflection is self-improvement. Before looking at another's fault, one must improve one's self. Many of the entries in Mingdao's diary are self-reflections. For example, in the entry for April 21, 1921, Mingdao recorded eight faults, including eating too many candies, being too parsimonious, telling lies, gossiping, telling jokes, looking at pornographic pictures, thinking too much about having a vehicle, and spending too little time on devotions (Wang 1997, 6-7). He was very strict and required himself to have disciplined thinking. One may find such discipline among Western monks or eastern Buddhist traditions; however, Mingdao is closer to the Confucian tradition. Ceng Zi (曾子), a disciple of Confucius, said:

> Every day I examine myself on three counts. In what I have undertaken on another's behalf, have I failed to do my best? In my dealings with my friends have I failed to be trustworthy in what I say? Have I failed to practice repeatedly what has been passed on to me? (*Analects* 1.4)

This self-discipline is what Confucius taught about *jen:* "To return to the observance of the rites through overcoming the self constitutes benevolence" (*Analects* 121.1). A *jun zi* is expected to have self-reflection practices like Mingdao did as a way of life in self-cultivation.

In fact, the fundamental difference between Confucianism and Christianity is the limitation on self-cultivation. The Confucian believes that there is no limit to self-cultivation. Everybody can become a sage through self-cultivation after exploring the principle in human nature. In contrast, Christianity stresses the fallibility and sinfulness of human nature. Wang Mingdao borrowed the concept of self-cultivation but used it differently. Repentance begins with self-cultivation. Only through repentance can a sinner receive the grace of God and begin a new life of sanctification. In Mingdao's terminology, true repentance meant being born again (Wang 1984b, 18-23). In other words, self-cultivation begins from being born again by the grace of God. Self-cultivation is not merely the human self working alone for personal growth but is a joint effort with the Holy Spirit. Mingdao believed that human corruption comes from the inner self (Wang 1984b, 10). Literally, self-cultivation can have no result unless one is born again. The Chinese churches cannot accept the concept of the unity of Heaven and human beings; however, the relationship between the Holy Spirit and the human beings in the practice of self-cultivation is a necessary step in spiritual growth. The work of the Holy Spirit is a must in the process of sanctification.

Faithfulness to the Mandate of Heaven

The Confucian seeks and lives a life according to the Mandate of Heaven. All misfortunes are the result of not following the Mandate of Heaven; therefore, a leader has the utmost responsibility to understand the Mandate of Heaven and lead the followers to live appropriately. Usually, people who live morally and benevolently are believed to be fulfilling the Mandate of Heaven. This expectation of the style of living is similar in Wang Mingdao's teachings. Even though his understanding of Heaven and the object of loyalty was different from the Confucian understanding, the requirement of personal faithfulness is the same.

Wang Mingdao was not concerned about social reforms, and he accused the church leaders who promoted the social responsibility of the church of being liberal. Liberal Christians, as defined by Mindgao, were people who rejected the literal inerrancy of the Bible, the virgin birth as a miracle, and the cross as a sign of God's wrath concerning human sinfulness. He used the terms *modernist* and *social gospel* to refer to these liberal Christians (Wang 1984d, 283-319). In Wang Mingdao's view, the church of Christ should concern itself mainly with the salvation of non-believers and the sanctification of believers. The Confucian who begins with self-cultivation ends by being the pacifier of the world, but the Christian who begins with self-cultivation ends differently. The ultimate target of a Christian on earth is to live a holy life and prepare for the inheritance of the kingdom of heaven in the future (Wang 1984d, 334-344). To Wang Mingdao, the kingdom of heaven was totally other-worldly, whereas the church leaders who believed that the kingdom of heaven could be achieved by human effort were following the social gospel. More seriously, Mingdao believed that the churches following social gospel were not true churches (Wang 1984d, 1-4).

In short, the teachings of Wang Mingdao clearly show that the Confucian cultural influence was strong in his life and ministry. He did not intentionally adopt the Confucian teachings into his sermons and publications, but he assimilated his own cultural tradition into his faith. Wang Mingdao did not explicitly write anything about the relationship between Christianity and Confucianism. He based his teachings on his Scripture reading, but whenever he found no contradiction between his faith and his tradition, he applied Confucian ideas to his teachings without hesitation.

Some of the main themes in Wang Yangming's philosophy are applicable to Wang Mingdao's teachings. Although a Christian cannot accept the Confucian concept of human nature as intrinsically good, the moral self as a starting point in the journey of moral perfection is acceptable. The expectation of morality as the key attribute of a leader is obvious. In fact, if the understanding of heaven can be transformed into the understanding of a personal God, even more similarities can be found between these religious traditions.

All in all, some characteristics of relational leadership were reflected in the life and teachings of Wang Mingdao. Morality and modeling are notable features of Mingdao's theory in developing Christian followers to become leaders. He was very pragmatic in his teachings in emphasizing the unity of knowing and acting. His concern was how to be a faithful witness for Christ. With his Confucian background, together with his understanding on the Bible, Wang Mingdao believed his practical teachings could educate the Chinese Christians to develop appropriate behavior in their daily lives. Because of the direct application of biblical teachings to daily lives, Mingdao's writings are among the most welcomed literatures to Christians even today. He did not intentionally develop many followers or disciples. Although he was in prison for over twenty-two years, there were still many of his former church members and coworkers who wanted to connect with him. They were proud of being the coworkers and disciples of Wang Mingdao even though he was a prisoner. He made a lifelong impact on the life and ministry for those Christians who were connected with him.

Jia Yuming's "Perfect Leader" and "Christ-Human" State

If Wang Mingdao gave practical and biblical teachings with strong Confucian characteristics, Jia Yuming supplemented with solid indigenous theological foundation in developing Chinese church leaders. Jia Yuming was one of the most important Chinese church leaders and scholars in the early twentieth century. Xie Longyi regards Jia as the "Irenaeus of China" because Jia was one of the earliest theologians, Bible expositors, and theological educators (2008, 28). Jia was involved in theological education for over 40 years. His books were used as text books in seminaries for at least half a century. Like many other fundamentalist theologians, Jia began his theology with soteriology (Ying 2001). According to the writings of Chinese pastors in Jia's day, spiritual growth is an essential element for leadership development. The expectations of a leader have only a qualitative difference with a lay Christian. If sanctification is a process leading to spiritual maturity, the process of leadership development is also a process of sanctification. The theme of sanctification is clearly present in the teachings on church leadership contained in Jia's biblical and systematic theological writings.

According to Jia Yuming, salvation is the main theme of both the Old and New Testaments. Salvation is not an event occurring only one time, but has different stages of development. In other words, salvation is a process of spiritual growth. Jia used characters in the Old Testament as metaphors to illustrate this process. For example, Abraham symbolizes justification, Isaac symbolizes sanctification, Jacob symbolizes victory, and Joseph symbolizes the glory of God. Based on these illustrations, salvation can be divided into four stages: justification, sanctification, victory, and glorifying God. The completion of these four stages is called total salvation. Jia termed this process the "moral progression" of the individual Christian because the signs of spiritual maturity was reflected by moral development (Jia 1959, 113-117). Salvation is therefore a process of moral growth, and spirituality is the same as moral maturity.

Moral growth as a reflection of spiritual growth is a distinct characteristic of Chinese theology. A leader is different from a lay Christian only according to the degree of maturity: a leader should complete the process of sanctification and become the role model for the followers to imitate. Three aspects of Jia Yuming's doctrine of sanctification will be discussed: the beginning, process, and result.

Sanctification Begins at Salvation

Accepting Jesus as a personal savior is only a beginning, not the completion, of the salvation process. According to Jia, salvation is the key word in the whole Bible. His theology is centered on Jesus Christ: "The essence of the whole Bible is salvation, which is the perfect saving method prepared by God for the salvation of human beings. Further, Jesus is the center and the cross is the main theme" (Jia 1959, 4). Justification by faith is the beginning of salvation. As the God we believe in is perfect, total salvation should include leading a person into perfection: "The saving method of Christ is not a plan for 'just-made' salvation, but he wants humans to become perfect. The real meaning of salvation is to lead a person into the richness of the Lord" (Jia 1992c, 247).

To be a role model for other followers, a leader is expected to achieve total salvation. The possibility of becoming perfect is not based on the Confucian assumption on human goodness but the love and power of Christ. Christ saves and leads human beings continuously into perfection through his abundant love and grace.

Redemption of Life

The first important step in Christ's salvation is the redemption of the human spirit. In Jia Yuming's terminology, life is not just a physical body, but includes spirit, soul, and body. This ternary view of human life was common among Chinese theologians in early twentieth century. The spirit is the most important part in this ternary view of human life (Kwok 2003, 69-70). The difference between human beings and other creatures is the spirit. Redemption of the human spirit is therefore equivalent to the renewal of the real life of a human. Jia usually used the term spirit-life (*ling sheng ming* 靈生命) to refer to the salvation of Christ.

Christ's redemptive work for humanity was done to save this spirit-life. In addition to the physical life which experiences birth, aging, sickness, and death, the spirit-life connects with God the creator. Jia insisted the journey of spiritual growth of a Christian is to pursue the spirit-life. In *A Perfect Salvation*, a book originally published in 1953, Jia mentions:

> Christianity is the experience of life. The only thing we gain when following Jesus is the spirit-life. Only those who have spirit-life are true Christians, those who do not have spirit-life are only nominal Christians, or are even not yet saved (Jia 1987, 211).

Many pastors of Jia's generation believed that salvation meant to save and develop the spirit-life of a person. Sometimes Jia uses only the word *life* to denote spirit-life: "A person who has real life should perform differently. . . . The temperament of a person reflects whether or not he or she has real life because temperament is the natural expression of life" (Jia 1987, 213).

The temperament shows the real self of a person. The behavior of a person reflects whether or not he or she is truly born again. This behavioral change cannot be achieved by human effort alone. True salvation will bring true behavioral change. Total salvation will bring complete change to the followers of Christ. The redemption of Christ brings a complete change to a person, which will lead him or her into perfection in behavior. Sanctification as a process leading to perfection is therefore possible. In other words, redemption of life is the beginning of the possibility in sanctification.

A Model of Perfection

Christ is the perfect model for Christians to imitate. In *The Life and Teaching of Jesus Christ,* published in 1921, Jia stated that Jesus developed deliberately the inner qualities of the disciples—faith, obedience, love, and wisdom—after they were called. The training Jesus gave the disciples involved neither ministry skills nor abilities, but behavioral and spiritual qualities. The purpose of the training was to equip them to become Christ-like evangelists (Jia 1990, 75-76). Jia studied the life and ministry of Christ from a practical perspective. In his theological education program, he followed Christ's model of emphasizing inner qualities. One important aspect that Jesus demonstrated through his life and ministry was servant leadership. The teachings in the Sermon on the Mount are the guidelines for the followers to learn from him. Jesus' sacrifice of himself for the sake of others was the highest performance of a servant leader (Jia 1990, 94-95). As faithful followers of Christ, pastors are expected to be the role model so that the congregation can follow them. Pastors have to learn how to shepherd themselves prior to teaching others (Jia 1988, 165-167). To be a good pastor, apart from teaching through lecturing, one has to teach through one's own life. A church leader's "behavior speaks louder than any voice" (Jia 1988, 211-212).

The basic lessons for developing church leaders come from the ways in which Jesus developed his disciples. In learning from Jesus, one ought not only to imitate his actions and good deeds, but also to invite him to live in one's mind. According to Jia Yuming, the first step to pursue spiritual maturity is to let "Christ live in me" (Galatians 2:20 NIV). The imitation of Christ should allow the indwelling of Christ in one's heart. The transformation of the heart precedes the changes in actions and behavior. Jia argued that spiritual maturity is only possible when Christ works in one's heart. It is not possible by human effort alone to achieve the ultimate goal of sanctification—perfection. The second step is to let Christ "fully developed in your lives" (Galatians 4:19 NLT). The birth and growth of Christ within a person's mind means letting him control the person's life. The Christian destiny is to own "the mind of Christ" (1 Corinthians 2:16). The Christian therefore lives like Jesus, thinks like Jesus, and behaves like Jesus. When Christ is fully developed in the mind, the third step is a natural consequence—to "put on Christ" (Galatians 3:27 NLT). To "put on Christ" is to develop the inner life so as to change the behavior from inside out. Following these three steps, the follower can live and reflect the spirit of Christ. Jia calls this the *Christ-human* state, which is the dwelling of Christ within and transformation of an individual so as to live a model life based on that of Christ (Jia 1992c, 278-282).

In addition to the imitation of Christ, the other aspect of establishing a leadership model is to follow the image of God. Similar to the ideal of the *Christ-human*, living out the image of God is the final destiny of a mature Christian leader. The beginning of sanctification is the dedication of one's life to God; the next step is a complete infilling by the Holy Spirit. The mind and behavior of a Christian therefore operate according to the guidance of the Holy Spirit. Jia Yuming named the goals of sanctification as having "God's divinity, ethic, and image" (Jia 1992c, 215-216). In other words, total salvation comes only with a life lived within the image of God.

The way Jia Yumaing interpreted the indwelling of Christ carries a meaning similar to "keeping the heavenly principle and removing the human desires" (*cun tian li, qu ren yu* 存天理, 去人慾) in the Confucian tradition. Jia borrowed the Confucian concept and interpreted it in Christian terms. Unlike the Confucian concept of principle, Jia maintained that the heavenly principle was the image of God. God created human beings according to the divine image and gave the spirit-life to human beings. Thus, Christ saves and lives in one's mind and heart in order that one may recover the spirit-life, which is damaged by sin. The *Christ-human* is thus the result of total salvation. In Jia's terminology, "removing human desires" is almost the same concept in Christianity and Confucianism. Both believe human desires should be wiped out. The moral standard of human beings must come from God.

Jia followed the Confucian understanding of human behavior to read and interpret the Bible. Confucians believed that the inner self was crucial and decisive in influencing a person's behavior. Jia replaced the natural born morality in the inner self with the image of God and indwelling of Christ. Developing the inner self in order to change external behavior is typically understood as an approach of "inward sageliness and outward kingliness" in the Confucian tradition. The better the relationship with God, the better one's moral behavior ought to be. As a result, better leadership is guaranteed. Jia's theory fit the Confucian understanding of human nature as well as the Christian one. Following the theological tradition of the Reformation, the theology of Jia Yuming emphasizes "Solus Christus" but not "Solus Fide" and "Solus Gratia." With his Chinese cultural concerns, Jia preferred to uphold the relationship between God and the human inner self. The union between God and human beings is one of the major characteristics of Jia's theology (Kwok 2003, 56-57). In this respect, relationship is the primary choice in Jia's theology.

Jia followed the Calvinist tradition, believed a future leader was predestinated. God takes the initiative to choose these potential leaders to be developed as *Christ-humans*. Jia mentioned some biblical characters as role models for evangelists; for example, Jeremiah in the Old Testament was a God-chosen leader in his time. Jeremiah's personal qualifications were not the concern of God; Jeremiah was a leader simply by his calling from God. Jeremiah was anointed by God, and his messages came from God. He worked together with God during his years of prophecy. Jeremiah was an influential leader because he was a holy person: he did not have a family so that he could work wholeheartedly for God. In the meantime, he was so passionate that he was willing sacrifice his life for God's people (Jia 1981d, 2000-2004). The leadership model demonstrated by the prophet Jeremiah is to live life according to the standard of God. The one who can be unimpeachable and willing to sacrifice his or her own interest for the sake of God is the leadership model for others to follow.

Sanctification as a Process of Becoming a Leadership Role Model

In Jia's view, redemption is only a beginning for the development of a leadership model. The final destiny of a leader is to become a *Christ-human*. In between redemption and becoming a *Christ-human* is the process known as sanctification. All Christians are asked to follow the role model of Christ in order to achieve spiritual maturity. The difference between a lay Christian and a church leader is a matter of degree in Christ-like character. Leaders are role models for their followers to imitate; therefore, they should live according to a higher standard and with higher expectations. The other difference between a lay Christian and a leader is the calling from God. Jia Yuming wrote,

> The office of apostle is a holy responsibility coming from the nobility of Heaven. If it were not given by Heaven and our Lord, no one could have the honor to serve him. Those fishermen from a village in Galilee were in and of themselves not able to serve in such a spiritual and heavenly ordained holy office (1990, 95).

Again, Jia borrowed the Confucian concept of heaven to represent God and the "nobility of heaven" (*tian jue* 天爵) to represent the office of apostle. The emphasis on calling represents Jia's belief in the sovereignty of God in the selection of a church leader. A leader is not the choice of any person by election or self-motivation but the decision of God. Since leaders are chosen by God, the followers will have higher expectations of and requirements for these leaders.

Sanctification and Moral Perfection

The responsibility of a church leader is to lead Christians to spiritually maturity. Spiritual maturity is measured by one's moral behavior; thus, a leader should live according to a higher moral standard. Jia Yuming understood sanctification and moral perfection as two sides of a coin. The spiritual maturity of a leader cannot be proven by any academic degree or certificate. The major differences between human beings and other living creatures are that human beings have spirit and are created in the image of God. To Jia, the image of God included "the original substance of righteousness, holiness, kindness, and goodness" (Jia 1992b, 112). Other creatures can never have "conscience" and "morality" like human beings (Jia 1992b, 113-114). To some extent, Jia's understanding of human beings is close to Mencius' definition of human nature—based on morality. Based on Jia's definition of human beings, morality is therefore an irreplaceable element in personal and spiritual growth.

The Chinese definition of sanctification means becoming holy. Holiness implies moral perfection. When one wants to imitate God, one is imitating

God's holiness: "The purpose of Christianity is to help human beings to become holy. This noble purpose is based on the holiness of God. God is the perfect spirit, therefore his holiness is also perfect" (Jia 1992b, 31).

One is unable to become holy by one's own efforts. Transformation to holiness comes only from the grace of God. The transformation happens when the personalities and moral character are changed by Christ (Jia 1992c, 314-316). Only through the work of Christ can a person become morally perfect.

The comments of Jia Yuming on some biblical characters reflect his view on sanctification and moral perfection as two sides of one coin. Jia affirmed Boaz in the book of Ruth as a man with faith. More importantly he perceived Boaz as a modest, peaceful, just, and humble person in dealing with his relationships with others (Jia 1935, 84-87). Jia did not explicitly deny that knowledge was a quality of a leader; neither did he recognize knowledge was as an important attribute. He explained that the knowledge which Moses learned in Egypt was a source of his arrogant and arbitrary behavior. In contrast, Moses learned to be patient and obedient in the wilderness, which brought out in him the noble characteristics of humility, love, trust, and total reliance on God. In the wilderness, Moses received the spiritual-moral training for being a leader. Jia insisted that Moses' experience in the wilderness was much more valuable than the knowledge he gained in the palace of Egypt. God gave the vision and mission to Moses only after he acquired such noble characteristics in the wilderness (Jia 1959, 163-167).

Jia compared the characters of the great Kings in Israel's history: Saul, David, and Solomon. King David had the "highest spiritual quality" as David was trained to have good qualities in spiritual life, faith and morality, and personal character (Jia 1981a, 786-789). All of these qualities are necessary for a good leader and none of them are related to knowledge. As Table 1 shows, Jia believed King David represented the best leadership qualities. Church leaders in all generations should model their lives after him. King Solomon was a wise man, whose intelligence represented some of the intellectuals in the contemporary church. King Saul loved himself more than anyone; therefore, he was a person who lived by his flesh. Three kings therefore represented three kinds of personae in the churches in Jia's days (Jia 1981b, 1105-1108). Based on his interpretation of these biblical characters, Jia described the spiritual quality as well as morality as the main essences of his leadership model.

TABLE 1: Great Faith Leaders of the Bible
(Jia Yuming 1981b: 1105-1108)

	King Saul	**King David**	**King Solomon**
Physical Appearance	Large Body	Great Spirit	Big Head
Spiritual Quality	Fleshly	Spiritual	Attached to the Soul
Religious Life	Society-oriented	Life-oriented	Liturgy-oriented
Attitudes	Selfish	Self-disciplined	Arrogant

Sanctification and Conscience

Another aspect of sanctification is its relationship with conscience. In Confucianism, the concepts of the innate knowledge of the good (*liang zhi*) and conscience (*liang xin* 良心) are used interchangeably although they are two different aspects of human mind-heart. Conscience is the operating system which governs a person to behave morally well. The innate knowledge of the good is the source of the moral self. Jia Yuming introduced the Confucian concept of the moral self into the Christian concept of sanctification. A Christian can become a morally perfect leader because God creates a passionate heart in human conscience. God does not use miracles to suddenly change a human being. God leaves this responsibility of becoming morally good to human beings because they already have the innate knowledge of the good. Human beings know what is necessary to satisfy the requirements of God because the conscience operates by governing their behaviors. All of this was part of the design when God created man and woman. Accordingly, one does not have any excuse not to be good. Human beings have an inescapable responsibility to become morally good individuals (Jia 1992b, 34-35).

In another passage, Jia pointed out the characteristics of Christianity as a religion with life, morality, and inner effort. He referred to the cultivation of spirit-life, moral behavior, and the *Christ-human* in the inner life of a Christian (Jia 1992d, 186-188). This illustration of the spirit-life has a similar connotation with the Confucian understanding of the mind-heart. The mind-heart exists where the heavenly principle resides and gives birth to morality. In other words, the mind-heart is the conscience. Jia reinforced the point that a conscience is a gift from God the creator (Jia 1992b, 34). Like Mencius, Jia affirmed morally good behavior as natural to human existence. The appreciation of others, material rewards, and fame are not necessary if someone follows his or her conscience to be a morally good person. Jia believed that God has given human beings the heavenly principle to be the moral standard in the human heart. The process of sanctification is therefore intended to develop the moral qualities given by the conscience:

> The human nature of the Chinese people is among the most kind-hearted in the world. Chinese people are morally good and peoples who love peace. Obviously villagers and farmers are morally good as they live close to nature. Their good hearts and behavior are actively shown every day. The moral and peaceful hearts of the farmers are also the good fields in the kingdom of heaven. Once the seeds of truth are laid, they grow fast, which brings a good harvest as well (Jia 1988, 158-160).

The major responsibility of the pastors is therefore to cultivate the seeds of good human nature. Jia borrowed the Confucian understanding of the role of Heaven in nurturing every creature on earth. He used the relationship between farmers and nature as an analogy to illustrate the human nature created by God. He combined the moral expectations of people with the universe created by God and assumed moral principles were found in physical nature. The natural growth of human beings thereby leads toward a direction of moral goodness. Sanctification, in this respect, is a process of the combined effort of human conscience and morality in the created universe. Sanctification is at the same time the process of exploring and developing human conscience. The Sermon on the Mount is comprised of the moral teachings of Jesus which record how he cultivated "the mind-heart of the people in the Kingdom of Heaven" (Jia 1990, 78). A church leader is therefore expected to be a person who lives out his or her morally good nature according to his or her conscience.

Victory as the Result of Sanctification

Salvation is only the beginning of a new life. The final destiny is victory in life. A Christian is assumed to continuously grow spiritually and not to stagnate. As sanctification and moral perfection are two sides of a coin, learning to live a holy life is naturally the most important element in the process of growth. In order to become a role model for others to follow, a leader must achieve the final goal of becoming a *Christ-human*. To become a *Christ-human* is the highest achievement one can reach on earth. Jia called it a victory in life (Jia 1992c, 255).

The Criteria of Victory

A victorious life for a Christian is to live a life of total union with the Lord. Jia believed a victorious life should have the following criteria: "Word becomes flesh and flesh becomes word;" "the Lord lives within me and I live within the Lord;" "from secular to holy and from holy back to secular" (Jia 1992c, 249-250). Jia described the ideal relationship between God and humanity as a unity. Although the wordings sound akin to Buddhism, the concepts are in fact borrowed from Confucianism. They carry a strong sense of "unity between heaven and humanity." Jia replaced the Confucian "heaven" with the Christian God, the Word, or the Logos. The real victory is to reflect the attributes of a holy God in a secular world. The newly converted Christians were not the main concern of Jia Yuming. His attention was on the Christians who wanted to have serious spiritual growth. The ways to develop disciples to live a victorious life were Jia's major concern.

Another category of criteria of a victorious life can be described as holiness, freedom, and rest. According to Jia's *Systematic Theology*, holiness means overcoming the desires of sin which comes from the worldly attractions and the self. Freedom means living without being controlled by sinful desires, enjoying life in the truth without any bondage, free to love and to recover the original goodness and beauty. Rest is the total peace of the mind and heart before the Lord—no frustration nor worry about one's daily needs in both body and soul (Jia 1992c, 251-252). In other words, the criteria of victory are decided by whether one has already entered into God's total salvation: true freedom and peace through believing in God.

Victory is a Process

The spiritual journey of a leader is as important as the final result. Without proper guidance and discipline in the process, final victory is not possible. A healthy spiritual growth requires a combination of three areas: knowledge, faith, and actions (Jia 1987, 256-260). Jia believed knowledge, faith, and actions are causally related. Faith without knowledge is superstition; however, having only knowledge of God but not total trust is not true faith. The process of spiritual growth is healthy only when a Christian acts according to what he or she believes is the truth.

This process of spiritual growth cannot be attained by mere human effort but only with the power of the Holy Spirit:

> The process of sanctification requires the efforts of spiritual discipline and cannot be achieved in a short period of time. Spiritual discipline does not occur through self-cultivation, but through the work of the Holy Spirit. This is a cultivation within the spirit, which means the Holy Spirit is a sculptor of one's spirit (Jia 1992c, 225).

Thus, Jia's expectations for church leaders are not concerned with their ability but with their behavior. The lifestyles of church leaders should reflect their faith and the works of the Holy Spirit. The achievement of the leaders cannot be the only criterion used to measure their success. The process of encountering God is also another important criterion to be included for consideration.

In summary, although the term *leadership model* does not appear in the work of Jia Yuming, the expectations for leaders are clearly defined. The concept of sanctification is understood as a journey of spiritual growth. All Christians should achieve spiritual maturity in order to attain the goal of total salvation. Church leaders should live an exemplary life and become role models for followers to imitate. To establish a leadership model, Jia began with the redemptive work of Christ. Only a fully saved person has the ability to become perfect. Perfection cannot be fulfilled by merely human effort. The moral perfection of humanity can only be achieved through the joint efforts of the Holy Spirit and the individual. The indwelling of the Holy Spirit makes perfection possible. In Jia's terminology, the *Christ-human* is the quintessential leadership model. In addition, human perfection can be seen through the moral life of an individual. Thus, the personality and social behavior of the leaders can reflect the attributes of God.

Jia Yuming's theology of sanctification is clothed with a Confucian understanding of human nature and the concept of Heaven. The most obvious feature Jia's doctrines have in common with Confucian relational leadership is the *Christ-human*, which is similar to the Confucian concept of the idealized human discussed in chapter three. The emphasis on moral leadership and the cultivation of the inner life qualities all lead to the development of the idealized human being.

Yang Shaotang's Pastoral Mentoring

If Jia Yuming provided a Chinese systematic theological perspective with Confucian characteristics, Yang Shaotang provided a practical theological perspective to the leadership development model for Chinese churches. Jia Yuming gave a Christian interpretation to the Confucian ideal leadership model of "inward sageliness and outward kingliness." Yang Shaotang provided practical guidelines for leadership in the Chinese cultural context.

Similar to Wang Mingdao and Jia Yuming, Yang Shaotang did not give a theoretical account of a leadership model; however, Yang's concern was primarily church development. According to Yang, there were two obstacles to developing a healthy church: the inferior quality of church workers and the absence of leadership teams. Church workers were actually the church leaders. However, the behavior of the church leaders was often not good enough for them to become the models for the congregation to follow. Yang pointed out a church leader should "go to the pulpit and preach the truth and come down from the pulpit and live as a role model. Preaching and leading are inseparable" (Yang 2005a, 79).[8] Role models are people who live what the Scriptures say literally. To become holy, they should be consistent in their beliefs and actions (Yang 1939, 104-106). The only way to become a perfect model is to imitate Christ, the highest standard of Christian life. The model Christ presents to human beings comes through his suffering and sacrifice on the cross; therefore, to follow Christ is to walk through his suffering every day (Yang 1939, 117-120, 1998, 282-283). The very first step in learning to be a leader is to learn from the model of Christ.

The second obstacle was unawareness of the necessity for developing coworkers of the leadership teams. Yang believed church workers should follow the model of the apostle Paul who worked together with Barnabas, Sirah, and Timothy in leadership teams (Yang 1939, 127-128). The church does not belong to any one person; therefore, not a single person can bear the responsibility for the whole church. Yang stated clearly that the biblical model was a model of team leadership. Without a team of coworkers working together, the church would not grow healthily (Yang 1939, 54).

Yang Shaotang assumed that the church was an organic organization. The church on earth is not perfect in the beginning and will grow and change in time. Only a holy church can become a useful tool to fulfill the purpose of God to all humankind. The work of the Holy Spirit is essential to lead and transform the imperfect church (Yang 1998, 132-134). The church will grow and change in relation to the quality of the church workers. Yang related church growth to the quality of the church leaders, which made leadership development the only solution to the problems of the church:

> Some of the churches today have sent students to theological seminaries. They think that the seminaries can help them to train pastors and teachers. These seminaries consider only the ability and academic degree of the students and assign them to various church positions. The seminary faculties are not really

---

8. The works of Yang cited here are coming from a combined and reprinted edition of Yang Shaotang's two books, *The Course of the Church* and *Church Growth*. These two books were first published in 1951 and 1957 respectively.

concerned with the spirituality and spiritual gifts of their graduates (Yang 1939, 71).

Yang Shaotang was more anti-intellectual than Jia Yuming. He emphasized the inner quality of the church leaders and denied the value of academic training in seminaries. Yang thought that the key attributes of good leaders were moral holiness and the spiritual insights (Yang 1998, 127). In addition, he believed that unity among the coworkers is the sign of a healthy church (Yang 1961, 11). With this background, Yang Shaotang founded the Spiritual Action Team to develop high quality church leaders according to his biblical standards.

In his works, Yang Shaotang emphasized three areas of leadership development: pastoral mentoring, character nurturing, and practical training.

Leadership Models and Pastoral Mentoring

The concept of pastoral mentoring comes from a relational understanding of mentoring. Walter C. Wright defines mentoring as "an intentional, exclusive, intensive, voluntary relationship between the leader and the follower. Mentoring is a relational experience in which one person empowers another by sharing him- or herself and his or her resources" (2000, 44). Mentoring is a one-to-one, or sometimes one-to-several, coaching and learning relationship.

In East Asian culture, a master-apprentice relationship carries a meaning similar to the Western conception of mentoring. The master-apprentice relationship has a long tradition in China. The apprentice learns the skills and personality of the master through living and working together with him or her. A good master carries the image of the parents as well; likewise, the master-apprentice relationship is similar to a parent-child relationship. The followers in the church expect their pastors to lead like the masters in Chinese tradition. I have thus termed this association a pastoral mentoring relationship. In this pastoral mentoring relationship, the pastor teaches the mentee the skills of leading and managing a congregation, cares about his or her spiritual growth, and gives advice in times of crisis in life and ministry as well. The pastoral mentoring relationship is fully reflected in Yang Shaotang's sermons and lectures.

The Church as the Extension of Family

The first and most important element of the pastoral mentoring relationship is the perception of family in Chinese culture. Yang Shaotang was born into a Christian family. His father had made at least two positive impacts on Yang's spiritual growth: he nurtured his faith in a Christian family and provided him a role model. In the *Record of Sermons of the East China Pastoral Retreat*, Yang said openly that his father was a good role model for him in learning what serving the church truly means (Yang 1941, 141-142). Yang understood the church as the extension of a family. Issues happening in the church are just like events happening in a family. The role of church leaders is similar to that of parents. In the church, a leader should likewise lead the family members to overcome the problems. Because of this belief, Yang founded the Spiritual Action Team in order to equip coworkers in a family-like institution (Yang 2005b, 237).

The relationship between the ministers and the congregation is similar to a parent-child relationship. In *God's Workmen*, Yang used family relationships to interpret the Corinthian epistles:

> What is the meaning of "spoken honestly" (2 Cor. 6:11)? There is nothing you cannot tell. "Hearts are wide-open" means that there is nothing you cannot forgive. Similar to the ways a father teaches his children, discipline comes from love (Yang 1961, 83).

Yang used family as a metaphor to illustrate the inter-personal relationship within a congregation. The pastor of a church is like a father as the head of the household; therefore, the pastor is the leader of the church. The main theme of the metaphor is the loving relationship in a church. The leader should love everyone in the congregation like the father who loves his children. A pastor, according to Yang, should have the heart of a father: teaching, encouraging, and nurturing the spiritual growth of the church members (Yang 1939, 70). Like a parent, a church leader therefore has the responsibility to love and educate the followers in the church.

The head of a household at the same time expects obedience from the congregation. The church members should give absolute obedience to the church leaders because the leaders are chosen and appointed by God. "The congregation can only recognize, accept, and work together" with the leaders (Yang 1939, 72). The congregation has no right to choose their pastor. Yang objected to all secular employment practices in the church. Ministers cannot bargain for their benefits with the congregation, and the congregation cannot treat the minister as an employee. As a servant of God, the minister represents and speaks for God. The decision he or she makes has authority. The only choice the congregation has is to "obey, listen, and accept [the pastor's] leadership" (Yang 1998, 36).

Yang Shaotang's exegeses were widely accepted in early twentieth century Chinese churches even though not many scholars accept his illustrations today. Yang mixed biblical principles with practice. In fact, the authority of the parents in a family is different from that of a leader in a church. The absolute obedience of the whole congregation to the leaders can lead to the abuse of authority. Having been born and raised in a good Christian family, Yang Shaotang was limited in his visualization of an idealistic role of a father in family. He applied only the positive use of power and authority in the church. Yang had experienced only loving relationships in a family and assumed the church was the same. A pastoral mentoring model can be applied to the master-apprentice relationship in a family-like situation. According to the observation of Yu Leekung, Yang's method was close to what William Carey (1761-1834) did with his coworkers: they lived and worked together like one extended family (Yu 2006, 129). The Spiritual Action Team Yang Shaotang established was evidence to support his theory.

Modeling as the Best Teaching and Learning Method
The second element of a pastoral mentoring relationship is modeling. Modeling is a teaching and learning method for both mentors and followers. The leaders and the followers can learn from one another in when they work together. Pastoral mentoring is a mutual learning process. The leaders should live exemplary lives so that they can be qualified to be role models for their congregations. At the same time, the followers are willing to imitate the leader's attitudes, behaviors, and lifestyle because the leaders are assumed to be the representatives of God. The leaders can be inspired

by the followers which will lead to his self improvement in leadership skills. Modeling is a common learning method in Chinese culture.

Yang Shaotang learned effectively through model himself on others. Yang Shaotang was willing to become a full-time minister because he met with some good examples of those who rightly modeled Christ (Yang 1941, 142). Christ is the ultimate role model for all Christians to follow. A leader who models him- or herself after Christ has also partaken on the spiritual authority from God. Under leadership representing the highest spiritual authority, church members take up "the same burden and the same passion" so that both leader and followers can accomplish the purpose of God together (Yang 2005a, 77).

Modeling oneself after Christ is the first priority. The apostle Paul was another model in Yang Shaotang's eyes. Paul functions as a model in the way he nurtured church leaders:

> Paul has given us a good example to follow. He has one young coworker working together with him, a son born from the gospel. They communicate intimately in spirit. Heart speaks to heart, and therefore they talk and work alike. This is the reason why Paul sent him as his representative to Macedonia and kept him at Ephesus to continue Paul's unfinished ministry (Yang 2005a, 86).

The coworker of Paul mentioned in this paragraph is Timothy. The ways Paul communicated, educated, and encouraged his coworkers constitute a model of leadership development. Church leaders should follow the model of Paul to equip more leaders. According to Yang, only those pastors who followed the footsteps of Paul could be named God's workmen (Yang 1961, 52).

Modeling is not simply following the behaviors and working habits of the mentor; it also necessitates the transformation of one's inner life. The "life of the apostles" is the standard church leaders should achieve. The apostles lived their lives with the sweet perfume of Christ which is exactly what the contemporary Chinese church leaders did not have, according to Yang. The sweet perfume of Christ is the holiness of Christ. A person who lives the holiness of Christ can naturally attract and change the lives of others (Yang 1961, 62). In other words, the transformation of one's inner life is meant to attract others to fear God (Yang 1998, 136). Thus Yang believed that modeling is an effective way to learn what Christ and his apostles demonstrated in the Bible. Such a leadership model is not simply an ideal but something that can be realized. To live like model leaders in history is more practical and attainable than merely learning the theory and doctrine about being a leader.

Long-term Relationships Among Leaders

Pastoral mentoring is to be understood as a long-term commitment for both senior and new leaders. The senior leaders are those who are older in age and have more experience as church leaders. In contrast, the new leaders are those younger in age or newer to the role of being a church leader. Both groups can actively learn from each other. Typically, the senior leaders are the mentors and serve as the role models for the new leaders. The new leaders are usually looking for people they can trust to be their mentors. They can grow into maturity when they find experienced leaders who are willing to help. Both the senior and new leaders engage actively in this pastoral mentoring relationship.

According to Yang Shaotang, the apostle Paul is a good example for leading the new and young leaders. Yang commented that the leaders of his day were short-sighted. Not many senior church leaders had learned from the model of Paul. They were concerned only about equipping themselves, and they neglected the newly emerging leaders. In Yang's eyes, those senior leaders were not "willing to nurture a potential Timothy" (Yang 1939, 126). Yang noticed one important criterion for pastoral mentoring: paying attention to the potential leaders in the church and guiding them to grow gradually into maturity. Yang had expectations for the potential mentors. He expected them to have patience as well as to provide encouragement and guidance to the new leaders. Control and manipulation were not allowed in this mentoring relationship. The senior leaders' task was simply to serve as role models for the young leaders to follow (Yang 1939, 46).

Pastoral mentoring was necessarily understood as a mutual relationship between the mentor and apprentices, and as such, the new leaders were expected show a humble attitude as they learned from the senior leaders. New leaders were expected to make progress through personal spiritual exercises they performed. Furthermore, the new leaders should not rely totally on the instructions of the senior leaders. Even though they were expected to learn from the senior leaders' experience and wisdom, the young leaders had to try their best to contribute to the leadership team (Yang 1939, 98; 1961, 12; 1998, 62). Yang did not believe that a single person could meet all the needs in a church. In fact, developing young leaders was one of the seven steps in building leadership team. According to Yang, inner life qualities, faith, spiritual gifts, and personality were the major areas in training young leaders (Yang 2005a, 75-100).[9] Team leadership must be composed of the senior and young leaders who would work together in building a healthy church.

Mentoring is relational in nature. Instead of functional and hierarchical relationships, the mentor-apprentice relationship seeks to benefit both the mentor and apprentice. Spiritual growth is the main purpose in this relationship. Following the role models described in the Bible, nurturing the spirituality of the young leaders is multi-dimensional. In addition to one's relationship with God, a young leader should learn the skills and techniques needed in leading church ministries and developing inter-personal relationships from his or her senior leaders. As a mentor, the senior leader bears the responsibility of a teacher, guardian, Bible instructor, and counselor at the same time. Sometimes, the mentor acts like a parent in order to nurture the inner life of the apprentices effectively. This model of leadership development combines the characteristics described in the Bible, Chinese cultural practices, and the roles of a pastor and parent.

Leadership Models and Character Nurturing

Anti-intellectualism was the main trend of theological thought in early twentieth century China. Anti-intellectualism rejected the interpretation of the Bible only through critical methods; however, it did not deny the value

---

9. The seven steps in building leadership team are: 1. All leaders are chosen by God; 2. All leaders should have unity in the Spirit; 3. A clear division of labor; 4. Recognition on the work of others; 5. Developing young leaders; 6. Accept team work in all areas of ministry; 7. Good inter-personal relationship (Yang 2005a, 75-100).

of knowledge as one of the gateways to know God. In contrast to the emphasis of seminary training, Yang Shaotang's teachings held that spiritual character was more important than the other qualities of a leader. He was repeatedly saying the moral and spiritual characteristics of a leader were far more important than his or her knowledge and ability (Yang 2005a, 85-86).

Yang was disappointed in seminary theological training. He denounced the training in seminaries as providing only academic knowledge but not the necessary inner qualities pastors should have. Thus, theological education through the seminary system cannot fulfill the need of the churches.

A Supplement to Seminary Training

The churches in China, according to Yang Shaotang, did not grow very steadily and healthily. A church leader should have higher moral and spiritual levels so as to become the role model for the congregation. Yang even said that what defined a good person according to secular standards could not be applied to the expectations of church leaders. Church leaders should have good behavior, know how to work with people, have a humble attitude, know the heart of Christ, and be filled by the Holy Spirit (Yang 1939, 129-139). Yang Shaotang stated that the ways the church recruited leaders were not biblically correct. He criticized the poor quality of spirituality and morality of the church leaders, writing that,

> The chosen leaders have some abilities and enthusiasm, but are not mature in spirituality. When they become leaders, they may think themselves as the masters of their congregations, always regarding themselves as having a higher status than other Christians (Yang 1939, 56).

Yang regarded those who had some abilities as already the more mature Christians in the congregation. It was not uncommon to find a selection of church leaders according to their interpersonal skill in the rural churches.

Yang also disagreed with the selection of leaders based on academic degree and/or diploma. To supplement the inadequacies of seminary training, Yang declared that the candidates for church leadership should go through a spiritual test—a study of their spiritual lives and an assessment of their morality and behavior (Yang 1998, 56). He objected to the graduates having a higher status, salary, and responsibility in the church compared with other non-seminary trained church workers. He even stated that seminary training was not a prerequisite of being a servant in a congregation. Learning to be a servant of Christ could be achieved through reading the Scripture and listening to sermons. In other words, Scripture saturation should be priority for a spiritual leader. The church leaders who appeared in the book of Acts did not have any formal, institutionalized theological education (Yang 1939, 93-94).

In view of the historical background of Yang Shaotang when he announced his theological perspective, many theological seminaries were founded by the Western churches with liberal theological traditions. Yang even criticized them as "social gospel" (Yang 2005a, 56). In this situation, Yang Shaotang rejected liberal theological tradition and denied that it had any potential value in providing appropriate theological training to the pastors.

However, even though Yang mistrusted the liberal seminaries, he was aware of the problems created by the free evangelists throughout China. The free evangelists traveled freely from one village to another preaching in the local churches. Many had not received any theological education but preached according to what they claimed was the vision given to them from the Holy Spirit. Sometimes, these free evangelists transmitted heretical teachings. With this issue in mind, Yang maintained that certain levels of theological education were important. As such, he was willing to accept and work with graduates from the fundamentalist theological training centers.

Whether one is with or without formal theological training was not the main issue to Yang Shaotang. One's spiritual journey with mature Christians or church leaders is more important in nurturing the spiritual life of a church leader. In this respect, Yang viewed seminary training as inadequate but not meaningless.

The Performance of a Leader

Determining the means by which to measure the spiritual and moral characteristics of a leader is no easy task. Since Yang believed that character is the most important criteria in deciding whether or not a person can be qualified as good leader, Yang Shaotang proposed the congregation find evidence of effective leadership through observation. Through the observation of a potential leader's behavior, one can find out which abilities and the spiritual gifts he or she has (Yang 1961, 37).

The first area of observation is the quality of work. The ability of a leader can be observed through the actual performance of daily operations in church ministry. The second area is the morality of a leader. People who "say one thing and doing another" are not qualified. Additionally, church leaders who work for their own benefit in the church are not qualified either. Yang criticized these bad leaders, saying,

> In spiritual terms, they understand and speak clearly the biblical truth and the ways one should behave; however, they behave falteringly and inconsistently. They have only the outside form of godliness but deny the power of God. All they have are the rules and laws but not the real life in Christ. Their Christian behavior is artificial, not naturally flowing from the heart (Yang 1998, 107).

Preaching and acting in daily life should bear witness together. The leaders should be consistent in what they say and how they act. Actions speak louder than words; as such, observation by the congregation is an effective way to find the evidence of God's calling overshadowing their leaders.

The third area of observation is the leader's attitude toward finances. The way they handle money can reflect their attitudes toward the materialistic world. The fourth area is their attitude toward physical desire; for example, how are they going to deal with relationships with the opposite sex? The fifth area is whether or not they are humble. In contrast to arrogant people, a humble leader leads his or her followers more effectively (Yang 1998, 59-62). Through observations in these five areas, Yang could determine whether or not the candidates were qualified as spiritual church leaders.

It is easy to see that as measurements, all five areas are quite subjective. Personal impressions and relationships with the potential leaders may affect the final judgment after the observations have been made. Observation is in fact an aspect of the Chinese intuitive decision-making process. Jia Yuming and Wang Mingdao shared a similar emphasis on observation as measurement.

Character First
Management skills are not included in Yang Shaotang's list of leadership expectations. The most important quality is not what skills one possesses, but one's moral character. Yang stated clearly that all kinds of skills and knowledge are not comparable to the importance of personal moral attributes. The increase in academic knowledge cannot be regarded as spiritual growth. Spiritual maturity should include the improvement and development of one's moral character (Yang 1998, 88-89). Character development comes neither naturally nor from academic training. Advice from senior leaders and self discipline are both necessary for this growth to occur. Three areas of spiritual exercises are needed.

Nurturing the inner life is the first exercise: "We can learn more working skills, understand more biblical truth, learn more evangelism methods, but we have to deal with our inner life in order to make progress. The outer life and inner life are all important" (Yang 1961, 60). Effective ministry comes only with a good inner life. If one does not have a good and influential life, relying on hard work alone will not bring fruitful results in ministry. A good church leader is therefore one who has a mature spiritual life with a good moral character.

Suffering is the second exercise to build up the attributes of a leader. Yang Shaotang agreed that Christ is the perfect and ultimate model for all church leaders to follow. Not only learning Christ's ministry skills and behavior, but also learning from his model of suffering is beneficial for leaders. Jesus Christ demonstrated servant leadership through his sacrifice on the cross. His life and ministry were characterized by his suffering, and as such, the success of the cross comes from the suffering of Christ. The attributes of the leaders are thus conditioned through hardships and adversity in life. The success of leaders is determined by their spiritual maturity, meaning they are not to conform to difficult situations just because doing otherwise is painful. Yang says,

> Suffering is the way of Christ's success. We are people who are following Christ; therefore, we must follow straightforwardly on the same way. The way to success is the way of bearing the cross. It is a delusion to dream of no cross, no suffering, no war, no sacrifice, and going to heaven peacefully (Yang 1998, 11).

Being filled with the Spirit is the third exercise. Character development is the fruit of the Holy Spirit. A good church leader is more than merely a good person. The virtues of Christ reflected in the life of a good leader. Only through the work of the Holy Spirit will the life of a person change in a godly way. When the leaders' attributes become more godly, the church will be transformed. Prosperity and growth come only with the work of the Holy Spirit in the life of the leaders. The final result is the glory of God through the churches (Yang 1998, 123).

In short, only a morally upright person can completely fulfill the requirements of being a good leader. According to Yang Shaotang, a good church leader has to be mature in his or her spiritual life as well. Only through the joint efforts of the Holy Spirit and personal discipline in spirituality will the inner life of a leader grow into maturity. Leading a healthy church requires a mature leader defined by his or her godly characteristics.

Pastoral Mentoring and Practical Training

Practical consideration is always a principle in the decision-making processes of Chinese pastors. Yang Shaotang addressed the practical needs of the church in developing church leaders. Having knowledge without practical experience is inadequate for someone who wants to become an effective leader. Through living and working together with the senior leader, one can develop practical leadership skills. When Yang was working in his hometown in Shanxi, he did not have enough church leaders working together with him in the thirteen congregations to which he was ministering. After noticing this need in the church, Yang established the Spiritual Action Team to address the problem of the lack of church leaders. He was at the same time serving thirteen congregations and developing church leaders through Spiritual Action Team. Learning through working together is highly recommended because working is also part of the learning process

(Yu 2006, 277-278). Pastoral mentoring is in fact one of the effective leadership development methods as it combines training and working together. Through actual ministering in the congregations, the potential church leaders gain valuable experience that cannot be learned simply by reading books and listening to lectures.

Experience is not limited to one's own subjective perceptions. The work of the Holy Spirit goes hand in hand with leadership development:

> Learning has two parts: knowledge and practice. The truth of the Bible and the ways of work are knowledge. Preaching in the pulpit and personal evangelism are practice. One has to learn that these two parts together are equally important (Yang 1939, 93).

In other words, Yang emphasized putting theory into practice. Even though both knowledge and practice are important, experience in the learning process has a higher priority. Practical skills are helpful to a church leader in leading him or her to work effectively. Experiences constitute more than merely acquiring skills. To experience the truth and promise of God is the most important value in the learning process. As God guides and helps those going through difficult times, a church worker will actually be experiencing the realization of God's promise. This process is known as "experiencing truth" in Yang's terminology (Yang 1939, 96).

The young leaders can learn from the senior leaders who have experienced the grace of God in the process of following Christ. This learning process is a pastoral mentoring process. The experiences the senior and young leaders share include difficulties, hardships, and, more importantly, solutions given by God. As servants of God, leaders should prepare for suffering as Christ did. Yang believed team work was beneficial to both the senior and young leaders as they learned and worked together. Through working together, they exchange experience, and each can inspire the other by sharing his or her perspective (Yu 2006, 278). The transfer of experiences is important, but the process is only a tool for the personal growth of the church leaders. Yang insisted transformation will happen in the process of working together, because the whole team will experience divine intervention in God's ministry. Most important of all, human efforts are in vain if they are not done through joint participating with God. God's intervention can be in the form of the inspiration of Holy Spirit, or revelation from the word of God (Yang 1939, 1).

The leadership development practices Yang Shaotang taught can be summarized as a leadership model developed through a pastoral mentoring relationship. The understanding of the relationship in the churches is based on the preconception of traditional Chinese hierarchical and loving relationship of a family. Similarly, teaching methods are comprised of modeling and transfer of experiences through cooperative efforts. The direction is to equip the inner spiritual life and moral character of the leaders but not to encourage managerial skills alone as theories from the West advocate. Yang valued the importance of the learning process. He insisted on maintaining lifelong relationships between the teachers and students as Jesus did. In addition, the most obvious feature of relational leadership found in Yang's theory is paternalistic leadership: the church as an extension of a family and the pastor as the undisputed leader with authority similar to that of a father in a household.

A Further Reflection on Relational Leadership in Chinese Churches

After studying the works of Wang Mingdao, Jia Yuming, and Yang Shaotang, a further reflection is made on relational leadership in the contemporary Chinese churches. All three pastors and theologians can represent the main stream of theological thoughts and practices in contemporary Chinese churches. Even though Chinese pastors may not be aware of or intentionally adopt the norms and values of Confucianism, their application of these values, especially regarding moral teachings, is high. Despite the fact that some of the differences between Christianity and Confucianism have not been resolved, pragmatic Chinese pastors are already living in a Confucian culture. With the increase in the knowledge about the common areas between Christianity and Confucianism, more possibilities exist in finding positive roles for Confucianism in developing church leaders and followers.

In chapter three, seven characteristics of Confucian leadership are concluded. They are an idealized human, moral leadership, modeling, extension of a family, paternalistic leadership, inner life quality, and pragmatic culture. After studying these three pastors, another summary can be made in order to reflect the centrality of relationship in Chinese Christian culture. They are the relationship with the divine, the relationship with the self, and relationships with others in the community. They are crucial aspects of Chinese relational leadership.

The Relationship with the Divine

In Confucianism, no space is available for a wholly other, divine being whom Christians call God. The mind is a principle, and the Mandate of Heaven is revealed directly to the human mind. Every person can become a sage through his or her own effort by self-cultivation. Despite the fact that the Neo-Confucians in the Song and Ming periods did not have the opportunity to hear about the personal Christian God, most of the Contemporary New Confucians who lived in late nineteenth century argue against the similarities between the Christian God and the Confucian heaven. Many of the early Contemporary New Confucians were born during in late eighteenth and early nineteenth centuries. They experienced the invasion of Western cultures and developed strong national and patriotic sentiments to protect Confucianism and Chinese culture against the Western culture represented by Christianity (Chen 2007, 200-201; J. Tang 1974, 56). Undeniably the belief in the ultimate goodness of a transcendent existence, which the Confucians call Heaven, shares similar attributes with the Christian concept of a transcendent God. In many cases, the Confucian concepts can be replaced with Christian terms without deviation from the original meaning (Tu 1985, 132). As Liu Shuxian points out, "Heaven was referred to as a personal God in ancient China" (Liu 1972, 45). In fact, in pre-Confucian China, Heaven was understood as a personal God (H. Yang 1981, 23-28). The understanding of God as Heaven at least reflects a common expectation of the Chinese Christians in bringing Christianity and Confucianism together.

On this common basis, faithfulness is also a common requirement of both Confucianism and Christianity. In Confucian philosophy, the

Mandate of Heaven is regarded as the ultimate standard of reference for human morality. The common goal of human development is to become a sage. A sage is expected to be the role model for a moral life according to the Mandate of Heaven. A Christian is also required to live a moral life, according to the standards given in the Bible and with guidance from the Holy Spirit.

It is easier for Chinese Christians to transfer the understanding of the transcendent Heaven into a transcendent God. Chinese Christians are familiar with the concept of a *Heaven-son* as a description of the leader. It is critical for the Chinese Christians to transfer this traditional faithfulness toward the human representative of heaven to the concept of a personal God. It is not unusual for Chinese Christians to have unrealistic expectations of a church leader because they have this unconscious idea of the Heaven-son. Chinese Christians have a tendency to idealize church leaders and ignore their imperfections (Leung 2003a, x-xii). The idealistic expectations of the Chinese pastors, the perfect morality in Wang Mingdao, and the Christ-human of Jia Yuming are coming from the belief in a total indwelling of the Holy Spirit through the power from the Divine. A human can achieve moral perfection through of the power of the Divine. This expectation of the possibility of becoming perfect remains an assumption about the development of human nature among Chinese pastors today.

The Relationship with the Self

The Confucian ideal is to become a sage. The Christian knows well that no sage can be found on earth. The fact that the Confucian relies totally on human effort, and the Christian relies on the guidance of the Holy Spirit is a significant difference in the leadership development process. The process of sanctification in Christian personal growth is a joint effort of the Holy Spirit and the human being. However, these differences aside, reliance on human discipline to become a sage or a better person is the bridge between Confucianism and Christianity.

The bridge is found in scripture-based learning cultures. Explaining and learning from scripture is not a new concept in China. The scriptures in the Chinese tradition are the Confucian classics, including the *Four Books* and the *Five Scriptures*. Many people began their schooling by reciting these scriptures before the introduction of the modern education system. Teachers were expected to be authorities in explaining the meaning of the scriptures. The influence of Zhu Xi lasted for several centuries because his exegesis on the *Four Books* served as the curriculum for civil examination. Chinese culture is a culture of exegesis that has used scriptural explanation to justify present action (Leung 2003b, 14-16).

Chinese church pastors may not be well aware of this exegetical tradition, but they apply it well in using the Bible together with the Confucian classics in their preaching and teaching. Wang Mingdao did not receive a formal theological education. He emphasized self learning through studying the Bible and prayers. He was a pragmatic pastor who applied the Bible to daily living. The Bible is a guide that helps Christians live a life pleasing to God (Leung 2003b, 24). In developing followers, leaders, or even sages, education based on the scriptures is the common method in China. The combination of Chinese traditional wisdom and Christian practices in using Scripture is one possible way of developing indigenous Chinese Christian leaders.

If becoming a sage is not the common ground between Christianity and Confucianism, then moral development should be the undisputable path of human development in both cultures. In line with Confucian culture, Christian churches in China emphasize moral development in sermons and other teachings. The selection of church leaders is based on their spirituality which has no objective criteria. Only through observable behaviors can the followers differentiate whether or not the leaders are spiritually mature. Self-cultivation in a Confucian Christian context is moral cultivation. The leader also teaches the followers that even a non-Christian can be a moral person. A Christian should uphold a higher standard. As a matter of fact, many teachings of Christian behavior are complementary with Confucian tradition. Moral leadership and followership are therefore the dominant characteristics of Chinese Christians.

The Relationship with Others

The morality requirement of Chinese tradition is relationship-oriented. Morality in the Confucian sense concerns the demonstration of appropriate behavior in living with others. The "Five Relationships" in traditional

Confucian culture is clearly an order of appropriate social relationships. A sage is also a person who organizes his or her relationship networks well. Because of the emphasis on relationships, Chinese culture is also known as a communal or collective culture. Self-cultivation cannot stand alone. The benefit of self-cultivation that is directed toward personal saintliness in turn serves to harmonize relationships with others (Tu 1985, 67). A mature person should be actively involved in society—including family, church, community, nation, and even the world (Tu 1985, 113-114). This concept is also the path laid down by the *Great Learning*. In Christian terms, salvation is the recovery of the original relationship with God the Father. Wang Mingdao quite often preached the sermon through applying Christian ethics into the "Five Relationships." The church as an extension of a family is also the platform for maintaining human "Five Relationships." A good leader in China should have good relationships with others. A good Christian leader should also have good relationships with others for the sake of his or her testimony as well as for effective ministry.

The purpose of having good relationships with others is to attract them to become Christians. In the meantime, good relationships are also the best way to develop followers. Because Chinese culture treasures concrete and applicable knowledge, modeling behavior is one of the most effective ways for followers to learn practically. Wang Yangming believed that the best two ways of teaching were through dialogue and example. Telling the truth is different than showing the truth. Yangming used the traditional wisdom of modeling in his development of followers. Modeling is not a systematic way of developing followers; however, it is an effective way because the multidimensional relationship with the followers is more effective than the transmission of knowledge through only a one-dimensional relationship (Tu 1976b, 141-143). Likewise, Wang Mingdao and Yang Shaotang give similar emphasis in developing church leaders. A church leader has the responsibility to lead by example: to live and to demonstrate what he or she preached to the congregation. A leader's personal holiness is related to the health of the church. Only a morally healthy leader can help the church of Christ develop in a healthy way (Wang 2005, 127).

Modeling oneself on a teacher or leader is the beginning stage of leadership development. The next stage is transferring the modeling from a human object to the Divine. The imitation of Christ is understandable in Chinese tradition because Confucianism also has the concept of imitating Heaven. Even though one can find the Mandate of Heaven in human nature, the human being is not totally identical with heaven. A sage is a person who has succeeded in imitating the way of heaven. He or she lives according to the standard laid down by the Mandate of Heaven (Liu 1972, 48). In view of leadership and followership development, leading by example is the most familiar model in Chinese tradition.

In summary, the theologies and practices of Wang Mingdao, Jia Yuming, and Yang Shaotang are highly indigenized. Relationship is the primary concern. The expectations and methods of leadership development all follow different forms of relationship. The relationship with the Divine helps to create idealistic expectations of leaders. Morality reflects the indwelling of the Divine in the Confucian context. The human development is therefore equivalent to the leadership development in terms of the cultivation of one's morality into maturity. Having a close relationship with the Divine makes it possible for a person to become holy or even morally perfect.

The cultivation of morality begins and ends with the cultivation of one's inner life. Beginning from developing the moral self, the leaders are characterized by their moral maturity observed in behaviors. As morality is observed and evaluated by the relationship with others, the effectiveness of the leader is then measured by the inter-personal relationship. Relational leadership is therefore the notable leadership style in the Chinese churches.

Summary

After the discussion of the situational factors in developing Chinese church leaders and the theologies of Wang Mingdao, Jia Yuming, and Yang Shaotang in this part, three implications for leadership development in Confucian context are found. A further discussion on relational leadership in Chinese church context, it is necessary to consider the situational factors in Chinese church context which is quite different from the Western society. An indigenous approach in leadership development is possible in Chinese churches as it has developed its own characteristics. In addition, some inadequacies of the works of the Chinese pastors are found in the process of incorporating Confucianism into Christian churches.

The Implication of Situational Factors in Chinese Leadership Development

The first implication for leadership development in the Chinese churches is the awareness of the impacts that historical, social, and cultural situations made in the church. The churches and church leaders exist in a specific environment which has an effect on them and vice versa. The strong influence of Confucianism has already been mentioned in the preceding discussions on the contextualization of Chinese Christianity. The influences of the missionaries faded away rapidly in early twentieth century. The anti-Christian movement in the 1920s and the TSPM in the 1950s sped up the process. The expectations of the qualities of a leader are largely shaped by Confucian culture; for example, moral leadership is the most popular type of leadership in the Chinese churches today. In a humanistic culture like China, the person and role of a leader, not the system nor the structure of the church, are most important.

Another important impact from the Chinese cultural and historical situations is fundamentalism. The daily practices of the Chinese churches today generally reflect fundamentalist beliefs. The theologies of Wang Mingdao, Jia Yuming, and Yang Shaotang reflected their anti-intellectual attitudes. They disagreed with the formal theological education of their day—not because of their educational level but their liberal theology. In their view, the purpose of leadership development is to meet the need of the churches in equipping the church leaders. Leading the congregation to grow in a healthy way is the primary responsibility of the pastors. The liberal tradition in seminary education in early- and mid-twentieth-century China was not able to fulfill their expectations.

The rise of Chinese nationalism also made a major impact on the churches. Concern for contextualization can be understood as a byproduct of nationalism. The anti-Christian movement was a major catalyst in speeding up the discussion of contextualization of Chinese Christianity. The TSPM was later developed under the slogan of anti-imperialism. "Christianity with Chinese characteristics" was a way to get rid of the image of foreign religions in China.

The Implication of the Indigenous Approaches to Leadership Development

The second implication for leadership development in Chinese churches is the collection of common features in the approaches of Wang Mingdao, Jia Yuming, and Yang Shaotang toward developing leaders. First of all, modeling is an effective way of learning to be a leader. Christ is the perfect model for all Christians to follow. Jia Yuming named the idealized human model as the *Christ-human* which meant a person can fully live a Christ-like life with a heart and mind united with him. This is clearly a Christo-centric theology. Second to Christ as role models are King David and the apostle Paul. In addition to biblical models, Yang allowed that some other church leaders or missionaries in history or even today can also be role models. The experiences of the senior leaders are helpful guidelines for the younger church leaders to follow. In a similar way, Wang Mingdao urged the church leaders to live an exemplary life so as to testify to the God they believed in.

Another common characteristic is the measurement of the inner quality of the leaders by their moral behavior. All three pastors required the congregation to discern whether or not a person was a spiritual leader through observing his or her behavior. Good deeds are no help in salvation, but good deeds can reflect the condition of one's faith. Since Confucianism upholds moral behavior as the standard to evaluate a person, having high expectations of church leaders is understandable. A church leader keeps a higher moral standard which is helpful for evangelism as Chinese Christians are still a minority in society.

The third characteristic the three pastors shared is their belief in the effectiveness of mentoring and developing leaders in China. None of them used the term *mentoring* explicitly; however, the concept is clearly shown in their works. Mingdao, Jia, and Yang valued the informal training of church workers in contrast to seminary education. Through working together with an apprentice, a mentor can help develop not only the necessary skills in ministry but also the apprentice's personality, spirituality, and morality. To achieve sanctification as a process of spiritual growth, the apprentice must overcome hardships and difficulties together with his or her mentor. By supplementing formal theological training with this informal leadership development method, the apprentice can apply theory to practice and thus benefit from the experience of an established leader.

The Implication of the Inadequacies

The third implication is that Wang Mingdao's, Jia Yuming's, and Yang Shaotang's theologies are inadequate in two areas: idealization and subjective observation. Thus, contemporary Chinese churches should approach their theories and practices with caution and revision.

Perfectionism is one of the common assumptions Mingdao, Jia, and Yang held about humanity. Although the Bible and church history contain many good role models, none of them are perfect, except for Jesus. Modeling is a necessary and effective way of learning, especially when the contents of learning are moral characters, behavior, and spirituality. In fact, Mingdao, Jia, and Yang idealized the biblical models as perfect human beings. In order to justify their claim of the possibility of achieving human perfection, the weaknesses of Abraham, David, and Paul are disregarded. Jia's concept of the *Christ-human* leads to the possibility of idolization of human beings. As Kwok Wailuen points out,

> The Chinese conservative churches use the functional approach in theological discussion which persuades Christians to believe in the possibility of achieving a "total sanctification" status. They look for a formula of a "higher standard of living" according to the "supreme" models presented by their leaders. The original version of "Christo-centric" is thus changed to "human-centric" gradually (Kwok 2003, 89).

Kwok has further explained the reason behind Jia Yuming's establishment of perfect biblical models. The quality of the Christians in early twentieth century China was not good in terms of spirituality and morality. Together with Jia and Yang, Wang Mingdao and John Sung's sermons and books show similar accounts in idealizing biblical models. The problem of the "human-centric" theology is therefore both a cultural as well as a historical phenomenon. Learning from human models is understandable. The problem is not the desire to become perfect but expecting perfection as a real possibility. The fallibility of human beings in the Christian tradition and the idealization of human beings in Confucianism are sometimes contradictory. In other words, even though the church leaders believe that becoming a perfect leader is possible, the possibility is low. The idealization of imperfect human beings is commonly found in the expectations of leaders. This may be the source of crises in today's churches.

In contrast to the use of quantitative measurement to evaluate leadership attributes in the West, Wang Mingdao, Jia Yuming, and Yang Shaotang all agreed to measure by observation. Observation is no doubt useful in the context of working and living together; however, it is too subjective. Hypocrisy becomes a constant challenge to Chinese churches with the lack of objective standards to measure morality. The negative consequences are unending criticism of the private life of leaders. Comments about others' lives and gossip are found commonly among church members.

The expectations followers have of their leaders in a collective culture like China's should be seriously noted. Living and working in a culture that values mutual relationships and expects them to be harmonious requires a high standard for interpersonal skills. These skills are not simply techniques in settling interpersonal problems; they also reflect the personality of a leader. The expectations of a leader are therefore not focused on ability and performance but on who he or she is and how he or she lives. Morality is therefore the major concern in Chinese leadership development.

Wang Yangming clarified the Confucian expectation of sagehood. The process of becoming a sage shares some similarities with Christian sanctification. When expectations are deeply rooted in a culture, people naturally perform according to those expectations. The culture drives the expectations of the followers in shaping the performance of the leader. In the meantime, the leader also expects him- or herself to perform accordingly. Studying the *Four Books* and *Five Classics* is no longer required in contemporary Chinese education systems, yet the influences of Confucianism remain strong. The Chinese government in mainland China is promoting the revival of Confucianism. In short the awareness of the positive and negative impact of Confucianism on leadership development is necessary. On the positive side, human potential will be released because of the optimistic view of human nature. On the negative side, human-made idols will repeatedly appear in Chinese history. The evidence to support the findings in this chapter will be illustrated through the field data collection and analysis in the next part.

Part III: Relational Leadership in Contemporary Chinese Churches

CHAPTER 6

Internal and External Situations of Urumqi, Sanyuan, and Fuzhou Churches

From the cultural and historical perspectives, the major elements of relational leadership are found in the Chinese churches. The specific Chinese situations in the twentieth century helped the development of indigenous Chinese leadership patterns. After the discussions on the characteristics discovered from the theoretical, cultural, and historical perspectives, it is necessary to find the evidence from the contemporary Chinese churches to support the theory of relational leadership. No theory of leadership development has been developed in contemporary Chinese churches; however, my case studies have discovered some effective practices of leadership development on the churches located in Urumqi, Sanyuan, and Fuzhou. These churches were selected because of their distinctive characteristics and representations in the PRC. The Urumqi church represents a Han Chinese church located in a Muslim community. The church leaders have a strong missional background. The Sanyuan church has a strong family network within its local county. Social ties are a typical phenomenon in Chinese society. The Fuzhou church represents one of the most influential Chinese indigenous church affiliations, the CAH. More details are given below. The case studies discussed in this and the next chapters reflect the current practices of the contemporary Chinese churches in developing followers as leaders. These case studies were conducted between 2008 and 2010. I stayed in Urumqi for a week in 2008, in Sanyuan for another week in 2009, and I visited Fuzhou three times between 2008 and 2009 to arrange and conduct interviews. Before the actual interviews, I had already built

TABLE 2: Interview Schedule

Case	Code of Name	Duration of Interview (minutes)*	Date	Remarks
Urumqi	HQZ	184	June 11, 2008	First met in 2001
Urumqi	FCG	155	June 12, 2008	First met in 2001
Urumqi	CXQ	144	June 11, 2008	First met in 2001
Urumqi	JQ	80	June 13, 2008	First met in 2001
Urumqi	CHB	52	June 12, 2008	First met in 2002
Urumqi	ZL	50	June 13, 2008	First met in 2008
Urumqi	ZSH	50	June 13, 2008	First met in 2002
Urumqi	LQF	40	June 12, 2008	First met in 2001
Urumqi	SJH	37	June 12, 2008	First met in 2008
Urumqi	YJ	25	June 13, 2008	First met in 2005
Urumqi	LWG	25	June 13, 2008	First met in 2008
Sanyuan	ZGR	72	July 28, 2009	First met in 2001
Sanyuan	ZFQ	71	July 28, 2009	First met in 2009
Sanyuan	YHT	70	July 28, 2009	First met in 1999
Sanyuan	YYL	53	July 29, 2009	By local interviewer
Sanyuan	YCQ	41	July 28, 2009	First met in 2001
Sanyuan	LXN	25	July 29, 2009	By local interviewer
Sanyuan	YHG	22	July 28, 2009	First met in 2001
Sanyuan	CYP	18	July 28, 2009	First met in 2009
Fuzhou	YZD	133	July 22, 2009	First met in 2008
Fuzhou	LDJ	79	July 23, 2009	First met in 2008
Fuzhou	CJ	43	July 23, 2009	First met in 2009
Fuzhou	YJY	41	July 24, 2009	First met in 2009
Fuzhou	LSQ	30	July 24, 2009	First met in 2009
Fuzhou	ZX	30	Nov. 10, 2009	By local interviewer

* The duration includes only the time during the interview with voice recorder. Some information was gathered before and after the interview in the form of casual talk.

the rapport with the informants. From these ethnographic interviews, participant observations, and life story interviews, I studied the background of the churches and the leadership development process. The influence of Confucianism and the legacies of the indigenous Chinese theologians are reflected in all these case studies. Before the analysis of the findings, the internal and external situations and their impact on the church leaders are discussed below.

General Information on the Churches in China in This Study

A total of twenty-five church leaders were interviewed. I interviewed all the church leaders in Urumqi and the major church leaders in Sanyuan and Fuzhou. I have personally known the old pastors in Urumqi and Sanyuan for about ten years. The life story interviews lasted for a few hours but the information had already been collected for some years. In Table 2, details of the schedule and the duration of the interviews are listed. The percentage of male and female pastors was 56 percent male and 44 percent female; which is a fairly accurate representation of the gender ratio in church leadership in the PRC even though female church members outnumber male members in the churches. According to a recent survey on Christianity by the Chinese government, around 70 percent of the Christian population is female; however, males still dominate the leadership of Chinese churches (Jin and Qiu 2010, 111-138).[1] Figure 3 shows the gender of the informants in all three churches. In the cases of Urumqi and Sanyang, I interviewed all the church leaders who serve as pastors in the area. The key leader in Urumqi now is a woman pastor who has the support of the old male pastors. In the cases of Sanyang and Fuzhou, the leadership is clearly dominated by men. To a large extent, leadership in general is dominated by males in China. It is more difficult to find potential male leaders when the percentage of male church members is only 30 percent. More female pastors are needed

---

1. The survey conducted by the government includes only the number of Christians in the official churches. The non-registered churches are excluded.

in the church because of the overwhelming proportion of female members. In fact, it is clear from the situation in these three churches that gender is an issue in Chinese church leadership. That church members expect male leadership in accordance with Chinese tradition is understandable. Further studies on the gender issue in Chinese church leadership are needed.

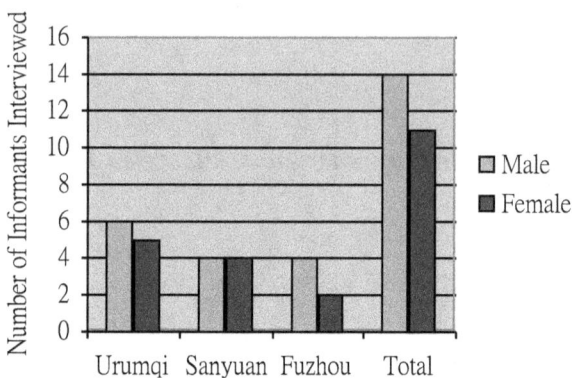

FIGURE 3: Informants: Male and Female

The other general phenomenon reflected in this research is the disparity in age groups of the leaders interviewed. A general characteristic of the churches in PRC is the absence of middle-aged believers. Due to the impact of the Cultural Revolution (1966-1976), certain generations have difficulty believing in or committing to the Christian faith. The major reasons for their resistance to religion seem to be a strong sense of mistrust of idealism and religion. From Table 3 it is clear that the age groups between sixty and eighty are missing in the leadership teams of these three churches. The majority of the young leaders are between thirty and forty years of age. This is the leadership gap in the churches in China. In the Urumqi church we found two old pastors who are still serving in the church without having retired which is very usual in China. In the Sanyuan church, the age group distribution is comparatively even because many of the informants grew up in Christian families. The relations among the church leaders are similar to three-generational family relationships. In my observations, the young leaders under forty regarded the old pastors as their grandfathers, and those between fifty and sixty as parents. The age group distribution is one factor that contributed to the family characteristics of the leadership in this church.

TABLE 3: Informants: Age Groups

Age\City	Urumqi	Sanyuan	Fuzhou	Total
21-30	0	1	0	1
31-40	8	2	4	14
41-50	0	2	1	3
51-60	1	2	0	3
61-70	0	0	0	0
71-80	0	0	0	0
80 or above	2	1	1	4

The third phenomenon of the churches reflected in this survey is the autonomy of the TSPM churches. The TSPM churches are the only Christian churches legally recognized by the Chinese government. The organizations representing these churches are the National Committee of the Three Self Patriotic Movement (TSPM) and the China Christian Council (CCC). The TSPM was founded in the 1940s while the CCC was founded in the 1980s. Their major responsibility is to manage and develop Chinese local churches.

According to government policy, every church is required to register with the Religious Affairs Bureau (RAB). If there is no TSPM or CCC organization in its city, the church leaders should organize and found these two organizations. If these governing bodies exist, the local church simply joins them as a member. The TSPM and CCC are divided into different administrative levels according to the corresponding political structure, namely, national, provincial, city, and in some occasions, county levels. The TSPM and the CCC are usually referring as "two associations" (*liang hui* 兩會) because they always exist together. Except at the national level, the two associations usually share the same office and some of the leaders hold joint positions in both organizations.

All three churches in this study are registered with the RAB. Other names used by foreign Christians to describe the TSPM churches are *government churches*, *open churches*, and *official churches*. People have the impression that the government has tight control over the daily operations of the church, such as the appointment and ordination of pastors, the content of the sermons, and the use of financial resources. As I travel extensively in mainland China, I notice that in some cases, the government has indirectly influenced the appointment of leaders. However, according to my interviews in these three TSPM churches, they are free to do anything they wish in their internal affairs without direct interference from the government. In each of these three cases, the appointment of church leaders is considered entirely an internal affair to be determined by the church itself.

Urumqi: An Expanding Church with a Harmonious Leadership Team

The first case study in the church in Urumqi, a city located in Northwestern China with a multi-ethnic background.

Geographical and Political Background

Urumqi is the capital city of Xinjiang, the farthest northwestern province in mainland China (Map 1). Owing to the racial policy of the Chinese government, many Han Chinese have moved to Xinjiang since 1949. Before the Communist government came to power, however, the majority of the population was Uyghur, a Muslim ethnic group with physical characteristics similar to Turks. Today, however, the Uyghurs are a racial minority in China. According to recent government statistics, only 47.47 percent of the population now are Uyghur while 37.58 percent are Han Chinese (People's Daily Online 2010). Urumqi was formerly known as Dihua. The name can be found in early missionary reports before 1949.

In the past few years, the Chinese government has been troubled by the East Turkestan Islamic Movement which claims that Xinjiang should be an independent Islamic country (Fletcher and Bajoria 2008). Foreign activities, especially Christian missionary activities, are regarded as a threat to the national and religious stability in Xinjiang because they have encroached on the Islam faith. The missionary activities will provide an excuse for the Muslims to revolt against the government as the government is not able to safeguard the Islamic faith as promised. Hence, most foreign Christian activities were suspended and foreign Christians were expelled from Xinjiang in 2008 before the Beijing Olympic Games. The TSPM churches in Xinjiang cannot reach out to the Uyghurs because of this religious sensitivity; therefore, the growth of the congregations comes from an increase of the Han Chinese Christians. I visited the Urumqi church again in June 2008, just two months before the Beijing Olympic Games. I saw many police officers and public security personnel patrolling the streets every day. Since I am a Chinese from Hong Kong, I did not have any problem with interviewing the pastors in the church located in the city center.

MAP 1: Location of Urumqi, Xinjiang

A Brief History of Christianity in Urumqi

The China Inland Mission (CIM) was the earliest mission to Xinjiang, which sent missionaries as early as 1876. In fact, the first gospel station was opened only in 1905 in Urumqi by George Hunter (Broomhall 1934, 61). The CIM later sent Percy Mather and Emil Fischbacher to Urumqi. The number of Christians did not increase in those years. One reason was the social instability caused by the continuous rebellions of the Muslims against the Chinese governor. The two missionaries Mather and Fischbacher were busy day and night in taking care of the wounded citizens in Urumqi, a city without any medical service. Both died in 1933 of overwork and typhoid (Lambert 2009, 3). Even though they did not bring many people to Christ, their sacrifice for the people in China was an effective witness for Christ.

The Urumqi church relocated their graves to the church cemetery in 1979, and the congregation visits the graves every Easter to remember the two missionaries' sacrifice (Q. Huang 2005, 3).

After the missionaries' deaths, the church had developed without any foreign help until the 1940s. According to Pastor HQZ, one of the old pastors I interviewed, some Christians from Henan province migrated to Urumqi between 1943-44. They became the foundation of the Han Chinese Church. Almost at the same time, Pastor Li Kaihuan and his wife responded to a call from God and moved to Urumqi from southwestern China in 1945 (Q. Huang 2005, 3). Li founded and became the first pastor of the Chinese Christian Church of Urumqi. Several indigenous mission groups targeting Xinjiang arrived between 1948 and 1954. The two most influential mission groups were the Northwest Spiritual Movement (NSM)[2] and the Chinese Christian Preach the Gospel Everywhere Band (usually translated as the Back to Jerusalem Evangelistic Band, BJEB).[3] All these missions were willing to cooperate with and assist those who had already begun their ministries earlier. CXQ and HQZ, the two old pastors I interviewed, came from the NSM and BJEB respectively. They worked together with different missionaries, and since the 1940s they have devoted themselves to developing the migrant's church in Urumqi.

As in churches in the coastal areas and other parts of China, all the activities in Urumqi church had to be suspended under the Communist government. Between 1953 and 1979, no church activity was permitted openly in Urumqi because of the political movements. Right after the Reform and Open policy launched in 1979, the pastors and elders were released from

---

2. The NSM was an indigenous mission organization founded in Wei Fang, Shangdong Province in 1946. Zhang Guquan (張谷泉, 1920-1956), the founder of the NSM who was a graduate of North China Seminary. Zhang followed the theology of Jia Yuming and the NSM was therefore regarded as an extension of Spiritual Institute. Between 1946 and 1948, different groups of forty-two members from the NSM arrived in Xinjiang (Fan 2005a, 21; Zou 2005, 23-24; X. Chen 2005, 9).

3. The BJEB was founded in 1943 by the vice-principal of the CIM's North West Bible Institute in Feng Xiang, Mark Ma (馬馬可, 1913-2008). A group of seminary students followed the vision of Ma and began a mission outreach trip to northwestern China in 1946. I had the opportunity to meet with He Enzheng personally in June 2001 in Kashgar. She was one of the members of BJEB who went to Xinjiang in 1947. She told me the story of how she came to Kashgar with her husband, Zhao Mecca. Their stories were later written and published in Taiwan by Wang Juichen (2003).

labor camp and began to resume church activities (X. Chen 2005, 11). In 1985, the original Xinjiang Chinese Christian Church was re-opened in the street Mingdelu which is located near the city center and was registered as a TSPM church. From 1985, the Urumqi church in Mindgelu has been the central church of the whole city. The term *Urumqi church* is not referring to a single church building with a group of pastors working together to serve the same congregation every Sunday. Rather, in addition to the main church located in city center, sixteen other churches (meeting points)[4] are registered and under the governance of the main church and the same group of church leaders. The same leadership team is responsible for the ministries of these seventeen churches. A single Urumqi church developed into seventeen churches in twenty years. The number of Christians has grown from 600 in 1985, to more than 20,000 in 2005 (Q. Huang 2005, 4). By the time I interviewed the pastors in 2008, the number of meeting points had grown to eighteen, and the members of the church had reached 25000. Including the main church located in the city center, there are now nineteen open churches in the city of Urumqi.

The provincial government in Xinjiang is so conservative that it does not allow the expansion and development of religions other than Islam, because the government does not want to stir up the religious and national sentiments in the Uyghurs; therefore, the two associations (the TSPM and CCC) of the Protestant church do not exist at the provincial level. Religions other than Islam are perceived as a threat to the social stability in Xinjiang. As a capital city, Urumqi can enjoy more freedom than can other areas of Xinjiang. The TSPM and the CCC do exist in Urumqi at the city level. The pastors in the two associations in Urumqi have the responsibility of taking care of the needs of the churches in Urumqi. All congregations in Urumqi are under the leadership of the two Urumqi associations. Because of the reputation and seniority of the old pastors, all the churches in Xinjiang outside Urumqi are actually looking for help and leadership from the Urumqi church.

---

4. A meeting point can be understood as a local congregation without its own TSPM committed organized. A meeting point is usually affiliated with a city or provincial TSPM. All religious activities and personnel are supposed to be approved by the TSPM church.

The Informants and Interviews

Most of the pastors I interviewed have leadership roles in the Urumqi TSPM and CCC. As mentioned earlier, sometimes the same person occupies joint positions in the two associations. Table 4 shows that the pastors HQZ, CXQ, and FCG have taken all the leading positions of TSPM and CCC. According to the church's records, the Urumqi TSPM/CCC was formed in 1994. Since then, HQZ, CXQ, and FCG have taken the leadership positions. Other positions have been filled by younger pastors or elders but not the chair and general secretary positions (Urumqi China Christian Council 2005, 27-28).

In response to my request, Pastor FCG selected the informants for this study. She is in charge of the church's daily operations. The old pastors CXQ and HQZ are only figureheads. My request was to interview the pastors; therefore, FCG did not arrange interviews with other committee members of the TSPM/CCC who are representatives from the laity. All these pastors, including the old pastors, are preachers, teachers, and senior pastors of the nineteen congregations. Some of them even have to look after two congregations.

TABLE 4: Positions of the Pastors in Urumqi TSPM/CCC Church

Name Code	Position in TSPM/CCC	Age*	Gender
CXQ	Chairman and President	90	M
HQZ	Vice-Chairman and Vice-President	87	M
FCG	Vice-Chairman and Vice-President, General Sectary	57	F
LQF	Committee Member	37	M
ZSH	Committee Member	38	F
ZL		36	F
YJ		34	M
SJH		37	F
LWG		35	M
JQ		39	F
CHB		38	M

*The ages listed in this table are at the date of the interviews.

As a result of the interviews, four important features were found in relation to leadership development. The first one is the family backgrounds of the informants. Among all eleven informants, only four were not born into Christian families (HQZ, LQF, ZSH, and CHB). In the beginning of each interview, I asked them why and how they became Christians.[5] All the responses began with statements telling whether or not they came from a Christian family. As a common feature, they were all prepared to share about their family background. Family background was an important contributing factor in each of their faith or at least showing some kind of linkage between family and church life. Some of them were even dedicated to God by their parents when they were still children (FCG and ZL).

The second feature is the relationship with foreign Christian churches and organizations. Unlike other churches in the mainland and coastal areas, the Urumqi church is located in a very remote province in northwestern China. Not many foreigners visited the Urumqi church each year compared with churches located in the mainland and coastal areas. The pastors cautiously keep a distance from foreign churches and organizations in all aspects of ministry cooperation. For example, the coastal churches welcome donations from foreign churches and organizations to support the church ministries and even welcome foreign scholars or pastors to come and preach to their congregations. In contrast, Urumqi is different because of the local political and religious sensitivities.

One reason for the conservative attitude of the Urumqi church is that the church is located in a city surrounded by Muslims. The other reason is the conservative theological background of the pastors. HQZ was trained under CIM Bible schools in the 1940s, and CXQ has not received any formal theological education. Based on my observations over the past few years, these pastors welcome visitors to come and share informally on a personal basis. In fact, they take a long time to observe a foreigner before they will accept him or her as a partner. Under these circumstances, the leadership development method and pattern in the Urumqi church is unique and purely indigenous because no foreign help is found in the process.

---

5. Please refer to appendices A and B for more information on interviewing questions in the interview guides.

The third feature is the mission background of the pastors. HQZ (appendix F) belonged to the BJEB which intended to carry the good news back to Jerusalem. CXQ (appendix G) joined the NSM in the 1940s, another group carrying a vision to plant churches in Northwestern China. FCG was deeply influenced by her parents who were members of BJEB. The open churches in China have been restricted by religious policies and therefore cannot really launch any cross-cultural mission targeting the Uygurs or the Kazakhs in Xinjiang. Instead, the pastors keep a strong sense of mission for the Han Chinese. The vision of the church is therefore not side-tracked by other ministries, for example, investing resources in social services as other churches do in the mainland and coastal areas. Local evangelism is the main focus of the Urumqi church.

TABLE 5: Background of Theological Education of the Young Pastors in Urumqi

Name Code	Age	Years of Study in Yinjing Seminary	Remarks
FCG	57	1985-1988	The first class since the re-opening of the seminary after the Cultural Revolution.
LQF	37	1997-2000	Did not finish his study because of health problem.
ZSH	38	1997-2001	
ZL	36	1995-2000	Wife of CHB.
YJ	34	1999-2003	
SJH	37	1999-2003	
LWG	35	1993-1998	
JQ	39	1997-2000, 2001-2002	Returned to Urumqi in 2000 because of a health problem. She continued and finished her study after a year.
CHB	38	1995-2000	Husband of ZL.

The fourth feature is the young pastors' background in theological education. Due to the policy of the CCC, only the Nanjing Jinling Theological Seminary and Beijing Yinjing Theological Seminary can recruit students from Xinjiang. All the young pastors, including FCG, are graduates of the Yinjing Seminary. In response to my question about the value of theological education, many of them named the same group of seminary teachers as those who had particularly made an impact on them. Table 5 shows the years the young pastors were studying in the seminary, which gives a clear picture of the similarities and differences in the comments on theological training. Except FCG, all other informants should have met one another at school in the year 1997. They all studied at Yinjing Seminary in the 1990s. They shared some similar experiences about the teachers and curriculum in the seminary.

These internal and external situations of the Urumqi church have created a unique environment for leadership development. The ministry is indigenous. A stronger influence from the personality and tradition of the old pastors is discovered.

Sanyuan: A Church Characterized by Family Relationships

The second case study is a church located in central China. Sanyuan is a city located near Xian, the capital of ancient China.

Geographical and Political Background

Sanyuan County is located in northwest China near Xian, the capital city of Shaanxi Province (Map 2). Even though it is a rural county with about an hour's traveling distance from Xian, Sanyuan was an early mission center in northwestern China. As early as 1876, the CIM sent missionaries to central Shaanxi where Sanyuan County was located (X. Wang 2007, 241). The population is mostly Han Chinese, but around Xian it also includes some Hui people, a traditional Muslim group.

MAP 2: Location of SanYuan, Shaanxi

A Brief Historical Background of Sanyuan Churches

According to ZGR, the first group of Chinese Christians came from Shandong Province in the east in 1889 during the late Qing period. The migration was initiated by the Qing government because of its wars with the Hui people in northwest China. The Qing government wanted to have more peaceful Han people move to the area in order to minimize the proportion of unfriendly Muslims in the overall population. The Christians in Shandong responded to the government and understood this migration as a mission opportunity. They named it "the gospel migration": migration in order to share the gospel.

In addition to the foreign missions working in this area, the Chinese Christian Church had established a parish in 1926, which included Sanyuan, Fuping, and other five counties together (X. Wang 2007, 263). Before 1949, Sanyuan was the mission center of the parish, and the pastors of the Sanyuan church were the leaders of the churches in those seven counties. The churches grew very fast in the early twentieth century. Some villages' population were 100 percent Christian and were therefore named "the Gospel Villages."

As the headquarters of the Chinese Christian Church in the area, Sanyuan suffered the most serious persecution during the Cultural Revolution. The churches were closed. The pastors were arrested and sentenced to labor camps. After the end of the Cultural Revolution, Sanyuan resumed its place as an influential church center in the 1980s. After the establishment of the TSPM in Shaanxi Province, the structure and practices of the churches had to change in response to government policy. The administrative center of the churches had to move to Xian. Interestingly, however, in 1983 ZGR founded a Bible school in Sanyuan instead of Xian. Even though the majority of the leaders of the TSPM were located in Xian, the impact of Sanyuan in Shaanxi remained (although the Bible school moved to Xian in the mid-1990s).

Before the Cultural Revolution, this parish contained only 3,000 Christians scattered across eight counties, but now the whole district has more than 80,000 Christians in registered churches. According to ZGR, Sanyuan County alone has around 6,000 Christians in twenty-four meeting points.

The Informants and Interviews

Local interviewers I trained, along with myself, interviewed eight informants in Sanyuan and Fuping counties. Five of them belonged to two families. ZBR and ZFQ are father and daughter. ZFQ, who has no formal theological education, works under YCQ in Sanyuan churches. YCQ is the father of YHT and YHG. YHG works under the leadership of his father. YHT, the elder brother of YHG, is the senior pastor of the Fuping church, a county next to Sanyuan, a 40 minute traveling distance by car. YHT, YYL, and LXN work together in the Fuping church while the others work and live together in Sanyuan. Table 6 shows the positions, ages, and genders of the informants.

As stated above, ZGR founded the first Bible school in Shaanxi Province in Sanyuan in 1983. When ZGR retired from the leadership position in the school, he kept the title of honorable president of the seminary. The school later moved to Xian and was renamed Shaanxi Theological Seminary. ZGR taught over 300 students in more than twenty years at the Bible school. He has great influence among the church leaders today throughout the entire Shaanxi Province. Five out of eight informants are graduates of the Shaanxi Bible School. YHT graduated from Nanjing Jinling Theological Seminary and ZGR received theological education from three different schools.

TABLE 6: The Major Responsibilities of the Church Leaders in Sanyuan and Fuping Churches

Name Code	Responsibility in the Church	Age*	Gender
ZGR	Retired Pastor	85	M
YCQ	Senior Pastor in Sanyuan church	57	M
YHT	Senior Pastor in Fuping church	35	M
YHG	Pastor in Sanyuan church	33	M
CYP	Pastor in Sanyuan church	40	F
LXN	Evangelist in Fuping church	28	F
YYL	Evangelist in Fuping church	44	F
ZFQ	Evangelist in Sanyuan church	56	F

*The ages listed in this table are by the date of interviews.

The life of ZGR is legendary. He was born in Henan. When his father died, he was only six years old. His family had a strong Confucian background. His grandfather and uncle were traditional teachers of the Confucian classics. When ZGR's father died, he was home-schooled by his grandfather and uncle. They used the *Four Books* and *Five Classics* as the text books to teach ZGR. In fact, ZGR's Chinese name carries a strong sense of Confucianism. The literal translation of his first name is "champion scholar." "Scholar" is *ru*, which is the original Chinese name for Confucianism. ZGR became a Christian in a revival meeting when he was thirteen years old. John Song, one of the most famous charismatic evangelists in early twentieth century, was the speaker at the revival meeting. ZGR followed John Song's style of preaching in the year after his conversion. He therefore was given the nickname "little Dr. Song" by a Christian newspaper in Shanghai.

In the period between 1920 and 1950, China was in chaos. ZGR went to theological seminary four times in different schools and locations. He attended the theological training school run by the Canadian Presbyterian Church and the American Mennonite Church. He also attended local theological seminaries—Guanzhong Divinity School in Shaanxi and Huaxi Theological Seminary in Sichuan—in the 1940s. When he returned to Shaanxi after the Sino-Japanese war and the civil war, he was ordained a pastor and became a church leader. He was the responsible pastor for all the churches in seven counties. Due to his connections with the foreign missionaries and his leadership role in the church, he was imprisoned and sent to a labor camp for thirteen years before the Cultural Revolution began in 1966. In those years of imprisonment, ZGR's mother and elder brother died due to serious sickness and pressure from the Red Guards. Under the Reform and Open policy, ZGR was released from prison. According to ZFQ, ZGR worked hard to regain the church property and resume the ministry right after he returned home. He later won the trust of the government and other church leaders and founded the Shaanxi Bible School. Before his retirement, ZGR had led the TSPM and CCC in Shaanxi province for over twenty years. In appendix H, the major life events of ZGR have been listed for reference.

A strong sense of kinship became evident during the interview process. Apart from previous cases, many family members or relatives serve in the same county or even the same church in Sanyuan. In addition to ZFQ, ZGR's other children are also active members of different churches. YCQ is a fourth generation Christian. YCQ's father was an ordained elder. YCQ and his two sons are ordained pastors. During the interviews, YHT told me that the active church members in Sanyuan County mainly come from two families, the Yangs and the Zhaos. He introduced me to some church pastors and volunteers whose family names are Yang and Zhao. The cultural setting of the rural churches is highly relational, which means the church members know one another and their family members well. Many families in the church emphasized religious education at home. As a result, many church workers belonged to the same family became one of the major characteristics of the churches in Sanyuan County.

Another characteristic of the Sanyuan churches is the predominance of local people in the church leadership. Another common phenomenon in rural churches in China is the lack of well-equipped pastors through formal theological education. As reflected in the imbalanced economic development in China, urbanization attracts many young people to work in the cities. Better income and future prospects are the main attractions for these young people, including seminary graduates. Many young church leaders leave their hometowns to work in churches in the cities after they graduate from seminary.

The informants are all local residents of Sanyuan County. YYL worked at the Bible school in Xian after graduation, but she chose to return to Sanyuan to work with ZGR. Churches in Nanjing, Xian, and Fuping wanted to recruit YHT as church pastor at the same time after he graduated from the Nanjing seminary. Until the time of interview, he was the only graduate who has returned from Nanjing to Sanyuan and Fuping counties. The young leaders' responses in the interviews revealed that calling and vision are important elements in their decision-making process; however, the personality of ZGR and the close relationships the young leaders are also significant factors attracting them to stay in the Sanyuan area.

The third characteristic of Sanyuan churches is the relationship between family and the journey of faith. Similar to the case in the Urumqi church, all informants mentioned their family backgrounds. YCQ, YHT, YHG, and ZFQ come from Christian families. The family impact on their life and ministry are strong. It is natural for them to connect their faith journeys with their families. The other four informants, ZGR, CYP, LXN, and YYL, are not come from Christian families per se, but they all mention the faith journey of their parents who came to Christ either before or after the informants themselves became Christians.

Similar to the case in Urumqi church, the old pastor has a strong influence over the younger leaders in Sanyuan. In such a rural setting, the inter-personal relationships are significant in the leadership decision-making process. The growth in spirituality and personality of the church leaders is inseparable from the role model of the old pastor.

Fuzhou: A Church in Transition

The third case study is a church located in Eastern China: Fuzhou in Fujian province.

Geographical and Political Background

Fuzhou is the capital city of Fujian province in eastern China (Map 3). The population is mainly Han Chinese. It was one of the earliest ports forced open for trade with foreign countries through the unequal treaties in the eighteenth century. Through the forced opening, many missionaries were sent to Fuzhou in the early nineteenth century. The Methodists, Anglicans, and the CIM were among those active foreign denominations and mission organizations.

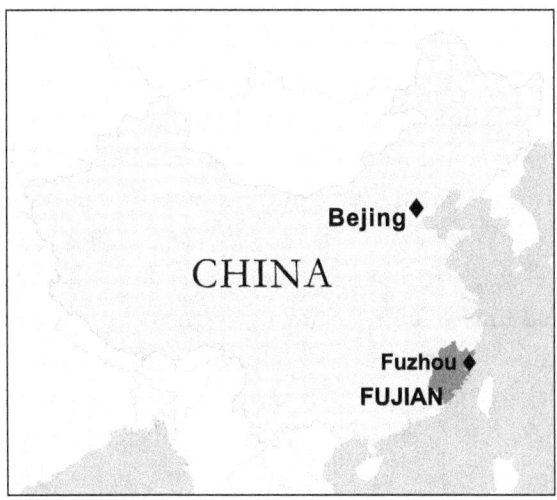

MAP 3: Location of Fuzhou, Fujian

A Brief Historical Background of the Zhong Zhou Church

The Zhong Zhou church, founded in 1949, is located in the city center of Fuzhou. The Zhong Zhou church originates from the CAH. The CAH is one of the largest indigenous churches in China. Watchman Nee was a Fujianese who began his ministry in Fujian; therefore, Fujian became one of the base camps of the CAH (Editorial 2009). Watchman Nee upheld the model of the church described in the book of Acts. In his view, the ordination of pastors and the title *reverend* were neither necessary nor biblical. He believed that denomination was a sign of disunity. Churches should be named after their geographical locations; therefore CAH is also called the Local Church. The church members call the church leaders elders, teachers, or simply brothers and sisters.

According the YZD, the old leader I interviewed, the Zhong Zhou church is where Watchman Nee began his ministry. During the Cultural Revolution, the Zhong Zhou church was forced to close down without exception. YZD faced persecution because of his faith. When the Cultural Revolution ended, the original members of the Zhong Zhou church merged with other churches in Fuzhou. As a result, YZD has also preached in non-CAH background churches for many years. Under the leadership of YZD, sixty members from the original CAH church came back from other non-CAH churches to Zhong Zhou, and the church resumed its services in 1990. Even though the original CAH members joined the TSPM, they keep the practices and characteristics of the CAH. For example, the church has no ordained pastor and no paid staff. All the church workers are volunteers who work full-time in the church. The Zhong Zhou church includes a central church with its own church building and twenty-three meeting points scattered around Fuzhou city and the surrounding villages. A hundred full-time volunteer church workers work and meet together in the central church every week. Not all the volunteer church workers can become preachers; only thirty of them are included in a core team which can preach the meeting points. As in the central church located in Zhong Zhou, only four of them can deliver sermons among the thirty preachers.

The volunteers in the church do not have any salary, and only some of them receive a subsidy of one to two hundred RMB per month from the church. Some of them are retired workers who live on their pensions, some of them are supported by their family members, and some of them may receive irregular support from other church members. This volunteer-based church structure is one of the major characteristics of the CAH. The Zhong Zhou church members believe that total surrender to God and living by faith form the model found in the Bible. The church leaders mentioned in the book of Acts received no income and therefore the CAH also believe such a way of nurturing their total reliance on God.

In the political movements between the 1950s and the 1970s, the CAH suffered from persecution because of Watchman Nee. The Chinese Communist government accused Watchman Nee of being immoral and the business run by him illegal. The church founded by Nee was therefore forced to close down because of its connection with him. As the members had donated all their money, land, and belongings to the church, the church was named a "big landlord" and was therefore accused of being a capitalist enterprise. Capitalism was not permitted before the 1980s (Leung 2003a, 19-29).

In the face of the requests from the government to register and join the TSPM in the 1980s, the church members had different responses. The first response was to refuse the requests from the government. The church will become part of the house church movement instead of registering and joining the TSPM. The second response was to merge with members of other denominations to form a TSPM church without keeping the CAH original identity. The third response was to use the TSPM church building and to keep its original structure. They would keep their own identity and practices in a separate worship service.

The Zhong Zhou church is the product of the fourth one. They built their own church and registered it with the government. They literally joined the TSPM but kept their own identity and practices. It was not necessary for the Zhong Zhou church leaders to take active roles in the TSPM and the CCC at both the city and provincial levels. As YZD mentions, the Zhong Zhou church is the only former CAH church that exists in this special form in China today.

The Zhong Zhou church's ministry is not restricted to a county or a city. The church can arrange for their leaders to preach in former and newly-developed CAH meeting points throughout Fujian Province. Sometimes the leaders of Zhong Zhou church even help other CAH or even non-CAH churches in other provinces through a short-term leadership training program and sermon CD distribution. As long as requests for assistance come from other churches, they are willing to help.

The Informants and the Interviews

I interviewed the founder of the new Zhong Zhou church, Elder YZD (appendix I). YZD was born into a Christian family and received training in music in a Christian elementary school. Before becoming a full-time volunteer church worker in the 1980s, he had been a music teacher in elementary and high school, and later in a college. Even though he worked together with Watchman Nee between the late 1940s and the early 1950s, he was not a member of the CAH before 1955. According to YZD, Watchman Nee invited him to go to Shanghai to be his coworker in 1950, but he refused. YZD preferred to stay in Fuzhou. The Zhong Zhou church was re-established and rebuilt by YZD in 1990. The original church from the 1940s had been closed and demolished. In this sense, YZD can be regarded as the founder of the new Zhong Zhou church.

I interviewed nine pastors in Fuzhou,[6] but only six of them are qualified informants and useful in this research.[7] Among the informants from the Zhong Zhou church was LDJ, a middle aged elder who is now the appointed successor of YZD. He is actually the one who lead the whole church in recent years. The selections of the other four leaders to interview are random following their time and availability when I visited them. More information about the informants in the Zhong Zhou church is found in Table 7.

TABLE 7: The Major Responsibilities of the Church Leaders in Fuzhou Zhong Zhou Church

Name Code	Responsibility in the Church	Age*	Gender
YZD	Preacher and Trainer	85	M
LDJ	Preacher and Trainer	49	M
CJ	Preacher and Multi-media Production	36	F
LSQ	Preacher, Driver, and Purchaser	35	M
YJY	Trainer, Chef, and Interpreter	34	F
ZX	Preacher and Computer Technical Support	33	M

*The ages listed in this table are by the date of interviews.

---

6. For the sake of consistency with other case studies, I use the term pastor in addition to elders, brothers, and sisters in describing the leaders of CAH churches even though CAH did not recognized the title pastor.

7. The others are pastors from the headquarters of the Fujian TSPM and CCC. They have no direct relation with the Zhong Zhou church.

Some features are found in the interviewing process. First, all informants in the Zhong Zhou church are Fujianese. All were born in Fuzhou except YZD and YJY who were born in other cities in Fujian province. YZD's father was an army officer. His family travelled in different parts of China in the 1920s. YZD and his family returned to Fujian when he was a teenager. Since then he had never left Fuzhou to live in any other city. YJY was born in a county near Fuzhou. She speaks the local dialect fluently and became one of the interpreters when preaching in the villages in Fujian.

Unlike some churches in other parts of China, the Zhong Zhou church is homogeneous in dialect and sub-culture. China is a country with many different ethnic groups. In *Operation China* (2000), Paul Hattaway distinguishes the ethnic groups according to their dialects. Chinese people may not agree with this method in differentiating the peoples within China; however, it reflects the reality that dialects have made some differences in subcultures within Chinese society. The language used during the worship in the Zhong Zhou church is Mandarin, but the leaders use Fujianese to communicate among themselves.

The second feature is the understanding of total surrender to God in Zhong Zhou church. Total surrender means to give up everything which means living a life of sacrifice (Ye 2006b, 442). Total surrender is reflected in the response of the leaders to the calling of God. They quit their jobs and went to work in the church full-time without salary. More than 100 volunteers came to the church to work in different areas. Full-time ministry does not necessarily refer to preaching and evangelism. It can include working in the kitchen, laundry, or doing office work. In this church, no one seeks to benefit him- or herself. The volunteers regard earning money from church work as a sign of loving the materialistic world. Through giving up their full-time jobs, they believe they are entering another stage of spiritual progression.

The third feature is the duties of the church leaders. Apart from teaching, training, and preaching, all of them have other assigned duties in the church except for the top leaders. As shown in Table 7, only YZD and LDJ concentrate on preaching and training church leaders. YZD told me that the church has thirty preachers who speak in the pulpit every Sunday at different meeting points. These preachers have other assigned duties in the church; for example, they are drivers, chefs, or provide computer technical support. The assigned duties are not directly related to the traditional understanding of pastoral responsibilities. Working in the church itself is living a holy life, but the nature of the assigned duties are not their concern.

The fourth feature is the same as in Urumqi church: the Zhong Zhou church has three generations of leaders. Although Table 7 shows only six out of their thirty leaders, the team composed of these three age groups: eighty-one or above, forty-five to eighty, and below forty-five. I visited their leadership team prayer meeting and gave a short speech in December 2008. In the meeting I saw YZD, the oldest member, four to five middle-aged men and women, and the rest of the team, who were under age forty. YZD and LDJ confirmed that the leadership team was composed of three major age groups. During the interview, YZD repeated that some members of the leadership team disagreed with him in the past and chose to leave. The remaining team members are faithful and support to YZD and LDJ; therefore, the present leadership team works in unity.

Some characteristics of the CAH tradition can be found in the Zhong Zhou church. The internal and external situations have already delimited the leadership development pattern in the Zhong Zhou church. The YZD's function as role model is significant in maintaining the tradition. Having senior leaders as role models tells the younger leaders that the doctrine of total surrender is practical.

Summary

Some similar characteristics of the internal situations are found in these three case studies. The significance of the role models, the family relationships among the church leaders, and the emphasis on personality instead of educational qualifications are all important features in relation to leadership development. To a large extent, these common characteristics reflect the impact of Confucian culture in the churches in China.

The history of development of these churches shows some significant impacts from the revival movement in the 1920s and the indigenization movement. The Urumqi church was founded by the early mission groups to Xinjiang, the development of Sanyuan church was affected by John Song and the ministry of the Chinese Christian Church, and the Zhong Zhou Church follows the tradition of the CAH. A missing generation of leaders is another common feature reflected in the history of these churches. During the Cultural Revolution, the church activities had been suspended and the pastors were either imprisoned or sent to labor camps. The absence of the generation between ages 60-80 is therefore problematic in the church leadership transition in China.

In facing the political and social changes after 1949, all three cases reflect some similar responses to the government's policies. The church leaders had accepted the fact that registration with the government can bring them opportunities to have public worship and to serve the community with an official identity. The Urumqi church, for example, cannot have cross-cultural ministry toward the non-Han Chinese people. In fact, what the church can do is to focus on the Han Chinese ministry and therefore develop a good team of young church leaders.

The social and economic settings of these churches are the rural areas and small towns even though two out of three are located in the capital city of a province. According to the informants, Sanyuan church is a rural church as the church members are mostly peasants. Even though Urumqi and Fuzhou are capital cities, most of the church members are not wealthy middle-class people. Apart from the metropolitan churches in Beijing and Shanghai, these case studies reflected the characteristics of the rural and small town churches in China.

CHAPTER 7

Findings from the Case Studies

The external situations of the contemporary Chinese churches affecting leadership development are the historical events in the first half of the twentieth century and the cultural root of Confucianism. Reflected from the works of the Chinese theologians, the attitudes of the leaders and the expectations from the followers are all influential elements in the leadership process. By adding the internal situations, which are the backgrounds and traditions of the churches under study, some further evidence is found to support the distinctive characteristics of relational leadership in Chinese churches mentioned in earlier chapters. The old pastors interviewed in the case studies from Urumqi, Sanyuan, and Fuzhou formed different ministries to develop the next generations of church leaders which resonates with the theories discussed in Part I. Two major areas are observed from these case studies: the historical impacts and the Confucian culture. A total of seven generations were concluded from these two areas. Chinese history is long enough to influence all aspects of the Chinese people's daily lives. The development of the church and society in the first half of the twentieth century had an especially important effect on the churches. These case studies illustrate the compatibility of Christianity and Confucianism in the daily operations of the churches. The beliefs and practices of the church leaders reflect a strong impact of Confucianism.

The Historical Impacts from the Early Twentieth Century

All the old pastors interviewed were born in early twentieth century China. They were educated under the traditional Confucian schooling system, experienced the missionary ministries, survived the two world wars, and faced persecutions after 1949 because of their Christian faith. In the last three decades they have experienced the Reform and Opening policy of the Chinese government and witnessed the flourishing of the churches as well. Three generalizations were represented in the interviews.

Experiences of Suffering

Suffering is one of the environments used by God to shape church leaders. As McKinley Johnson agrees, God uses environment as a tool to develop leaders in specific situations (2006, 42-45). The political and social environments were harsh to Christianity until the late twentieth century in China.

The old pastors had concluded that several lessons they have learned from the suffering experiences. The first lesson was spiritual maturity. HQZ, CXQ, ZGR, and YZD all experienced different kinds of suffering or persecution: HQZ and ZGR were sent to labor camps for nine and thirteen years respectively, CXQ was imprisoned for three years, and YZD suffered from cancer in the 1950s. All of them said that the suffering experiences were good to their spiritual growth. They interpret the suffering experiences as valuable lessons from God. During the experiences, they learned patience, humility, and faithfulness. These suffering experiences led them into spiritual maturity so that they could sustain a harsh environment in later years. They believe suffering is an honor given by God because it is a sign of spiritual maturity: they are now "qualified" to face suffering. As Christ is their role model for suffering, they believe that their own suffering experiences cannot be compared to Christ's. They are honored because they can be part of the suffering church founded by Jesus.

Together with other old Christians, the old pastors experienced suffering from persecution during the Cultural Revolution. Hardships and poverty are the signs of the spiritual lessons they had to learn. What they experienced has become a norm or a standard for being a good leader. ZGR literally proclaimed, "A pastor should prepare to suffer. Without the willingness to suffer, he or she is surely not a good church leader." Being prepared to suffer for the sake of winning people to Christ is one of the expectations ZGR has of church leaders. Many of the informants accept and follow this standard when examining themselves.

The young pastor YHT from Fuping takes it for granted that a pastor should suffer in order to serve God wholeheartedly. He rejected the offers from the city churches and returned to the village. The villagers did not accept him in the first year he arrived at Fuping. Even though Fuping and Sanyuan are so close physically, the church members in Fuping did not accept YHT as a local resident. YHT thinks that a servant of God should suffer in the name of Jesus. He waited for a year until the church members in Fuping began to accept him. In the beginning of his ministry in Fuping, the church did not have money and human resources to support him. He served thirty-three meeting points alone with weekly visiting and preaching. As a consequence, his physical health collapsed. He thought that his predecessors, for example, ZGR and foreign missionaries, had been the role models of suffering. YHT was therefore willing to tolerate the situation. He mentioned to me that he over-emphasized the value of suffering as a symbol of a good church leader during the beginning years of his ministry in Fuping.

The second lesson the old pastors learned from suffering was the necessity of looking after the church workers. The suffering experience of the old pastors was a reason for them to insist on the improvement of the conditions for the young pastors. CXQ and HQZ suffered from poverty and persecution when they were traveling to Xinjiang. Unlike other prevailing ideas that the younger generation should follow in their seniors' footsteps by experiencing suffering, they have tried hard to fight for the benefit of the pastors. Since they are retired volunteers in the church and work full-time without receiving salary, they are not fighting for their own benefits but for the young pastors. As HQZ constantly said throughout the interview, "We do not want our next generation of leaders to experience the hardships we have." Even though some of the elders in the church have disagreed with them, they have spent time explaining and sharing their ideas with the congregation. It is rare in China for anyone to insist on the importance of the welfare of the pastors. The majority of the churches are willing to spend as many resources as possible on church building construction and ministries but not for the benefit of the pastors.

Political Sensitivity

The other distinctive characteristic of the Chinese churches is the political sensitivity. Almost all the pastors in China have different levels of political awareness. The Chinese government intends to control every aspect of the society in order to maintain the Communist rule.[1] Even though Wang Mingdao intended not to involve himself with politics in the very beginning of his ministry, eventually, avoiding politics became impossible. Through tight control over media and other public activities, the government wants to maintain the stability of the society. Religion is understood as one of the ways to maintain the stability of the society; therefore, the government keeps an eye on the development of all the recognized religious organizations to make sure they carry out the policy of the government. All the leaders of the official religious organizations are automatically appointed to be members of the Chinese People's Political Consultative Conference (CPPCC), a consultative body made up of delegates representing different political parties, national minorities, religions, and even business organizations.

Political sensitivity is a basic criterion for a church leader. This does not mean that the church leader should strictly follow orders from the government, but he or she must understand the rules of the game in order to maintain his or her position in leading the church and to protect the status of the church. The church leader should know how to develop church ministries even without the blessing of the government and how to handle relationships with other religions when sharing the gospel with people of other faiths.

In relation to the political sensitivity, the structure of the TSPM church is another influential element in shaping the church leadership. The TSPM

---

1. The scholars in political science called this tight control from the government to all aspects of the society as political totalism (Tsou 1994).

is a religious organization supported by the government in order to manage Christian activity under the government's supervision. The leaders of the TSPM are nominated or elected according to a joint consensus of the government and the church. Different administrative levels, like the national, provincial, and county levels, have their own TSPM leadership team. All these leaders have to handle church administration and government relations at the same time. On some occasions, the RAB sends a representative to become a member of the TSPM's leadership team. Even though some of the TSPM leaders are not eager to connect themselves with the government officials, they have to establish a day-to-day working relationship with the government. Political wisdom and good inter-personal skills are the essentials of good leadership for TSPM church leaders.

In Xinjiang, the TSPM limits church leaders from outreach to the national minorities. The church is therefore focused on developing an indigenous Han ministry. As Xinjiang is located on the northwestern border of China, several parts of the province are governed by the Xinjiang Production and Construction Corps, that is, the army. The army's major responsibility is to maintain political and social stability along the border. The army is the most conservative sector of the Chinese Communist government. Ministry in the church is therefore limited to within the church buildings, and no ethnic minority members are allowed in. Besides, the Urumqi TSPM can only manage the needs of those Christians in Urumqi city, not in the other parts of Xinjiang. The ministry in the Urumqi church is therefore conservative in terms of expanding the influence of the church to the society. With these limitations, the old pastors concentrate on developing the infrastructure of the church. The Urumqi church invests heavily in leadership development, for example, increasing the benefits of the pastors, sending young people to receive theological education, and having weekly prayer and consultation meetings with them. As a result, the loyalty and quality of the young leaders are very high.

As members of CPPCC, some of the TSPM church leaders have a higher social status than other church leaders. Some of them may make use of this higher status to seek more opportunities for church ministry, while others may look for more power and benefit for themselves. Social status is a temptation for some of the TSPM church leaders. The old pastors I interviewed are all good examples of overcoming the temptations of power and social status. They have a high social prestige among the CPPCC members and give Christianity a good reputation because of their personal integrity. Their faithfulness has become the model for their followers to imitate. HQZ, for example, told me how he handled the relationship with a Taoist representative when he attended a CPPCC meeting several years ago. He was assigned to stay in the same hotel room with a Taoist representative. The Taoist got sick during the conference and was unable to bathe and eat by himself. HQZ helped him eat and even washed his feet. The Taoist was deeply touched by HQZ's actions of love. Before they left the conference, the Taoist recognized that the Christian God is a loving God, and HQZ gave him his Bible. Since then, HQZ and the Urumqi church has gained high reputation in the government, because HQZ has become a role model for promoting a harmonious society through the actions of love.

The church leaders in China are very aware of the suspicious attitude of the government toward the churches' foreign relationships. The history of foreign missionary connections before 1949 is surely one important reason. In addition, the collapse of the Communist governments in Eastern European countries in the early 1990s was another important and unforgettable lesson. The churches behind the scenes in Eastern Europe were perceived as a major force which intensified the democratic movement, which led directly to the collapse of the Communist regimes. Thus, the Chinese church leaders are very cautious in dealing with foreigners. In Urumqi and Sanyang, the pastors are highly sensitive when Westerners visit their churches. They prefer to keep a low profile when working with foreign Christians even if they do want to have partnerships with them.

Since China is a vast country, the political sensitivities of the church leaders are different according to region. The coastal cities are more open when compared with churches located inland. The inland church leaders are more conservative in their relationships with foreign visitors. The pastors in Urumqi, for example, are very wary if a Westerner comes to the church and offers them a leadership training program. Leadership development programs, for example, should be programs developed by the local church leaders. In today's China, the practice of the Urumqi church of not allowing foreign pastors to preach in their church is unusual. The only way to introduce a new ministry to the Urumqi church is to work together with their leaders to develop a new program. The more participation from the local pastors, the more chance the program has of being implemented successfully. This practice is in fact beneficial in intensifying the formation of indigenous leadership development programs within the church.

Leadership development in the Chinese churches is never simply an independent church issue. The church leaders have to deal with social and political issues in addition to the internal situations of the churches.

The Church Tradition

As discussed the chapters 4 and 5, the first generation of local church leaders and the foundation of the indigenous church ministries were developed in the early twentieth century. Even though all the denominations were forced to join together under the TSPM, some of their original denominational characteristics have been maintained. The Urumqi church was founded under the Chinese Christian Church with a strong theological influence from the CIM. Many of the founding members came from the BJEB and received theological training from the CIM-run Bible school. Their theology was developed along with the CIM tradition. For example, the emphasis on developing indigenous leaders and ministries are closely related to the theological tradition of the CIM.

The church most obviously influenced by its denominational background is the Zhong Zhou church in Fuzhou. The background of Zhong Zhou church is the CAH, one of the largest contextualized Chinese church networks that began in the 1920s. Watchman Nee was no doubt the most influential person in the CAH. Even though YZD declared that he did not agree with Watchman Nee in certain doctrines, he has kept most of the CAH's tradition. The other members of the leadership team quoted the works of Watchman Nee several times. LDJ even used Watchman Nee's work twice during the interview. Obviously, YZD had taught Watchman Nee's theology.

The Zhong Zhou church is different from other TSPM churches in several ways. In addition to following the ordination and church structure models described in the book of Acts, it does not have a rigid management structure in church administration. Under the leadership of YZD and LDJ, most of the decisions are made by the whole team. Further, spirituality can be measured through the level of willingness to give up one's possessions. Working in the church as a full-time volunteer is described as faithfulness to the Lord. Obedience to authority is encouraged because the leaders are chosen by God. They are the representatives sent by God to lead and govern the church. In YZD's sermons, he emphasizes absolute obedience as a virtue described in the Bible (Ye 2006b, 384).

YZD mentions one of the reasons why the Zhong Zhou church joined the TSPM is that they shared the same attitude against denominationalism. He said the CPC wanted to get rid of all the foreign missions to develop a truly indigenous Chinese church, and therefore it founded the TSPM in the 1950s. As the CAH also disagrees with denominationalism, YZD discovered a common ground between the CPC and the CAH. He believes a true indigenous Chinese church can only be developed without the intervention from foreign missions.

In addition to denominational background, leadership development in the Chinese churches was largely impacted by local revival movements in the early twentieth century. Fundamentalism became the cornerstone of the Chinese theology at the same time. In all three case studies, the old pastors were influenced by the indigenous church leaders in the 1920s and 30s. The old pastors are the agents who continue the fundamentalist church tradition developed before 1949. For instance, the doctrine of total surrender advocated by YZD came from the theology of the CAH. In fact, the works of Wang Mingdao and Yang Shaotang shared similar ideas. In addition, CXQ was influenced by Zhang Guquan, who followed the theology of Jia Yuming. ZGR was converted in a revival meeting where John Song preached.

The theological development of the Chinese churches has been deeply influenced by the conservative missionaries in the twentieth century as well. The missionaries of the CIM penetrated into the interior of China and shared the gospel with their conservative faith. They influenced the church leaders in the 1920s and 30s, who assimilated and developed Chinese fundamentalist doctrines. Since the major church growth is observed in these areas, fundamentalism is therefore the dominant theological perspective in China today.

The important elements of leadership development in these churches are largely influenced by their historical background. The interactions between the old pastors and their historical environment shaped their attitudes and practices of leadership development. Furthermore, the young leaders observed and learned from the role models of the old pastors and chose to follow them. The historical situations have established the framework while the cultural background provides the substance of leadership development.

The Cultural Impacts of Confucianism

Many Chinese Christians struggle with their identities when living out of a Confucian tradition and at the same time accepting a new life in Christ with Christian norms and values. As an external situation influencing Chinese Christian leaders, the assimilation of Confucianism into Christian living is an essential step of inculturation. Four cultural generalizations are discovered from the case studies: Confucianism and human development, collective culture and team development, community as an extension of family, and experiential learning in leadership development.

Confucianism and Human Development

In Confucian understanding, leadership development is human moral development. The difference between a leader and a follower is only on the maturity level in becoming a sage, that is, maturity in moral life. According to Wang Yangming, everyone has the potential to become a sage. The one who becomes a better person is a role model for others to follow. Human development is therefore equivalent to leadership development in terms of moral maturity.

Cultivation of Morality

Personal integrity is one of the basic expectations on leaders. In order to cultivate a good personality, HQZ encouraged the young pastors to read Chinese classics. He gave every pastor a set of *Guwenguanzhi* (古文觀止), a collection of Chinese classics from the eighth century B.C. to the fourteenth century A.D. HQZ pointed out that the qualifications for pastors should include whether or not their personal behavior in daily living is consistent with what they preach.

> A pastor should combine knowledge with his or her daily life. When he or she preaches about "loving one another," people will ask: how about you? Theory and practice should come together. A pastor should preach faithfully and live a pious life (HQZ).

When I asked about the expectations of a leader in the Urumqi church, LQF, JQ, ZL, and CXQ, as well as HQZ pointed out immediately that personality is one of the basic criteria for a good church leader. ZL even stated clearly that HQZ is her role model to learn from because of his knowledge of Chinese culture. She expects that a good Chinese pastor should also have good knowledge of Chinese culture.

Compatibility between Christianity and Confucianism

ZGR in Sanyuan does not have the problem or frustration of being a Christian and living in a Confucian culture at the same time. From his life-style, personality, and ministry, he successfully merges the two identities into one. ZGR's grandfather and uncle taught him the philosophy of Confucianism when he was young. His grandfather and uncle were at the same time the first group of villagers who converted to Christianity. Under this family and educational background, ZGR has never doubted the compatibility of Christianity and Confucianism.

A poem hanging in the wall of ZGR's office shows that Confucianism gives him the direction of life and ministry. The calligraphy of the poem was written by ZGR's friend. He keeps it as a reminder in his office. Four major instructions have been mentioned in this poem: holding one's heart (*chi xin* 持心), establishing oneself (*li shen* 立身), handling issues (*chu shi* 處事), and dealing with people (*dai ren* 待人). ZGR explained that the moral ideal and the philosophy of daily living in Confucianism and Christianity are similar. This poem reminds him that a leader should cultivate his or her own self in order to become an influential person. In classical Confucianism, equipping one's self will lead to social and political achievement. ZGR applies this philosophy in his sermons, which teach the congregation to nurture their spiritual lives and live harmoniously with others, so as to become good Christians (Zhang 2009, 73).

According to Confucian tradition, a good leader should first cultivate his or her inner life. Likewise, the twentieth-century Chinese theologians emphasized not the leadership skills, but the inner qualities of a leader. Half of the informants mentioned that cultivating a good inner life was a must for a church leader. ZGR said, "Having the inner life of Christ, one can naturally live in the manner of Jesus Christ" (Zhang 2009, 70). He directly related the cultivation of the inner life to Christ's example in order to develop one's own personality and morality. The leadership attributes related to management and communication skills are less important when compared to the cultivation of the inner life. This is typically the Confucian path to sagehood.

Personal Behavior of Church Leaders

Thus, the expectations for the quality of the church leaders follow the virtues advocated in the Confucian tradition. ZGR insisted a good family relationship was important to a church leader because the Bible teaches that one should manage his or her own family well before managing the church. Confucianism teaches that a good leader should begin from his or her personal development and family relationships.

Inner life qualities are reflected through the morality and spirituality of a person. What ZGR taught and practiced in the past became the spiritual and theological foundations of the Sanyuan church today. His cultural and educational background shaped his expectations of the church leaders. The mission of the church is to attract more people to come to know Christ. The best strategy is to develop the behavior of the church leaders. The purpose of being a person with moral behavior is to attract non-believers to come to the church. ZGR said, "Numerous pieces of evidence prove that a congregation which emphasizes ethics and applies them to daily life will attract people to the church. A great cohesion and attraction can therefore developed" (Zhang 2009, 154-155). The church with a moral leader will become a church of victory. LXN's expectation of a holy life and YHT's expectation of a good reputation as requirement for good leaders are based on what they heard and learned from ZGR.

Leaders and Guanxi

In a less competitive rural society, human relationships are highly valued by the church. Over the past decades, people coming to China learned what *guanxi* ("relationship" or "connection") is when dealing with the Chinese people, especially in business. No matter how good one is, without *guanxi* there is no way to begin what one expects to do. Similar situations happen in the church. A rural church even more obviously relies on relationship. In the rural churches, human relationships are more important than profound knowledge. Therefore, in developing church leaders, having a good relationship with the potential leaders is much more important than what the teacher teaches. YYL commented that she enjoyed her relationships with the teachers in the seminary. Students learn more effective when they have good relationships with their teachers. YHT said that good leaders should have good reputations as reflected in their relations with others; their behavior should be consistent with their teachings. YYL responds that the most important qualities of a leader are humility and respecting others in inter-personal relationships. LXN was concerned with the personal holiness of a leader. One should demonstrate what one believes before teaching others. All these are also the virtues advocated by Confucianism.

Confucian characteristics are clearly found in the leaders in Urumqi and Sanyuan. The leaders in the Zhong Zhou church in Fuzhou agree with the importance of developing inner life qualities as important elements in personality maturity. YZD is the one who has good morality and won the support from the whole church.

Collective Culture and Team Development

Another characteristic of Chinese culture is collectivism. In contrast to individualism, collective culture is the term used to describe the right of the community or the state to override the rights of the individual. Each individual is ready to sacrifice his or her own right for the benefit of the community. In the process of decision making, the perceptions and expectations of the community supersede all other considerations. In Urumqi,

Sanyuan, and Fuzhou, under the guidance of the old pastors, the younger leaders work together as leadership teams who agree on a higher priority of the rights of the community over the individual rights.

Team Approach in Management

All the case studies show the trend of developing leadership teams. The young leaders work and learn together under the guidance of the old and middle-aged pastors. As Chinese culture is relational and collective in nature, the team approach in organizational management is culturally familiar. As the congregation expects the leader to help them in every aspect of daily living, only through a team approach can the spiritual gifts of different leaders function together well. The tradition of top-down decision making faces challenges when there is a generation gap in leadership transition. After the old pastors, leaders between ages 60-80 are missing. Through team leadership, a better model for the power structure may develop in the future when the old pastors have passed away. A new generation of leaders who have already developed the habit of working as a team may bring transformation of the traditional top-down power structure. The danger of perfectionism and total reliance on a single person as the representative of God can be overcome by team leadership.

Team leadership is not only a division of labor, but also a means of working together to achieve the common goal. A regular phenomenon in China is the splitting of a church because of the disagreement among the leaders. The respect for seniority exists in the churches in China; however, unity will be gone together with the old pastors when they pass away. Successful team leadership may be a possible solution to the leadership problem in China. The role of FCG in the structure of the Urumqi church is significant. HQZ praised her as a good manager of relationships. Not everyone is equal in terms of ability, charisma, spirituality, and popularity in a team. FCG serves as a bridge between the old and the young. At the same time, she leads the younger generations in the ministry and daily operations of the church. She can work in a team with the old pastors and with the younger team respectively. A structure without a culture of unity cannot be sustained for long.

The relationship between the two old pastors in Urumqi is an excellent model of team leadership. The fact that they have worked together for over fifty years has already demonstrated a unity that many churches do not have. As LQF pointed out, this phenomenon is something extraordinary. The young pastors model themselves after the old pastors in order to work in unity. LQF and ZSH mentioned that they enjoy a good working relationship with the elders and deacons. Unity is an essential element of team leadership. In the responses to my question on the expectations on leadership, three out of nine young leaders in Urumqi explicitly said that unity is the number one concern. HQZ pointed out three reasons for the success of their team leadership:

> Firstly, work in unity among the old, middle, and young generations. Secondly, respect the leadership of the deacon board because the deacons are selected by the congregation. Thirdly, define clearly role and responsibilities of different positions (HQZ).

The Structure Favorable to Team Leadership

The intention of developing team leadership is obvious and clear in Urumqi. Compared with the churches in other provinces, the Urumqi church has a better foundation because the pastors have intentionally connected the young leaders to work together. FCG said she planned to retire from her leadership position at the age of sixty-five. Even though it may not be realistic in the Chinese church context, she has the intention to develop and organize the younger leaders to take over her responsibilities. In many cases, disunity comes with a sudden change of leadership when there is no preparation. In my observation, the young leaders had simple hearts and minds. They loved one another and treasured the time together in their Monday prayer meetings. The real challenge to the team leadership has not yet come because the moment of leadership transition has not yet arisen. In a few years' time when the two old pastors pass away, the real challenge will come.

In the case of the Fuzhou church, the culture of the CAH emphasizes the practices of team leadership in the church structure. The thirty leaders who can preach in different meeting points belong to the leadership team. They meet every Tuesday in a prayer meeting and on some other occasions for learning and discussion. YZD founded a church management committee that the thirty leaders are included. They make all important decisions together. The issues decided by this committee have included: who can become a preacher, which coworker needs special financial support, and even who YZD's successor can be. In the church structure, this committee has the highest authority. In practice, YZD and his successor LDJ have the greatest influence in the decision making process.

It is necessary to clarify that team leadership is not collective leadership in this case. In the leadership team of the Zhong Zhou church, not all the members have equal status and power. The nature of this team is to support the top leader. The CAH emphasizes that the authority of the leader comes directly from God. The leaders should be chosen not based on their relationships and performance but on the work of the Holy Spirit. Although YZD stated clearly that obedience is only given to God, the leadership team obeys and follows the decisions of YZD and LDJ without hesitation. As a result, the top leader has the sole authority to make decisions. When I asked YZD about the criteria for the selection of his successor, he did not give a direct response. He told me that the other potential leaders had left. Only LDJ remained. Since he was the oldest on the leadership team, he was selected to be YZD's successor. Seniority in age and experience is one of the main concerns in selecting a top leader. Even LDJ said that YZD had not planned to make LDJ his successor. LDJ was chosen only because others had left the Zhong Zhou church, which made him the only candidate. The decision was not made by the leadership team decision in practice but by the old leader.

In addition, the division of labor and unity of the leadership team are clear. Interestingly, when I asked the informants whether they knew their spiritual gifts, everyone's responses were clear and firm. LDJ affirmed that his gifts were leadership, administration, and preaching, which are necessary qualities of the top leader in a church. This situation demonstrated that the teaching about spiritual gifts is strong and that the division of labor among the team members is clearly connected to their spiritual gifts. The team then decides how to allocate responsibilities in the church among themselves according to the spiritual gifts they have perceived in each member.

The hierarchy of the church is clear. Three layers of authority and responsibility in Zhong Zhou church were divided: YZD and LDJ at the top, the thirty preachers in the middle, and the 100 volunteers below. Team leadership in this sense operates under the leadership of a senior leader. Good relationships with mutual trust are the necessary element in developing strong leadership team. A clear division of labor and a structure that promotes unity are necessary as well.

Community as the Extension of Family

Family is the center of all social relationships in Chinese society. The perception of universal brotherhood and paternalistic leadership are also based on the understanding of family relationships. Community is the extension of family relationships. In Chinese Christian churches, the universal love among the church members is interpreted as family love in Christ. The church members are related to one another like the relatives in an extended family.

In Zhong Zhou church, ZGR emphasizes the importance of family in his sermons and lectures in the Bible school. He has repeatedly expressed his regret to his family when he was imprisoned during the Cultural Revolution. His wife was responsible for taking care of the whole family of six people when ZGR was in the labor camp. She earned only thirty-six RMB a month in the 1960s, which was the sole income of the whole family. Based on his personal experience, he said outright that taking care of family members is the first priority of a church leader. In this respect, having good family relationships is one of the requirements of being a good leader.

The Impact of Christian Families on the Leadership Team

Apart from ZGR's teaching, some good role models demonstrate the importance of good family relationships. ZGR's children are all devoted to serving God in the churches. One of his daughters became part of the leadership team in Sanyuan church. The testimony of the Yang family is a good illustration as well. The father of YCQ was an ordained elder. Before he passed away, he gave his final blessing to YCQ. YCQ said,

My father blessed me before he died: "Though the mountains be shaken and the hills be removed, yet the love of the Lord will not be leave you." After he blessed me, he stopped breathing. He had a great impact on me because he was faithful to God even in the times of persecution (YCQ).

The blessing from his father motivated YCQ to serve God wholeheartedly when he was young. YCQ belonged to the generation that was most affected by the Cultural Revolution. This age group in China contains a comparatively low percentage of Christians. Good religious education within a family can help to overcome the adversity outside. The Yang family maintained their worship of God even during the Cultural Revolution when Christianity was banned. YHT and YHG, the sons of YCQ, are also influenced by their family. Their grandmother, the mother-in-law of YCQ, was a student in the Spiritual Institute founded by Jia Yuming, the popular theologian in early twentieth century China. She taught her grandchildren biblical knowledge as well as laid the foundation of their spiritual lives. YHT and YHG followed their father's footstep in dedicating themselves to serve God before they finished high school. As the Zhang and Yang family role models show, the Sanyuan church can be characterized as a church with family love.

Paternalistic Leadership in the Christian Church

The old pastors have the image of father or grandfather which provides the foundation of paternalistic leadership. In Urumqi, Sanyuan, and Fuzhou, the old pastors have a strong intention of developing young leaders. In the case of Urumqi, the two old pastors—CXQ and HQZ—worked together with the elders and some old lay leaders in the 1940s. When the church was re-opened in the early 1980s, they were eager to find potential church leaders to receive theological education. Even though there were objections, two pastors insisted on sending out the first student to Yinjing Theological Seminary in Beijing when it resumed its function as a seminary in 1985. FCG was therefore enrolled as the first and only student from Xinjiang.

Further, the resistance of the Urumqi church to sending students to seminary remained strong even after FCG returned from Yinjing. A Youth

Fellowship was founded in 1993 after FCG listened to the suggestion from JQ, who shared the bitterness she felt because of working alone without youth coworkers in the church. One of the contributions of this Youth Fellowship was to identify and recruit potential church leaders (Fan 2005a, 31). CHB was the first one recruited from the Youth Fellowship who was later sent to seminary in 1995. All the young pastors are related to the Youth Fellowship in different ways.

The establishment of the Youth Fellowship has been an important channel for developing church leaders. In addition to the Youth Fellowship, all the pastors come together every Monday to pray and share together. They called this meeting a pastoral-devotional meeting. This meeting in fact has multiple functions. The old pastors listen to the problems and difficulties of the young pastors but try not to give concrete suggestion to them. HQZ said clearly that the young church leaders should take responsibility themselves to minister in a church. The problems which arise are lessons they should learn. As the heads of the TSPM and the CCC, the old pastors have the authority to give instructions and intrude into the daily administration; however, they choose to give a free hand to the young leaders. In 2001, CXQ, HQZ, and FCG nominated LQF and ZSH to be the committee members of the TSPM and the CCC. This was a further step to empower the young pastors to take the leadership positions in the Urumqi church. The intentions are not restricted to the minds and hearts of the old pastors; the church follows up by empowering the young pastors with responsibility.

The old pastors had such strong intentions in developing next generation leaders, difficulties were identified. According to HQZ, four major inadequacies in developing leaders in Urumqi church were identified: love, the power of the Holy Spirit, good preaching, and management skills. In response to these inadequacies, he prays and seeks short-term and long-term training opportunities to upgrade the quality of the young pastors: FCG has finished a post-graduate degree at Nanjing Seminary, and CHB is attending a post-graduate class at Beijing University. In the meantime, the Urumqi CCC organizes some short term training classes for the pastors and lay leaders.

The intention of the old pastors to develop the young leaders in Urumqi church is similar to a father who wants his children to receive better education. Most young leaders respond that the old pastors are their spiritual parents or grandparents. The ways of work and love of the old pastors have increased the sense of belongings felt by the young leaders in this church. The young leaders share a feeling that they are now working and living in a spiritual family in Urumqi.

Experiential Learning and Leadership Development

Experiential learning is adopted by all the churches interviewed as one of the methods in developing followers. Experiential learning refers to a process of learning, which associated with "internships, apprenticeships, work/study programs, cooperative education, outdoor education, studio arts, laboratory studies, and field projects" (Hedin 2010, 108-109). In these three case studies, the old pastors give advice and consultation to the young church leaders through working with them and meeting regularly. Many of the informants show that they have put into practice what they heard in the seminary through working with the old pastors. Only after they work in the churches under the guidance of the old pastors, they finally learn what they heard in their classes. Clearly, experiential learning is popular and effective in contemporary Chinese churches. A mentoring relationship is in fact an effective way of experiential learning.

Role Models in the Urumqi Church

Throughout the interviews, the informants keep referring to the leadership models established by the old pastors, missionaries, and other spiritual leaders in history as their role models in the learning process. Consistent with Wang Mingdao, Jia Yuming, and Yang Shaotang, the old pastors always say that a Christian leader should live an exemplary life for the sake of witnessing the Christian faith. A Christian leader is a role model for the congregation to follow and imitate. Modeling is therefore one of the best method of teaching and learning in the Chinese churches. Confucius established a role model of being a good teacher. He did not have great success in his political life. He became a role model because of the consistency between his teaching and way of life. The Chinese churches are looking for leaders who live according to what they teach.

Mentoring and modeling are inseparable in leadership development as well. If modeling is a voluntary learning pattern which requires self-discipline and self-learning motivation, mentoring requires the active participation of both the mentors and apprentices. I use the term *apprentice* instead of *mentee* because the former is more culturally familiar in Chinese tradition. Apprentice is a follower who acquires the technical skills and personality from the master through living and working together. A Chinese saying, "one day is the master, whole life is the father," is the best description of the master-apprentice relationship in Chinese tradition. I use the term *mentor* instead of *master* because the relationships between the old pastors and young church leaders involve more than acquiring technical skills. The mentoring relationship is a two-way relationship, each one helping the other to grow spiritually.

The mentor-apprentice relationship is not new to the Urumqi church. HQZ began his career as an apprentice to learn acupuncture, a traditional Chinese medical treatment which uses needles. HQZ's master was a Christian minister, who led him to Christ through teaching him acupuncture. HQZ's role model helped him to grow in both technical skills and spiritual life. CXQ has not received any formal theological education in seminary. He is self-taught through reading the Bible and the sermons of other pastors. Zhang Guquan, the founder and president of NSM, was CXQ's role model and master who worked together with CXQ for several years before Zhang was imprisoned in 1951.

CXQ has repeatedly showed his respect for Zhang. When I interviewed CXQ, he could not wait to tell the story of Zhang: how he inspired CXQ with his vision of "Back to Jerusalem," and how much he impacted CXQ's life and ministry. In the meantime, HQZ also told the stories of the CIM missionaries. When he entered the Bible school run by the CIM, his first impression was not of the facilities. He said, "The most impressive thing was not the facilities nor the building but the teachers. They all looked like holy people. The way they spoke and the things they did were very different from those of ordinary people" (HQZ).

HQZ was especially inspired by the school's vice-president, the Rev. Mark Ma, to come to Urumqi in the 1940s. The first time I visited the Urumqi church in 2001, HQZ told me the story of the first CIM missionaries

Percy Mather (1884-1933) and Emil Fischbacher (1903-1933). HQZ did not know them personally. After hearing their stories and how they died because of their love for the people of China, HQZ affirmed their contribution to Chinese churches even though they did not even found a church. HQZ told me that the two missionaries are the role models of love and mission for the Chinese pastors to learn from. Thus, two old pastors have used modeling as a way of learning ever since they came to Xinjiang.

As FCG recalled, CXQ and HQZ usually attend and listen to the preaching of the young leaders. They give comments to them and instruct them carefully on how to improve their sermons. As a result, the young leaders conclude that they learn much more while putting their lessons into practice in the church. This is a typical example of the mentor-apprentice relationship in the Urumqi church. Every Easter the pastors and lay leaders visit the graves to Percy Mather and Emil Fischbacher, as well as those of the founding pastors of Urumqi church. HQZ told me that the visit and memorial service are part of the young leaders' education process. They have to learn the sacrificial spirit of their predecessors and remember how they suffered for the sake of the gospel.

As recorded in the *Xinjiang Chinese Christian Church 60th Anniversary Special Thanksgiving Issue* (2005), among the thirty-four articles, twelve of them tell the stories of the missionaries, pastors, elders, and some lay leaders in previous generations. As a matter of fact, FCG plays an important role in helping create the tradition of honoring and following the early models. She is spends the most time with the young pastors. Every young pastor from the Urumqi church—LQF, ZSH, YJ, SJH, JQ, and CHB—talks to FCG before applying to seminary. She said,

> I believe that the old pastors are the servants of God, who have offered themselves totally to the Lord. They live according to what they were called to be, and they live lives of total commitment to serving the Lord. These old servants practice what they teach. Their lives are role model for us to follow, and they have a great impact on us (FCG).

As a good communicator, FCG helps the old pastors to build up the foundation of following models in their ministry.

The other reason for the adoption of mentor-apprentice relationships in developing leaders is the limited choices in Urumqi. The churches in China lacked all kinds of resources, including Christian books and training opportunities, before the year 2000. In addition, Xinjiang is far too remote from any of the opportunities available in the coastal regions. The knowledge and experience of the old pastors are important as they are the only role models for the younger generation to learn from. The parents of FCG were the coworkers of CXQ and HQZ. The two old pastors and FCG's mother live on different floors in the Urumqi church building above the church facilities. They live and work together as an extended family. FCG treats the two old pastors as if they were her father. In the same way, the two old pastors also treat FCG as their daughter. FCG said, "Pastor HQZ teaches us like a father teaching his children, very straight." Under the guidance and protection of the old pastors, FCG and the other younger leaders are maturing in life and ministry.

During the interviews, HQZ and FCG are the names mentioned by other informants most frequently in the discussion of mentoring relationships. LQF and CHB have explicitly declared that FCG is their mentor who gives them advice and encouragement in life and ministry. FCG encourages LQF and CHB to receive theological education while they are still volunteering in the Youth Fellowship. JQ said repeatedly that FCG is her mentor in life and ministry. JQ has devoted herself to serve the younger generations because FCG comforted and encouraged her before she went to seminary. Acquiring knowledge through the life experiences of others is a gateway to spiritual maturity. JQ even calls FCG "elder sister" instead of pastor when no other church member is present.

ZL and SJH are attracted by the personalities of the old pastors. The loving and caring relationship in the leadership team is the major reason why they went and later returned to Urumqi to serve wholeheartedly without thinking of moving to the coastal cities. As a mentor, HQZ does not limit his care and concern to the coworkers only but extends his care to their family members as well. When he heard that ZL's parents were upset when she decided to go to Urumqi instead of staying in Shanxi to work in the church, HQZ flew to Shanxi in central China to comfort her parents. At that time, HQZ was eighty-two years old. This is one example of how the old pastors show their love and care to the young leaders. They win the hearts and loyalty of the young leaders.

In addition to the willingness of both the old and young to establish this informal mentor-apprentice relationship, the structure of Urumqi church has also created a favorable environment for such relationships. The young pastors are very eager to learn from the old pastors as well as from other old and pious Christians. Almost all young pastors name some characteristic of the two old pastors and FCG that they can learn from. For example, LQF wants to learn from their faithfulness, LQF and ZL want to be as knowledgeable as HQZ, CHB would like to learn from their servant hearts, JQ wants to learn the way they develop their inner spiritual lives. Besides the pastors, the parents of FCG and other old Christians are also role models for the young leaders. Obviously, modeling comes naturally in their learning practices.

As mentioned earlier, the Youth Fellowship provides a way to recruit and equip young leaders. The weekly prayer meeting provides a platform for leadership development. All the pastors should attend the weekly prayer meeting on Monday. The meeting lasts for several hours. One of them will share a biblical message for the group devotions. They then share their difficulties and pray together. The old pastors and FCG give some words of encouragement in response to their situations. The old pastors also share their own visions or some important message they have received from God recently. In my last two visits in 2006 and 2008, I heard that their vision was to pray that 100 high-quality church leaders would arise throughout Xinjiang province. As an outsider, I found it very impressive and interesting that all church leaders were speaking the same language about the vision of the church. They were not saying that it was the idea of the old pastors but was the vision God had given to Urumqi church. At last I found out it is the contribution of the weekly prayer meeting where they had communicated the vision for a long time.

Teaching Through Personal Relationships in the Sanyuan Church

Similar to the case in Urumqi, mentoring-apprentice relationship is the most impressive method in developing church leaders in Sanyuan. ZGR was influenced by many teachers and pastors through personal relationships. ZGR was not educated in the modern educational system with classes of different subjects. He began his journey of learning with a traditional mentor-apprentice relationship. He followed his grandfather and uncle in learning Confucian classics. After finishing a two years of theological training at the age of eighteen, he worked with a senior pastor in Henan. A mentor-apprentice relationship is an effective learning method especially in the chaotic social situations ZGR faced during his youth. China experienced the Second Sino-Japanese War (World War II) and civil war in the 1930s and the 1940s, so ZGR had to move from province to province. To finish a standard seminary curriculum was almost impossible when they need to move from time to time due to safety reasons.

Even though ZGR has retired from the school he founded—Shaanxi Bible School—he keeps good relationship with his former students. His former students are now church leaders in different cities and counties. Some of them contact ZGR when they need advice. They often invite him to preach in their churches. In the summer of 2006 when I visited Urumqi, the pastors told me ZGR had just left after a week long pastoral training program. The Urumqi church had invited ZGR to be the keynote speaker in the summer pastoral training camp.

The other informants said that ZGR was their mentor. CYP mentioned that ZGR was her mentor, and she follows his example of serving in the church. CYP has learned most from ZGR's personality and the way he handles interpersonal relationships. YCQ mentioned that he follows the example of ZGR who teaches him and nurtures his spiritual life. He said, "When I feel frustration, I visit these old pastors. It is not necessary for them to speak to me comforting words; merely by watching them go about their daily lives, I have been blessed (YCQ). ZFQ intends to learn from her father the attitudes of a faithful servant of God. She quoted ZGR's words, "fight to live, prepare to die, obey the Lord, focus at work." She has taken this statement as her motto to encourage herself to serve the Lord like her father has done. Another church leader, YYL, is deeply impressed by the life of ZGR. She said, "His style of living, spiritual discipline, and other areas of life can deeply influence others. His sermons and lectures are all very practical, not merely theoretical knowledge in a textbook" (YYL).

As the senior pastor in the Sanyuan church, YCQ has also a good mentor for the younger church leaders to follow. YHG is attracted by the humble spiritual of both pastors ZGR and YCQ. CYP also mentioned that these two pastors are good encouragers who motivate the followers to serve wholeheartedly.

The mentoring relationship between ZGR and YCQ came into effect during the leadership transition of the churches of Sanyuan County. ZGR is now a figurehead in the churches in Sanyuan. He preaches every Sunday even though he is eighty-five years old. His leadership influence remains not because of his position, but because of his personality and relationship with the congregation. Chinese people have a tradition of respecting seniors. A good senior person is usually the mentor of the followers. People come to seek his advice and blessing when making important decisions. Since ZGR lives in the church, he has retained his influence on the congregation even though that was not his intention. In this case, his successor may live in his shadow, which will make it difficult for him or her to exercise his or her leadership authority. In my observation, YCQ, the successor of ZGR in the Sanyuan churches, does not have obvious difficulty in leading the churches. YCQ is responsible for the daily administration of the churches and meeting points in Sanyuan County. He divided the county into three major districts and empowers the other pastors to take care of the needs of the churches and meeting points. I noticed that YCQ allows some of the meeting points to introduce some new ministries that the main church in Sanyuan does not have. It would not be possible if YCQ is defensive against the followers for fear of their challenges to his position. Like ZGR, YCQ is a gentle and humble person. He has good relationships with other pastors in Sanyuan County. His son YHG and ZGR's daughter are working under his leadership. The harmonious relationship among the leadership team shows the powerful result of mentoring relationships involving different generations of leaders. ZGR and YCQ worked together closely in early years, and now ZGR has given YCQ a free hand to empower him to take the leadership role. ZGR limits himself to the position of a retired pastor and is responsible for preaching only. As YCQ concluded, the old pastor gives him direction in church development and helps to nurture his faith and spirituality. In turn, YCQ is the mentor for the younger pastors. He has not created any formal structure for communication and training like the Urumqi and Fuzhou churches have done, but worked closely with the younger pastors to deal with the needs of the different congregations.

The mentoring relationships between ZGR and the younger pastors have come from the long years of education received by the old pastor. ZGR had learned the leadership models from the messages in the book of Acts, including the role models of Peter, Paul, James, and Barnabas. He expects a leader to be the role model for the congregation to follow. The role model is a servant who models after what Jesus did to his disciples (Zhang 2009, 143, 203-204). YCQ and other pastors have repeated ZGR's saying about the role model of a church leader: "To win people by virtues; to move people by love." The mentoring relationship and the use of modeling for effective learning in the leadership development process do not come naturally from human nature but only from a long-term cultivation of heart and mind.

Moral Leadership and Modeling in the Zhong Zhou Church

In Fuzhou, YZD and LDJ did not mention modeling and the mentoring-apprentice relationship explicitly; however, the way they live and the comments from others reflect the relationship. From my observation, everyone in Zhong Zhou church respects YZD. All five young leaders in the interviews called him teacher Y. However, at the very beginning of the interview with LDJ, he denied that YZD had influenced his life and ministry. Even YZD said that nobody but God has made an impact on his life and ministry. Interestingly, they do not ignore those who really are their mentors, but it is the tradition of the CAH to downplay the significance of human influence. The CAH believes that to praise the contributions of human beings is to steal the glory from God. The help of others is also the work of the Holy Spirit, not merely human efforts.

Undoubtedly, leadership in the Zhong Zhou church has developed around the person of the old elder YZD and the theology of Watchman Nee. Some counterparts left the church because of a disagreement with YZD many years ago. He remains as the only authority as well as the role model in the Zhong Zhou church. In the interviews, all five young leaders responded that YZD's identity as the role model is important. LDJ mentioned how he began his ministry in the Zhong Zhou church:

> I was helping to monitor the construction project of the Zhong Zhou church. I observed the attitude of teacher YZD and found that he really worked wholeheartedly for God. My heart was settled then when I saw YZD's true character. I would like to stay here to serve the Lord (LDJ).

Before coming to the Zhong Zhou church, LDJ was an independent evangelist who travelled around and preached in different churches. When YZD invited LDJ to come to the Zhong Zhou church, LDJ was touched by the passion and vision of YZD. ZX also said,

> The sermons of YZD, his behavior, and personality are all have made a great impact on me. The message he preached and inner life he lived are essential to me. Without his teachings, I cannot live the faith until today. The message of the pastor influences me even though I was not aware (ZX).

The sermons and behavior of YZD have indeed attracted and made an impact on many leaders. In addition to LDJ and ZX, CJ is another one who was deeply impacted by YZD's sermons and behavior. She decided to give up everything to serve in the church because of the messages YZD preached. Together with YZD, LDJ is also very well received and was recognized as one of the role models in the Zhong Zhou church even though he was just a middle-aged leader. ZX and CJ said explicitly that LDJ and YZD are the models they can learn from. Although they do not want to give honor to human beings, they in fact recognize YZD, and even LDJ, as mentors.

The expectations of a leader can more or less reflect the importance of modeling and the mentoring relationship. The work of the Holy Spirit, absolute obedience to God, and a pious life are all listed by YZD as the qualities a leader should have. As a leader, one should live and work according to the will of God. Only with these qualities can one become the role model for the congregation. As LDJ commented, a church leader is a morally good person and a role model for others to follow. LDJ and other leaders have learned from YZD as a role model, and therefore they expect that a leader should also live and work like YZD. In addition, the young leaders' lists of expectations of a leader are similar to what YZD has said. LSQ stated clearly that he wants to have the knowledge and qualities of YZD. All these can be regarded as effects produced by modeling. YZD strongly believes that leadership gifts and qualities cannot be learned through formal theological education and training; instead, they are inspired by the Holy Spirit. Only through daily observation and experiences of working together in the church can one's spiritual gifts be discovered and affirmed by other coworkers. In short, this is a process of peer mentoring as well.

Formal and Informal Training

Modeling and the mentoring relationship do not come out of an intentionally developed leadership development program but from a combination of the Chinese cultural tradition and the personality of the leaders. None of the informants even know the term *mentoring*. The belief that a leader is a role model for others to follow is already deeply rooted in their minds and hearts. In contrast to the theological education through seminary, all informants welcome mentoring as a form of informal training. From the responses of the informants, they gave no sign of tendency to suggest a replacement of formal theological education by the informal training. Formal theological education refers to the seminary training of church workers.[2] It

---

2. Under the structure of the TSPM and the CCC, only one seminary can accept students from all the provinces in China: Nanjing Union Theological Seminary. Five regional seminaries can accept students from surrounding provinces. Yinjing Seminary, which is mentioned later in this section, is one of the regional seminaries which covers the north and northwestern provinces in China. Most provinces have their own Bible schools which provide two to three years of theological training. Many counties and cities have local training centers which provide a few weeks to a few months of pastoral training.

is widely accepted that the church leaders should be trained in theological seminaries, Bible schools, or local training centers where biblical knowledge, theology, and the ministry practices in the church were taught. In fact, most church workers who can preach in the local meeting points were trained in some of these training centers.

In Sanyuan, YCQ commented on the different roles of formal and informal training: "Seminary education gives us theological knowledge. The old pastor builds up our relation with God." In comparing the knowledge with relationship with God, YCQ admitted that the latter is more important than the former. LXN puts spiritual growth prior to learning in the seminary. She pointed out that the seminary training is not practical enough. She believed that the spirit of a leader can be nurtured through serving in the church and having a stable devotion time.

Receiving formal theological education in seminary is a common way to equip potential church leaders. The old pastors in Urumqi and Sanyuan have intentions to develop more young church leaders through formal theological education. However, if the purpose of theological education is to equip potential church leaders, seminary should not be the only place for training leaders, and its curriculum should not be the only program through which the students can learn and grow.

In the specific situation of China, seminary teachers and curriculum may change suddenly with the changes in seminary leadership. In Urumqi, students who graduated in different years in Yinjing Seminary have different sorts of feedback on seminary education. Interestingly, five of the young leaders (CHB, JQ, ZL, YJ, and LWG) stated that formal theological education has opened their eyes widely. As the theological background of these young leaders is basically fundamentalist, some of them find difficulties in adjusting to the academic requirement of the seminary in the beginning. When they encounter some new theories and schools of thought, they respond positively and conclude that their knowledge is being enriched.

One of the reasons why they can accept new theories without problem is the lifestyles of the teachers. The personalities and spiritual lives of the teachers are very important in the seminary. They demonstrate how a spiritual church leader should behave; which attracts the students to learn from them. As ZL reflected, "I like to learn more biblical knowledge in seminary, but I really hope to learn from those teachers who live out their faith." In addition, LWG stated that the personality of the teacher made an even greater impact on him than the knowledge he learned in the seminary. He experienced the help from a seminary teacher in taking care of his sick sister while he was a seminary student.

FCG summarized the most important element of seminary education in her experience: "Those old pastors in the seminary know almost everything about the Bible. They are highly respected and are the treasure of the churches in China. Their lives are also good role models for us to follow" (FCG). The teachers in Yinjing Theological Seminary in the 1980s and the 1990s were the old pastors who had experienced suffering from the Cultural Revolution. Most of them were retired or had passed away by the end of the 1990s. Therefore, FCG has reflected the situations in the 1980s and early 1990s.

Another common feedback was that the seminary provides theological theories, and putting these theories to real situations of the churches is highly important. Yinjing Theological Seminary accepts students from north and northwest China. Application of the theories the students learn varies because many of them come from different backgrounds. SJH and YJ both commented that the seminary education cannot provide adequate practical training; therefore, they had learned from FCG, applying what she learned in seminary to the Urumqi church. LQF repeatedly emphasized the importance of practical experiences in theological education. Practical experiences include personal reflection on what one has learned, how to apply theories to actual situations, and how to develop the habit of self-learning.

The comments from the informants enrich the perspectives on the role of theological education in developing church leaders. Seminary training cannot stand alone in developing church leaders. It has to be closely connected with the lives of the teachers and their practical experiences.

Unlike other churches, the CAH did not sent any of their church workers to seminary to receive formal theological education. They did not trust the denominational institutions to serve their own purposes in developing the church leaders. As YZD commented,

> Leadership training is not dependent on seminary education. We observe the progress of learning through daily practices in ministry. The knowledge of the Bible, the knowledge of the truth, and the actions that are performed are considered in the observation process. Different people will serve naturally according to their gifts (YZD).

YZD assumes that leadership is a gift already given by God to those he has chosen. Seminary education does not help to find nor distinguish a person's leadership talents. Only through working together for a long time, can the old pastor observe the performance and quality of work of the young leaders. YZD believed that the God-chosen church leader will emerge naturally. Observation is the main means of discerning who is a leader.

Human efforts are needed in order to develop a leader even though he or she is chosen by God. The biblical knowledge and the nature of church ministry are necessary for equipping a person to become a leader. The Zhong Zhou church is different from other churches in leadership development. It equips leaders by itself in a small group and informal settings. YZD views theological knowledge as only one part of the leadership development process. The CAH tradition believed that a few years of learning in an institution is not the only way to develop church leaders. The internal leadership training at the Zhong Zhou church can be divided into the areas of Bible study and ministry consultation. YZD said,

> We equip the church workers only with Bible knowledge. We have many gatherings and meetings every day. The first one is a prayer meeting in the morning. After the prayer meeting, we have Scripture reading together. All the church leaders come together to read one chapter of the Bible each day. The leading brother or sister is responsible for explaining the meaning of the selected text. We begin with the book of Genesis and continue until Revelation. In addition, some special topics are taught, for example, "The Gospel of the Kingdom of Heaven," "The Eternal Plan of God" Bible study series, and "Foundational Truth." We also have evangelistic meetings (YZD).

LSQ responded that he benefited most from the weekly Bible study session. The leadership team members are selected to take turns in leading the Bible study. Training in Bible study and preaching happen at the same time. All of the four young leaders (CJ, YJY, ZX, and LSQ) responded positively that the meetings in the church were learning opportunities. They learn Bible knowledge and preaching, and share the vision of LZD. During the meetings, they share their difficulties and others respond. These kind of problem-solving meetings are found in the Urumqi church as well. They are a kind of ministry consultation.

This informal way of learning has undergoing a transformation in recent years. LDJ received one year of training for pastors organized by the Fujian provincial CCC in Fujian Theological Seminary. He responded positively, and therefore the Zhong Zhou church started a training center in Jin Shan in 2007. When I visited the Jin Shan training center, I noticed that the students with varied backgrounds came from rural churches. Not only were students from the former CAH attending these two-year training courses but also other Christians from the house churches as well as those from TSPM churches. In addition to the students in Fujian province, the Jin Shan training center accepts students from other provinces like Henan, Anhui, and Shanxi. In other words, the model of leadership development is changing in the Zhong Zhou church. The church leaders of CAH in Zhong Zhou church no longer restrict themselves to the traditional informal training but are now open to a formal seminary style of theological education. They are not only serving their own tradition but serving other non-CAH Christians as well.

This important change came as a result of the attitude of the old pastor YZD. In general, the CAH did not accept foreign pastors to come to their church to preach. In training church leaders, they run their own training institution inside their churches. In this exclusive environment, the traditional CAH churches want to guarantee that the church leaders follow their own doctrines without being "polluted" by denominationalism and other non-biblical doctrines. YZD told me that one of the differences between him and Watchman Nee is in the acceptance of teachers outside the CAH tradition. YZD invites non-CAH speakers to come and teach their students in their internal meetings. Even though all foreign speakers must be endorsed by either YZD or LDJ, the acceptance of foreign teachers is already a breakthrough. YZD did not receive any formal theological training, but he learned by reading books from a variety of backgrounds. He said that his reading list has included the classics of different denominations and theological traditions and even the books from cults and heretical teachings. He encourages the young leaders to read extensively so that they will know what the congregation is facing. When heretical ideas come to the church, the leaders know how to respond.

In addition, YZD sent LDJ to Fujian Theological Seminary to receive a year of pastoral training. LDJ benefited from the theological training. He said, "In thirty years of experience in serving the Lord, my knowledge is accumulated through continuous ministry. Now we have systematic training, which is a better and more efficient way of training and learning" (LDJ). The leadership team came to accept formal theological education as an effective means of developing the church leaders. The Zhong Zhou church was therefore established in the Jin Shan training center. LDJ does not intend to replace the informal training with this training center. When YZD said that spiritual gifts are discovered by experience, ZX said that through formal education, the process of finding spiritual gifts becomes faster and more effective.

YZD and LDJ were not trained through any formal theological education system. YZD emphasized the work of the Holy Spirit in every individual's heart and mind (Ye 2006a, 92). LDJ agrees with YZD's emphasis on the work of Holy Spirit, who gives each individual a special gift to use in serving the church. Through working together, the leadership gifts of the church leaders can be discovered through observation. Although LDJ is the only one who benefited from formal theological training, he did not downplay the value of informal training. Daily communications among the leadership team is still an effective means of leadership development in the Zhong Zhou church.

The trend in the Zhong Zhou church in developing leaders is to add a formal theological education style to the informal training method. At this stage, formal theological education is one of the training methods in developing leaders. The benefit of this method is that students can acquire knowledge in a more systematic and effective way. Traditional informal training, in contrast, puts emphasis on practical experience which cannot be learned in the classroom effectively. Through working together, the leadership team can discern the work of the Holy Spirit among one another by observation. In this respect, the work of Holy Spirit is perceived as relational, intuitive, and sometimes subjective. It is possible that the Zhong Zhou church may discover a good combination of the strengths of both formal and informal training in the near future.

Experiential teaching and learning methods have been adopted in all the churches in these case studies. The intention of developing a leader as a role model is the primary target of the experiential process. The inner life qualities, including morality and spiritual maturity, are the focus of attention in leadership development. A connection with the formal and informal training methods is the future pattern of leadership in Chinese churches.

Summary

Based on the case studies in Urumqi, Sanyuan, and Fuzhou, seven generalizations were identified: suffering experiences, political sensitivity, the significance of church traditions, Confucianism and human development, team development in a collective culture, community as the extension of family, and the use of experiential learning methods. These characteristics sketch out the leadership development pattern used in contemporary Chinese churches. External situations have shaped the basic framework of church leadership development in China. Some of the external situations have been internalized and become part of the internal culture of the churches. The churches and church leaders today are linked closely with Chinese church history and their cultural heritage.

What happened in the past determined certain characteristics in leadership development: the value of suffering experiences, political awareness, and some specific church traditions. Obviously, the historical situation in early twentieth century China is significant for the churches today. One cannot disregard the fact that another external influence—the Chinese Confucian culture—has shaped the perceptions and expectations of both the church leaders and the followers. The cultivation of human nature, the team approach, the importance of family relationships, and the methods of developing followers are all essential elements in developing Chinese church leaders. Relational leadership which includes all of these seven characteristics can be the most suitable practice within the Chinese cultural context.

CHAPTER 8

Missiological Implications of Relational Leadership in Chinese Churches

The characteristics and contextual framework of relational leadership are found in the case studies of this dissertation. Relational leadership is the common practice of leadership style and leadership development pattern of these churches in contemporary China. A summary of the major characteristics of relational leadership and its missiological implications for contemporary Chinese churches are discussed in this chapter.

The Characteristics of Relational Leadership

Relational leadership in a Christian context is a leadership style focused on developing followers through establishing mutual relationships between the leaders and the followers. The major purpose of the leader is to lead the followers into spiritual maturity and develop their ministry capabilities through working together with the followers for a certain period of time. Six major characteristics of relational leadership can be identified in the various outlooks of biblical studies, Western theories of leadership, cultural and historical traditions, and contemporary case studies. Some common features are consistent throughout this study.

Relational Leadership is a Response to Situational Factors in Leadership Development

Relational leadership is a process of interactions among the leader, situations, and followers to achieve some common goals. The decision making process of the leader is influenced by both the expectations of the followers and the situational impacts. Culture as an external situation has formed the perception of the leader and the expectations of the followers at the same time. In a Confucian society, interpersonal relationship of the leader is a means to achieve individual interests and the communal interests. The communal interests themselves are the products of the specific cultural contexts. A relational leader is sensitive to the needs and interests of the followers. Changes in the situations will bring changes to the expectations of the followers. The relational leader need not change his or her decisions in response to these changes but should be sensitive to the impacts from these changes in situations.

The political sensitivity of the Chinese pastors in the contemporary PRC context is one of their unique characteristics. The church leaders have to think and behave wisely in facing the requests and expectations from the government officials. In addition, the positive responses these leaders show toward experiences of suffering is another unique characteristic. The works of Wang Mingdao and the life experiences of the old pastors being interviewed have given theoretical and practical justifications to the value of suffering experiences. All the old pastors believe that suffering is a spiritual lesson given by God so as to bring those he loves into spiritual maturity.

In view of the participation on the world mission of the Chinese churches, two areas are worth for more attention by a Chinese relational leader: the international community and cross-cultural missions. In this age of globalization, followers coming from different cultural backgrounds are not unusual. A relational leader who is sensitive to these cultural differences will enhance his or her ability to lead. In a Christian context, a missionary is supposed to be a bridge between different cultures. Cross-cultural missionaries who have a relational leadership perspective will be sensitive to the different expectations of their coworkers in the mission field as well as the local converts. A successful collaboration among workers from different cultures requires sensitivity to changes in various situations.

Relational Leadership Recognizes Leadership Development is a Process of Spiritual Growth

Relational leadership emphasizes the process of development. Leadership development is understood as a process of spiritual growth in the Chinese churches in this study. As reflected in the theology of Jia Yuming, the process of spiritual growth is sanctification, and the final destination for spiritual growth is to become a Christ-human. A Christ-human is a spiritually mature Christian who is a spiritual leader as well. A Christian leader is characterized by his or her spiritual maturity and becomes a role model for others to follow.

In all the churches in this study, the cultivation and development of inner life qualities is recognized as a lifelong developmental process. Especially in the Zhong Zhou church, most of the informants said that spiritual maturity is the work of the Holy Spirit. The church leaders expected a total reliance on the work of God during the process. Relational leadership in a Chinese Christian context should begin with the relationship with God. The growing process is the reflection of the work of God in human.

The process of spiritual growth takes time and effort. Therefore, leadership development is understood as a lifelong process accompanied by divine intervention. The process of development is meaningful because divine intervention appears without human preparation. Even if the perceived goal is a vision given by God, the ways leading to the final destiny may be totally different from what human beings can expect and predict. A relational leader has patience, spiritual insight, and beliefs on the process of spiritual growth. He or she knows well that only God can make the followers grow.

Developing Role Models is the Major Goal in Relational Leadership

Relational leadership develops role models. All three case studies showed modeling as the major component in developing followers. On the one hand, all the young pastors said that the old pastors are their role models who live exemplary lives. The old pastors, on the other hand, are aiming to develop the potential of the young pastors and help them to become role models for the congregation to follow. All the informants agreed that the ultimate role model is expressed in the life and teachings of Jesus.

The major lesson for the followers is the development of inner life qualities during the process of learning to become role models. A relational leader is concerned that the followers acquired not only the leadership knowledge and skill but also the inner life quality. Thus, to supplement the seminary paradigm of formal teaching and learning, the leader needs to live and work with the followers. In a Christian community, inner life quality is understood as moral and spiritual development. Other leadership attributes are less important when compared with the morality and spirituality of a Christian leader. From the case studies of the Chinese churches, all respondents said that the significance of these two aspects of inner life qualities were important.

A relational leader is a person with good inner life qualities who is willing to commit him or herself to develop the morality and spirituality of the followers. In the Chinese cultural context, morality is a reflection of the Mandate of Heaven. A sage as a leadership model is defined by the morality of a person. This concept implies that a moral person has an intimate relationship with heaven. The Chinese pastors equate the concept of heaven with the Christian God; therefore, a moral person has an intimate relationship with God. The ultimate goal is to achieve spiritual maturity in the process of sanctification.

One of the emphases of relational leadership is to develop the followers through a mentor-apprentice relationship. Inner life qualities can only be developed through a continuous interactive relationship with the role model. Attraction to the spiritual maturity, the personality and the knowledge of the old pastors are the reasons the young pastors perceived them as role models.

Experiential Learning is the Major Method in Developing Relational Leader

The best way to develop inner life quality is not through studying theory only but also putting theory into practice. Therefore, relational leadership emphasizes experiential learning as the major teaching and learning method. Relational leadership encourages the team members to learn from one another through their working relationships. Experiential learning is a teaching and learning pattern based on relationship. Through guidance and working relationships with experienced seniors and peers, one can put theory into actual practice. As the findings from the case studies show, experiential teaching and learning methods are widely adopted in different churches.

According to the philosophy of Wang Yangming, Confucianism is a pragmatic culture which emphasizes the unity of knowing and acting. As a result, learning practical knowledge is more important than knowing merely theory. Wang Mingdao's main concern in his teachings was how to live the exemplary life according to the biblical ethical standards. A true Christian is identified through the application of biblical values to his or her daily life, which is also a true reflection of the grace experienced by a born-again Christian.

The weekly meetings of the Urumqi and Zhong Zhou churches are the actual places where experiential learning is realized and where the old pastors respond to the issues raised by the young pastors. An ideal human model is meaningless when it is unachievable. Christian values are necessary elements in developing potential leaders to become role models. A potential leader should be shaped into a role model. The followers then are supposed to imitate the attitudes and behavior of the leader who reflects the perfect image of God.

In addition, a mentoring and coaching relationship is a learning process that involves two or more people, in which the transfer of knowledge and experience from the mentor to the mentee is the core contents. Other usual practices in mentoring relationships include encouragement, empowerment, counseling, review, and assessment. They are major components in experiential learning process. Experiential learning is in fact a supplement to the seminary-type education in raising church leaders.

Relational Leadership Performs Well with Good Interpersonal Skills

Relational Leadership emphasizes good interpersonal relationship skills. As the case studies show, the Chinese churches emphasize the importance of interpersonal relationships. In the Zhong Zhou church, having good interpersonal relationships is even regarded as a sign of spiritual maturity. In Urumqi and Sanyuan as well, having good interpersonal relationships is perceived as one quality of good leader. Organizational effectiveness, the motivation of the followers, and trust relationships are built on good interpersonal relationship abilities. Having good interpersonal skills is a pre-requisite for effective leadership in today's Chinese society. Relational leadership assumes that having good, sincere relationships is a means to achieve organizational goals as well as an end which enables the working team members to enjoy brotherly love with one another.

A relational leader relates him or herself to the followers with love and emphasizes the harmonious relations in the working team. The personal growth of the follower is an important goal for the relational leader as well. In the practical theology of Yang Shaotang, the church is an extension of a family. In practice, the Urumqi and Sanyuan churches emphasize the leadership team as a family unit where the old pastors are the parents and guardians of the congregations. A clear sign of paternalistic leadership is found in these churches. In such circumstances, harmonious relationships in the working environment are encouraged. The personal growth of the followers is the responsibility of the church leaders.

A relational leader creates the opportunity to promote good relationships among the team members and develop a community of love. The followers enjoy a culture and atmosphere of friendliness, honesty, and trust among themselves. Within the Christian community, good interpersonal relationships are based on the love of God and the role model of Christ; therefore, the obvious observable feature of relational leadership is the establishment of a community of love. The universal love promoted in the Confucian tradition aligns with the love community emphasized by Christianity. The Chinese churches enjoy a favorable environment in developing the community of love. A relational leader is therefore good at enhancing good inter-personal relationships.

Relational Leadership is Effective Leadership Team Development

In addition to good interpersonal relationships, a relational leader develops a team working together to achieve a common goal. Relational leadership improves leadership effectiveness through transforming the leadership team. The development of the team has two major purposes: the fulfillment of the organizational purpose and individual achievement. A leadership team is not a temporary working group which will be dissolved after completing a short- or long-term project. Instead, the relationships among the team members will continue even after the organizational goal has been achieved. The main concern of a relational leader of a team is the personal development of each individual in the team. Team development leads to individual personality development through the members working together. The team members benefit from and learn through the strength of the other team members.

The team development approach adopted by Jesus of Nazareth and the old pastors in the three churches appears consistently in biblical and Chinese cultures. The common belief is to develop human potential, which is a mission given by God. A relational leader finds satisfaction in expanding and developing the potential capabilities of the whole team.

For example, the founding of Spiritual Action Team by Yang Shaotang was an attempt to realize his theory of leadership team development. The old pastors in Urumqi church intentionally use a team approach to develop the young leaders. The two old pastors are in fact a good demonstration of team leadership as they have work together for fifty years. The young pastors in the Sanyuan church, for example, the brothers of YHT and YHG have the intention to develop the next generation leadership team for the preparation of the future needs of the churches. In the eyes of the old pastors, the success of the young leadership team is the success of the church.

Both the theories and case studies have reflected these six characteristics of relational leadership. It is therefore fair to conclude that relational leadership is applicable to the Chinese cultural context at least in the churches in this study.

The Missiological Implications

Relational leadership is applicable to these Chinese churches located in different parts of China: Urumqi and Sanyuan County in northwestern

China, and Fuzhou in eastern China. The results of this study suggest six important missiological implications. The Chinese churches are undergoing a transition from being a mission field to becoming missionary sending churches. In order to participate actively and constructively in world missions, the Chinese churches have to develop mission leaders through culturally adaptable and effective leadership development methods. It is hoped that these implications can enrich the future development of the Chinese church's mission.

The Encouragement of Developing Indigenous Approach in Leadership Development

The first implication of relational leadership in the Chinese churches is that it is the beginning of developing a culturally familiar approach. A truly indigenized church should have indigenized leaders and leadership development methods. The discussions of the indigenization of Christianity in China have a long history but most of them are focused on metaphysical concepts. Relational leadership is a product of biblical and Chinese cultures. It is a practical aspect of the interfaith dialogues between Christianity and Chinese culture. A new paradigm for interfaith dialogues can be introduced because of the successful implementation of relational leadership. Relational leadership is not the only approach to developing Chinese church leaders; rather, it encourages the scholars and practitioners of leadership training that the Chinese culture has favorable elements it holds in common with the Western leadership theories. If it is a beginning research on indigenous approaches to develop followers, future research studies on this topic can be expected.

An Affirmation of the Study of Leadership Attributes

The Western leadership studies begin with the study of leadership traits, which are the abilities and personal qualities of an individual. Leadership traits studies believe the abilities of a leader can determine the performance of an organization. The focus of research has shifted from the person called leader to the interactions among the leader, situations, and the followers. The personality and ability of a leader are less important in these recent studies. The situational factors are believed to have stronger influence on both the leader and the followers. In the Chinese leadership development process, the personal behavior of the leader remains a core element in attracting the followers. In this respect, leadership attributes are still the core component in developing Chinese leaders. Even though the leadership attributes no longer dictate the leadership performance, their importance cannot be underestimated.

In the Chinese churches, leadership attributes can be replaced by the concept of inner life qualities. Inner life qualities are the core contents of moral leadership. The Chinese pastors believe that only through the work of the Holy Spirit can one truly behave as a good moral person. The spirituality of a person governs his or her moral behavior; therefore, spiritual maturity and morally good behavior are two faces of a coin. Inner life becomes a collective term to include spirituality and morality at the same time. The cultivation of an inner life is not possible by only gaining knowledge about the inner life through a formal class but only with guidance and coaching through long-term relationship in non-formal setting.

Moral leadership is especially important in China where Christianity is a minority in the society. The churches, including the TSPM churches and the house churches, both fundamentalist and liberal, are expected to bear the witness of Christ to non-believers. The good moral behavior of the church members is the best evidence and witness to support the existence and expansion of Christianity. Even though people witness the moral decay of the Chinese society today, people still expect good moral leaders. In order for the church to exist and expand, good moral leadership is helpful in persuading the majority of non-believers to accept Christianity as a solution and a future for Chinese society.

A Possible Consensus on Human Nature

The third missiological implication of relational leadership is that it brings a new perspective in the understanding of human nature among the Chinese Christians. One of the most contradictory themes in Christianity and Chinese culture is the understanding of human nature. A Christian believes that human nature is fallible, that is, corrupt and sinful. In contrast, the Confucian believes in the possibility that a person can become a perfect leader through self-cultivation. Relational leadership provides a bridge between the two contradictory views on human nature.

The Chinese churches attempt to incorporate both contradictory views through the doctrine of salvation and the work of the Holy Spirit. Human beings need the salvation of Christ to redeem the fallen humanity. The grace of God is reflected in the redemption of fallen humanity. Through the work of the Holy Spirit, the inner life qualities of individual Christians can be transformed. The Confucian concept of perfect humanity can be incorporated as the ultimate goal of becoming a morally good leader through the imitation of Christ. As human beings are created according to the image of God, salvation is therefore to redeem the fallen humanity and recover the lost image of God. Moral perfection is therefore retained as a possibility in human development. The whole process of achieving moral perfection is possible through the active participation of the human beings and the grace of God.

The Chinese churches have a tendency to fall into the trap of perfectionism: believing human beings can be perfect and literally expecting the leader to be a perfect person. A balanced perspective on human nature is therefore necessary in the process of leadership development. The fallibility of human nature sets the boundaries on the development of the human self. No one can become perfect, and therefore, no perfect leader is possible. The infallibility of human nature actually does not exist; however, the Confucian tradition provides a possibility of human development according to the image of God. The doctrine of fallibility alerts people to the limitations on human development whereas the possibility of achieving the role of an idealized moral leader gives people hope and encouragement to pursue higher moral behavior. The old pastors interviewed in all three case studies have given views of human nature that are balanced between Confucianism and Christianity. As mentioned earlier, Asian cultures value the process of development. It is important to try and keep the motivation to learn and grow. Even though the goal of moral perfection is unachievable on earth, the spiritual maturity that leads a person to become a Christ-human by the grace of God is believed to be achievable. Jia Yuming's Christ-human is still the hope and goal of many pastors.

Awareness of the Negative Aspects of Relational Culture

The fourth implication of relational leadership is the awareness of the negative side of relational culture. As mentioned earlier, successful businessmen in China rely highly on good *guanxi*, interpersonal relationship and social networks. With good *guanxi*, one can have more business contracts at better terms, higher revenues, or even better social prestige. Similar situations are found in the churches as well. A relational leader has to base his or her relationships on Christian value, not personal interest. Moreover, this is indeed a challenge to most Chinese pastors as they have grown up in this *guanxi* culture.

Giving presents to one another during many traditional festivals is regarded as a cultural practice. The purpose is to consolidate better relationships with superiors, neighbors, relatives, and friends. The Chinese pastors need to have the wisdom to teach and practice differentiating between bribery and fellowship as they keep good relationships with others through giving presents. The Urumqi, Sanyuan, and Zhongzhou church leaders have set good examples by having good relationships with the RAB without using bribery. The positive use of relationships is one of the best tools for evangelism in China. In developing followers, it is necessary to raise the awareness of the negative side of giving presents which misuses relationships for personal interest.

A Balance between Theory and Practice in Leadership Development

The fifth implication of relational leadership is evidence that a balance can be achieved between the theory and practice of leadership development. The Chinese Christians think and act pragmatically. Chinese people treasure practical knowledge to the extent that if something is practical but not understandable, they still adopt the practice. For example, Chinese pastors use the term *Heaven* to represent the Christian God and *liang zhi* to represent the God-given conscience. Whether or not these concepts are the same is still debatable, but the Chinese pastors adopt what they experience as terms that are communicable to the audience. Under this criterion of pragmatic value, experiential learning and modeling are effective methods for developing leaders. Followers are eager to follow those who can practice what they teach.

Jesus of Nazareth gave practical guidance to his disciples. He lived and worked together with the disciples, the abstract knowledge became concrete and practical. The experiential learning methods adopted by the Chinese pastors are a true reflection of this balance between theory and practice. Wang Yangming's philosophy on the unity between knowing and acting is the foundation of this cultural tradition. The young leaders who were interviewed are all attracted by the personalities of the old pastors as well as the the personalities of teachers in the seminary. The old pastors live what they teach. It is not knowledge that makes the old pastors different from other Christians; it is their consistent behavior in daily life.

Effective leadership does not require academic degrees but consistence between what the leader says and acts. All the practices of leadership formation which bring the theory into practices are welcomed in the Chinese churches. The mentoring relationship, for example, is one effective means of developing Chinese church leaders as it can balance theory and practice in the developmental process.

The Compatibility of Relational Leadership with Other Theories

The sixth implication of relational leadership is the incorporation of other leadership theories in developing Chinese church leaders. The relational leadership theory is not the only leadership theory applicable to Chinese culture. Relational leadership does not exclude the value of other leadership styles. Collaboration with other studies on leadership is needed. For instance, the relational leadership theory is based on the studies in situational theory. The relational leadership comes into effect through handling the interactive process among the leader, situations, and the followers successfully. In the concluding remarks in chapter 2, relational leadership is calling for collaboration between the leader and followers in this diversified world. In order to achieve organizational goals and personal success, working together is the only workable choice.

As Chinese culture is inclusive in nature, it borrows and absorbs the strengths of other cultures and re-develops into its own indigenous theory and practice. Relational leadership admits the value and importance of leadership attributes. The personal quality of a leader is important. Relational leadership recognizes the essential contributions and needs of the followers; therefore, ability to work with people becomes one of the essential attributes of the leader. In view of the paternalistic leadership in Asian cultures, relational leadership explains the core value of relationships which come from an understanding of family relationships. Community as an extension of a family is a gateway to understanding why relationship is important in Asian culture. Relational leadership can therefore be a possible bridge between East and West in the aspect of leadership development.

Summary

The study of leadership theory in the Chinese Christian context is new. The relational leadership theory is an attempt to consolidate what already is practiced in the Chinese churches. Through this study of the practices in the contemporary Chinese churches, some concluding remarks can be made. The characteristics of relational leadership and its missiological implications are drawn from the case studies in Urumqi, Sanyuan, and Fuzhou churches. As they represent TSPM churches with different backgrounds, the implication is that relational leadership can be applied into other TSPM churches in China as well.

In summary, this study shows some important areas which were missed in the past in the discussion of leadership development in China. The impacts of culture on leadership development were underestimated. It is clear that the cultural influence of Confucianism is so strong in the Chinese churches that the leadership expectations are shaped accordingly. The old pastors live out a good combination of being good Christians and faithful Confucians. In this tradition, relational leadership is the best summary of what has been found in these Chinese churches.

Part IV: Conclusion

CHAPTER 9

Conclusion

This research study has compared and contrasted the approaches to developing followers in biblical, contemporary Western, and Confucian Chinese cultures. The conclusion is clear that relational leadership is a bridge between the three different cultures in developing leaders. The contemporary Chinese churches can attempt to adopt the relational approach in equipping church leaders. This study concludes with a discussion of five areas of significance followed by suggestions for reexamination of existing practices in leadership development. Recommendations for further studies are also suggested.

Areas of Significance in this Research Study

This research study is one of the very few attempts to compare and contrast practical aspects of Christianity and Chinese culture. This study fills the gap left by most of the previous studies, which have compared only the metaphysical aspects of Christianity and Chinese culture.

Second, this study is significant because it is the first step in the study of leadership theory in a contemporary Chinese Christian context. More reflections and consolidations are needed before a widely accepted Chinese Christian theory of leadership development developed.

Third, this study has opened the way for research into the non-political aspects of the TSPM churches. Almost all the studies of the TSPM churches after the 1980s are focused on church and state relationship. No matter whether the subject is the impact of the Communist government on the church or the suffering experiences of the church pastors, every topic is related to government religious policies. The discussions of the daily practice of Christianity in the lives of eighty million Christians in the PRC are inadequate. Leadership development is one area worth studying in depth. Many other areas need more investigation.

Fourth, this study has begun an examination of the relationship between Wang Mingdao and Confucianism. The previous studies about Wang Mingdao focused on two major areas: his ethical teachings on Christian living and his resistance to the TSPM. It is important to analyze how Confucianism impacted Mingdao's teachings on Christian living when he did not receive any formal theological education. This research study focuses on the moral teachings of Wang Mingdao. I hope that some other areas of Mingdao's theology can be discussed in near future.

Fifth, Jia Yuming and Yang Shaotang have been introduced to Western scholars. Both Jia and Yang are well known in Chinese churches. Their books are widely published and used in both house and TSPM churches as textbooks in theological education. However, their contributions were neglected and none of their works has been translated into English. I hope that, in the near future, more works of important and influential Chinese pastors can be translated and studied in order to cover a wider area of Chinese indigenous theology.

Reviews of Existing Practices in Leadership Development in Chinese Churches

To Review the Existing Leadership Training Program in the Chinese Churches

The churches in China were reopened in 1978 after the end of the Cultural Revolution. The churches grew rapidly in the past three decades. Many of these newly developed churches do not have enough church pastors and leaders. In response to the need, the seminaries and Bible schools were reopened and many local pastoral training programs have been conducted. In addition, foreign Christians brought their familiar leadership training programs into China. These leadership training programs are being widely used without consideration for the differences in education levels, church traditions, and political situations between the original context of the program and the contemporary Chinese context.

Based on the present study, a review on the adoption of leadership development program is suggested. Leadership development programs used in China have been developed by Western Christians. Moreover, local culture cannot be neglected in the process of absorbing foreign and new ministries into Chinese churches. It is necessary to review the adaptability of Western programs to what has already existed in Chinese church. Four areas in particular should be considered.

First, the new leadership development program should be introduced together with the consideration for and even incorporation into the existing church tradition. As discussed in this study, the perceptions and expectations of leadership are largely shaped by the church traditions. The new program is not necessarily a replacement but rather a transformation of the old tradition.

Second, foreign programs have their strength and limitations. The previous research studies provided favorable foundations in developing training programs; whereas, the indigenous inputs provide what the foreign programs are missing in facing different culture. Indigenous inputs include the understanding and adaptation of local teaching and learning practices, educational philosophy, and perception and expectations of church leaders.

Third, long-term planning for leadership development should be a collaborative effort between foreign organizations with the local church leaders. In the past, due to the sensitive nature of foreign Christians working with the local churches, foreign workers would come and go within a few days. Leadership training programs were usually conducted in a hurry without long-term planning and goals. In response to the urgent need for more church leaders in the expanding new churches, a lay Christian who is willing to serve can become a church leader with only two to four weeks of intensive training. Some of them are even taking up leadership responsibilities without guidance. As this research study indicates, genuine leadership involves the lifelong development of the inner life qualities of the followers. To become an effective leader requires a process of long-term learning and practice through acquiring knowledge and building relationships with the followers. Without a long-term development plan and program, it is not easy to cultivate an effective leader.

Fourth, the cultivation of the inner life qualities should be a priority. Like the requirement for long-term development plans in leadership development programs, the inner life qualities require a long period of time to cultivate. An influential leader has personal qualities that attract people to follow and support him or her. Leadership skills are less important when compared with the morality and spirituality of a leader. Not many of the existing leadership development programs emphasize the development of inner life qualities; therefore, inner life qualities can be regarded as a forgotten but important area of leadership development in Chinese churches.

To Review the Existing Curriculum of the Seminary

The leadership development programs in Chinese churches can be conducted by the TSPM seminary or foreign Christians in both the TSPM and house churches. Both the TSPM and house churches have established different levels of leadership development. Formal and informal, academic and practical, and open and non-open leadership development programs can all be found in the churches.

The seminaries in China are not strong in theological research. Their theological education concentrates on developing church pastors in practical areas. The academic qualifications of the teachers and students are another limitation of the seminaries. Most seminary students have only a high school education level when they apply to the seminaries. In the 1990s, some debates arose in Hong Kong about on the role of "cultural Christians" in Chinese theological development (Fallman 2008, 21-40). *Cultural Christians* is a term used to describe Chinese intellectuals who have research interests in Christian theology. Some of them are converted Christians while others are literally non-Christians. Many universities have departments of religions and culture which have published research papers on Christian theological discussions. As a result, the church has less influence over the process of indigenization in theological development as it does not produce any scholastic research on Christian theology.

In the past few years, the situation has changed. More seminary teachers are studying abroad for doctoral degrees. In the meantime, a growing number of university graduates in eastern China are applying to study in the seminary.[1] It is a time to reexamine the seminary curriculum and increase academic research on subjects like indigenous leadership development so as to meet the needs of the churches.

To Review the Recruitment and Internship Arrangement of Seminary Students

Until nowadays, the Chinese churches do not have any difficulty recruiting adequate number of seminary students. However, in addition to the limited seats available for applicants, another problem is that the education levels of the applicants are varied: from junior high school to university graduates. Some of them find difficulty understanding the theological doctrines in the translated textbooks. Before graduation, the students can select a church for their internship. Some of them will go back to their home church, but most of them will move to a new church. In many occasions, they will stay in the internship church after graduation.

This arrangement is common among the churches in mainland China as well as in overseas Chinese churches. The problem is the disconnection between the seminary graduates' home churches and the new churches where they begin their ministry. It is hard to implement the system of mentorship in relational leadership. Leadership development is a lifelong process where the mentor and mentee should have a close connection at least in the beginning of the mentee's ministry. To develop from a seminary student into a mature pastor, guidance and encouragement from a senior pastor are necessary. To implement the mentoring relationship is necessary for a student to have a mentor in his or her home church before entering into seminary. After graduation, the mentor is able to connect with the graduate in the beginning years of his ministry. He or she will help the graduate to overcome ministry difficulties and frustrations.

---

1. The TSPM seminaries have noticed the need for academic research; however, the inadequate academic qualifications of the seminary teachers hinder the capacity for academic research. The recent trend of increasing numbers of university graduates applying to the TSPM seminaries has put greater pressure on the teachers to improve their qualifications. This information was given by Rev. Hu Yingqiang, the Vice Academic Dean of East China Theological Seminary in a recent private conversation in Hong Kong (January 11, 2010).

In the case studies of the churches in Urumqi, Sanyuan, and Fuzhou, the old pastors are able to give advice and encouragement to the young leaders. The mentoring relationships have been developed according to the intention of the old pastors. A mentoring relationship between a mentor and a mentee comes naturally from the context of the Chinese churches. It is necessary to develop a system in the church to encourage more churches to adopt mentoring relationships in leadership development. The system should include the design of the curriculum and the arrangement of internship with the seminary and the Bible school.

These recommendations are made for the purpose of implementing systematically the theory and practice of relational leadership. The immediate need is to review the current practices of foreign Christians especially in their participation in leadership development programs. Likewise, the seminary curricula and internship arrangements need revision in order to serve the long-term needs of the Chinese churches.

Recommendations for Further Research

The recommendations I have just made for the practice of relational leadership in Chinese churches are significant for a healthy development of the churches with healthy church leaders. Because of the limitations in the present study, I have seven recommendations for further studies of leadership development in Chinese churches.

Seminary Education and Leadership Development

A usual practice of leadership development in the churches in China is to receive theological education. As this research has shown, many informants responded that their most impressive experience in seminary was the impact the lives of the teachers made on them. An effective way to evaluate the impact of the seminary on leadership development is to study the curriculum and the performance of the graduates. As this research has shown, the young leaders learned most from working together with the old pastors. In fact, the knowledge they learned from the seminary should be another influential factor in shaping the leadership styles and expectations of these young pastors. Further research on the curriculum, internship arrangement, and the performance of the graduates after a few years of service is therefore suggested to evaluate the effectiveness of seminary education on leadership development in the Chinese churches.

Possible Negative Aspects of the Old Pastors

I have only interviewed those leaders who work closely with the old pastors. The result shows only the positive side of the mentoring relationship and the effectiveness of the leadership development method of the old pastors. This is one limitation of the research methods in this study. I have no access to those who disagree with the old pastors. Building rapport with one side becomes an obstacle to establishing relationships with those who disagree with them. Another suggestion for further research is to collect information from those leaders who cannot work with the existing old or younger church leaders. Their reasons for leaving the church can supplement the findings of the present study. Finding the negative aspects of the existing leadership can further improve the theory of relational leadership.

Ethnicity in the Leadership Development in Rural Churches

The third area discovered in this study that is worth further research is the influence of ethnicity and kinship in rural churches. Urumqi is a migrant city. The church leaders come from different parts of China. The leadership in the Sanyuan church is significantly dominated by two families. The Fuzhou church composed only Fuzhou people who speak the same dialect. Further study is needed in order to find the relationship between ethnicity and church development. China is a multi-ethnic country with fifty-six different racial groups living and working together. The study of ethnicity is important especially in future investigations of church leadership in racial minority churches.

The Gender Issue in Chinese Leadership Development

The fourth area recommended for further study is the gender issue in Chinese churches. The number of female church members is high; however, the church leadership is dominated by males in China. Many female laypeople serve in the church but only a very few can become key leaders or even senior pastors in the churches. In what ways has the church forbidden or discouraged female leadership to emerge? The ordination of women is accepted in the TSPM churches. Is the situation in the rural areas different or similar to the urban churches in allowing female to lead the churches? In addition, is a female leader more relational than a male leader? Are there any gender differences in building relationships within the leadership team? All these questions are important to the future leadership development especially when female followers are predominant in Chinese churches.

Other Influences of Confucianism

This research focused on the understanding of human nature in leadership development. Confucianism has other elements that require more in-depth study. For example, how is the Five Relationships in Confucianism influence the structure of the church? In what ways does the advocacy of harmonious relationships hinder or favor unity in the church? Confucianism, a dominant cultural and moral system in Chinese society which has recently received encouragement from the government, has increasing influence over most of the daily lives of Chinese Christians. This study is limited to the area of leadership development. Many more areas are worth further study.

Liberal Traditions in the TSPM Churches

I have studied the fundamentalist tradition in the TSPM churches here. It is the dominant theology in the most of the local churches. Some of the senior leaders in the TSPM churches are regarded as followers of the liberal theological tradition. Bishop Ding Guangxun is one obvious example as he strongly promotes process philosophy in his theological reconstruction. To some extent, the contextualization process is also a process of compromise with Western Christianity. The difference between fundamentalist Christians and liberal Christians is the degree of compromise. The impact of liberal theology in leadership development in the special situations of the Chinese churches also requires further study.

The House Churches and the Third Churches
The churches in China are diverse because of their attitudes toward the government in addition to their different church traditions. The seventh recommendation for further research is to study the rural house churches and the newly emergent "third churches" in the cities. The traditional rural house church networks are believed to have the most Christians in proportion to the other churches in China. The third churches are believed to have increasing influence over the future development of Chinese churches. The members of the third churches are composed of urban professionals. They are friendlier toward the TSPM churches leadership and the government. They are willing to register but not to join the TSPM because their spiritual needs may not be fulfilled. The third churches do not want to incorporate with the traditional house church networks because they do want to worship God publicly. Under these circumstances, the leadership development pattern may vary according to the backgrounds of these different types of churches.

A Summary and Final Conclusion

This dissertation covers three major areas in its study of leadership development in the Chinese churches. The first area is the theoretical foundations of leaders and leadership from different cultural perspectives. The teaching and practice of Jesus of Nazareth gives the biblical foundations of relational leadership. Western research findings in studies of leadership theory have proposed the interactive dynamics among the leader-situations-followers as the foundation for relational leadership. The Confucian understanding of human nature and human development reflected in the philosophy of Wang Yangming is the cornerstone of Chinese leadership theory. It discloses the gateway of bridging Christianity and Chinese culture in leadership development in the area of cultivating human nature.

As the first part of this dissertation shows, culture as a situational factor is decisive in shaping the expectations of the leader and the pattern of leadership development. The second part therefore covers situational factors affecting leadership development in the Chinese churches. The theological foundations of contemporary indigenous Chinese churches were laid in the early twentieth century when the historical, social, and political situations shaped the understanding and expectations of the church leaders. In the works of Jia Yuming, Yang Shaotang, and Wang Mingdao, some practices of Confucian Christians were discovered. Both in theory and in practice, the Chinese pastors practice relational leadership even they did not know the name. The Chinese leadership development patterns are found in the combination of Confucian and Christian cultures at the same time.

The third part of this study examines the contemporary Chinese churches through case studies. The interviews and participant observations in the churches in Urumqi, Sanyuan, and Fuzhou revealed illustrations of the influences of Confucianism on the Christian churches. In these case studies that focus on leadership development practices, the church leaders tell their experiences of how to develop effective church leaders. The characteristics of relational leadership are therefore concluded from these research findings.

The conclusion of this dissertation sheds a new light on future research on Chinese leadership development. It is possible to have indigenous approaches in developing local church leaders using some culturally familiar methods. Even though not many research studies had been done in the past, the elements for indigenous methods existed. The theory of relational leadership is a culturally familiar leadership development paradigm which can be adopted in the Chinese churches. Relational leadership is a product of the combination of the strength of biblical values, Western leadership theories, and Confucian Chinese cultural characteristics. As this is the very first research study of Chinese relational leadership, I look forward to seeing more studies in the near future.

APPENDIX A

Interview Guide for Old Pastors

About family and social context:
1. Please give me your personal information, including your age, your family, and how long have you been serving in this church.
2. During the Cultural Revolution, where were you and what happened to you?
3. Can you describe how you came to this city? How did you begin your work in this church? How long have you been working in this church?
4. Can you tell me about your family? Are they all Christians? How and in what ways have they impacted your life as a Christian as well as your full-time ministry? In contrast, how have you impacted their lives as Christian?

About calling, ministry and life destiny:
5. Can you tell me how you became a Christian?
6. Are there any important people who shaped your faith? In what ways?
7. Can you share about the process/story of how you were called as a full-time minister?
8. How long you have been working in this church? How did you begin your service here?
9. In your long service to the Lord, is there anyone who impacted your ministry in attitude, ministry skills, strategic direction, and faith in the Lord?
10. What are the most important ministries you have developed in this church?
11. Have there been any difficulties or obstacles in your ministry so far?

About spiritual gifts:
12. What kinds of spiritual gift do you have?

13. How did you discover and become trained in using these spiritual gifts?
14. How did/will you train your coworkers to develop their own spiritual gifts?

About theological education and training:
15. When and why did you receive theological training? How did the training in seminary impact your ministry?
16. What have you found to be most significant in your theological training?
17. Do you think the training in seminary is adequate for your ministry, both the knowledge and skills? Are there any other areas that need more follow-up training? Why?
18. Which teachers or pastors have had the greatest impact on you? In what ways?
19. What are the most valuable experiences you have had in working in this church?
20. What are the most unforgettable experiences from the past in which you learned something? How have these experiences impacted your ministry until now? How did/will you share the lessons you have learned with the young church leaders?

About developing successors:
21. Have you started any forms of theological training in this church/city/province? What are they?
22. What subjects have you taught? What are the durations of the course? What is your role in these training programs?
23. Did you train/teach any coworkers in your church? How? Can you share some of the valuable experiences in training coworkers?
24. How did you delegate responsibility to the next generation leaders?
25. What do you think is the most important element for being a church leader today?
26. If God gives you an opportunity to develop a new generation of church leaders again, which areas you think are most important?

APPENDIX B

Interview Guide for Younger Church leaders

1. Please give me your personal information, including your age, your family, and how long have you been serving in this church.
2. Can you tell me how you became a Christian?
3. Are there any important people who shaped your faith? In what ways?
4. When and why did you receive theological training?
5. What are the most significant factors in your theological training?
6. In what ways has your previous theological training helped shape your ministry today?
7. How do you compare the learning experiences in the seminary and in the church?
8. Which teachers or pastors have had the greatest influence on you? In what ways?
9. Can you describe how you have begun your ministry here in this church?
10. What are the most valuable experiences you have had in working in this church?
11. What do you think is the most important element for being a church leader today?
12. Do you think you are using your spiritual gifts to serve right now?

APPENDIX C
The Life of Wang Mingdao[1]

1900	Born in Beijing during the Boxer Rebellion. His father committed suicide because he was a pastor associated with Western missionaries.
1914	Became a Christian and was baptized in a church run by London Missionary Society in Beijing.
1919	Worked as a teacher in a Christian school.
1920	Decided to give up his dream of becoming a politician and committed himself to Christian ministry. Changed his name to Mingdao.
1921	Insisted on the sole validity of baptism by immersion and was rebaptized with other five students. Employment terminated by the school.
1925	Started a church in his home with 100 members.
1927	Began to publish the quarterly journal *Spiritual Food*, which later circulated all over China.
1928	Married Liu Jingwen, a pastor's daughter.
1937-45	Refused to join the Japanese-led Chinese Christian Federation of North China when Beijing was under Japanese occupation during the Sino-Japanese War.
1955	Taken to prison after he refused to join the Communist government-approved Three Self Patriotic Movement.
1958	Released from prison after signing a confession. He later repudiated the confession and returned to the prison.
1973	Finally released from prison with one eye blinded and lived in Shanghai.
1991	Organized house church meetings at home since the 1970s until his death at the age of ninety-one.

---

1. In addition to the information I presented in this paper, *The Biographical Dictionary of Chinese Christianity* is one of the basic references (Team 2009).

APPENDIX D

The Life of Jia Yuming[1]

1880	Born in Shandong Province.
1901	Graduated in Tengchow College.
1904	Graduated from a seminary run by Presbyterian Church and was ordained a pastor.
1915	Became a teacher at Nanjing Jinling Seminary.
1921	Became the vice-principal of the North China Theological Seminary in Tengxian, Shandong. Published *Systematic Theology*.
1926	Published *Pastoral Theology*.
1930	Became principal of Jinling Women's Theological Seminary.
1936	Started the Spiritual Institute in Nanjing.
1948	Attended the World Gospel Conference in Holland and nominated vice-chairman.
1954	Became vice-chairman of the committee of the Three-Self Patriotic Movement.
1956	Spiritual Institute was forced to close down in Shanghai.
1964	Died at the age of eighty-four.

---

1. In addition to the information I presented in this paper, *The Biographical Dictionary of Chinese Christianity* is one of the basic references (Li 2009).

APPENDIX E

The Life of Yang Shaotang[1]

1898	Born in Quwo in Shanxi Province.
1912	Entered a junior high school run by a church mission. Principal Rowland Hogben mentored him to become a devoted Christian.
1923	After graduating from high school, he enrolled in the North China Theological Seminary in Shandong.
1925	Graduated from seminary and went back to Shanxi and worked together with the missionaries from China Inland Mission.
1934	Started Spiritual Action Team in Shanxi.
1938	Spiritual Action Team was forced to disband because of the Japanese occupation of Shanxi.
1946	Moved to Nanjing and started a church in Huang Nigang.
1948	Preached before Jiang Jieshi (Chiang Kai-shek). Moved to Shanghai and taught in Jiangwan Theological Seminary.
1949	Refused to move out of mainland China and joined TSPM in Shanghai.
1952-57	Persecuted in the political movements; suspended from preaching in the church.
1966	Died of heart attack when persecuted by the Red Guard during the Cultural Revolution.

---

1. In addition to the information I presented in this paper, *The Biographical Dictionary of Chinese Christianity* is one of the basic references (Li 2009).

APPENDIX F

Major Life Events of Pastor HQZ

1921	Born in Qingyang County, Gansu Province.
1935	Began to learn Chinese medication at the age of fourteen.
1938	Began to attend church after meeting a Christian medical doctor.
1939	Imprisoned together with his younger brother for four months by the Kuomintang because his village was friendly to the Communist Party of China.
1942	Became a Christian and was baptized by James Hudson Taylor II. Applied and attended the CIM's Northwest Bible School in Fengxiang, Shaanxi Province.
1946	At the age of twenty-five, became a pastor in a church in Guozheng, Shaanxi.
1949	Went to Xinjiang with his wife and daughter after joining Back to Jerusalem Evangelistic Band, which was organized by the teachers and students of Northwest Bible School.
1950	Worked in Urumqi hospital as medical doctor and served as a pastor in Urumqi church at the same time.
1955	The church was closed by the government.
1966-72	Persecuted during the Cultural Revolution. His home was raided several times, and he worked in labor camp for some time as well.
1979	The church re-opened. Worked part-time in the church as a pastor and part-time in the hospital.
1970-80s	Served as a committee member of the Chinese People's Political Consultative Conference in Urumqi.
1984	Retired from the hospital and worked as a full-time volunteer pastor in Urumqi church.
1985	Ordained as pastor in Urumqi church.
1994	Elected as the first vice-chairman of the Urumqi TSPM and vice-president of the Urumqi CCC.

APPENDIX G

Major Life Events of Pastor CXQ

1918	Born into a Christian family in Gansu Province.
1935	Graduated from high school and worked as a teacher in a primary school. Became a Christian and was baptized together with his wife.
1937	Attended revival meetings and Bible study classes organized by John Sung in Xian.
1941	Served as a minister in a church in Xian, began contact with James Hudson Taylor II and the Rev. Mark Ma at the CIM's Bible school near Xian. Was influenced by their vision to go to Northwest China later.
1944	Decided to bring his family west, and arrived at Hami, Xinjiang Province, and the same year he began to plant a church in Hami.
1947	Ordained as an elder.
1948	One of the founding members of Northwest Spiritual Movement.
1951	Northwest Spiritual Movement forced to disband by the government.
1951	Accused by the government of being "anti-revolutionary" because of his membership in the NSM. Sentenced to labor camp for three years and four months.
1954	Released from labor camp and returned to Hami to bring his family to Urumqi. On the one hand, he worked in a transportation company, on the other hand he served as a minister in the Urumqi church.
1955	The church is closed by the government.
1970	Sentenced to rural labor camp during Cultural Revolution.
1979	Released and returned from labor camp after Cultural Revolution. The church re-opened.
1980	Retired from his work and worked as full-time volunteer minister in Urumqi church.
1985	Ordained as pastor in Urumqi church. Appointed representative to Provincial People's Congress. Served as committee member of Chinese People's Political Consultative Conference in Urumqi for fifteen years.
1994	Elected as the first chairman of Urumqi TSPM and president of Urumqi CCC.

APPENDIX H

Major Life Events of Pastor ZGR[1]

1924	Born in Anyang, Henan Province.
1930	His father died, and he went to church with his uncle.
1936	Repented at a revival meeting where John Sung was the speaker. Baptized in the same year and read the whole Bible within a year.
1937	Because of the Second Sino-Japanese War, could not continue his education in a middle school run by the Canadian Presbyterian church. Returned to his hometown to workI on the farm, learned the Confucian classics from his grandfather, and read the Bible himself.
1938	Began to preach in the church imitating the style of John Sung. Nicknamed "little Dr. Sung."
1940-42	Studied in Henan in a Bible college run by the American Mennonite Church.
1946	Went to Sanyuan County in Shaaxi Province because of the civil war. Finished a three-year theological program in two years at Guanzhong Divinity School.
1948	Went to Sichuan Province and worked with the Canadian United Church in its hospital and rural church. Later continued his studies in Western China (Huaxi) Theological Seminary in Chengdu.
1952	Returned to Shaanxi after liberation.
1955	Ordained as pastor in Sanyuan church. Responsible for the churches in seven counties.
1958	The church banned people from collecting donations and offerings. ZGR set up the Sanyuan milk product factory with other pastors in order to finance church activities.
1966-79	Branded a counter-revolutionary during the Cultural Revolution and sent to labor camp.

---

1. Information comes from the chronological summary in *The Gentle Pastor with Rock Solid Faith* (L. Yeung 2006, 54-56)

1980	Released from imprisonment and returned to his original job in milk factory. Worked in the church at the same time.
1982	Resumed full-time duties as church pastor.
1986	Co-founded the Shaanxi Bible School in Sanyuan.
2006	Officially retired from administration but keeps the title of honorable chairperson of TSPM/CCC.

APPENDIX I
Major Life Events of Pastor YZD

1925	Born in Shanxi Province in North China. Mother was a Christian in the Anglican Church. Father worked in the army.
1941	Returned to Fujian after travelling with his parents and was baptized (partially immersed) in an Anglican Church in Fujian. Later began his career as a music teacher in elementary school.
1948	Declared himself born again after attending a revival meeting and received a call from God to be a preacher.
1950	Received a letter from Watchman Nee who invited him to join the Little Flock, but he refused. After five years, he changed his mind and joined the Little Flock in Fuzhou.
1952	Baptized (total immersion) again in Zhong Zhou church, but did not join the Little Flock.
1955	Recovered from cancer miraculously and began to work in Zhong Zhou Church.
1978	After the Cultural Revolution, became a music teacher in university until 1982.
1980	Got a call from God to work full-time in the church again and to rebuild a church in Fujian. Later resigned from his position at the university and worked full-time in the church.
1990	Worked in other TSPM churches as pastor before returning to Zhong Zhou Church, the former headquarter of Little Flock.
1993	Appointed senior pastor of Zhong Zhou Church

Glossary

Ceng Zi	曾子	
Chao Tianen	趙天恩	
Chen Chonggui	陳崇桂	
Cheng Jigui	成寄歸	
Cheng Jingyi	誠靜怡	
Cheng Yi	程頤	
Chi Xin	持心	Holding one's heart
Chu Shi	處事	Handling issues
Cibei	慈悲	Mercy
Confucius	孔子	
Cun Tian Li	存天理	Keeping the Heavenly principles
Da Xue	大學	The Great Learning
Dai Ren	待人	Dealing with people
Ding Guangxun	丁光訓	
Ding Limei	丁立美	
Dong Zhongshu	董仲舒	
Gao Zi	告子	
Ge wu	格物	Investigation of things
Guwenguanzhi	古文觀止	
Han Yu	韓愈	
Huang Zongxi	黃宗羲	
Jen	仁	Benevolence, kindness, or love
Ji Zhiwen	計志文	
Jia Yuming	賈玉銘	
Jian Weizhen	焦唯真	
Jing Dianying	敬奠瀛	
John Song	宋尚節	
Jun Zi	君子	A gentleman, a profound person, or a sage
Li	理	Principle
Li Jian	李既岸	
Li Shen	立身	Establishing oneself

Li Xue	理學	The School of Principles
Liang Hui	兩會	Two associations
Liang Xin	良心	Conscience
Liang Zhi	良知	Innate knowledge of the good
Lin Jingkang	林景康	
Ling Sheng Ming	靈生命	Spirit life
Liu Jin	劉瑾	
Liu Zongzhou	劉宗周	
Long Chang	龍場	
Lu Xiangshan	陸象山	
Lun Yu	論語	Analects
Ma Mark	馬馬可	
Meng Zi	孟子	Mencius
Nei Sheng	內聖	Inward sageliness
Nie Ziying	聶子英	
Qu Ren Yu	去人慾	Removing the human desires
Shei Xinwo	石新我	
Sheng Ren	聖人	Sage
Shun	舜	
Tang Junyi	唐君毅	
Tao	道	The way, truth
Tengchow College	文會館	
Tian	天	The Heaven
Tian Jue	天爵	The nobility of Heaven
Tian Li	天理	Heavenly principle
Tian Ming	天命	Mandate of Heaven
Wai Wang	外王	Outward kingliness
Wang Chunfu	王純甫	
Wang Mingdao	王明道	
Wang Yangming	王陽明	
Wang Shouren	王守仁	
Wang Zai	王載	
Watchman Nee	倪柝聲	
Wu Leichuan	吳雷川	

Xie Fuya	謝扶雅	
Xin	心	Mind, or mind-heart
Xin Ji Li	心即理	Mind is principle
Xin Xue	心學	The School of Mind
Xing	性	Human nature
Xu Ai	徐愛	
Xun Zi	荀子	
Yang Shaotang	楊紹唐	
Yao	堯	
Yin-yang	陰陽	
Yu Leekung	于力工	
Yu Yao	餘姚	
Yu Cidu	余慈度	
Zhang Guquan	張谷泉	
Zhang Xuegong	張學恭	
Zhao Junying	趙君影	
Zhao Shiguang	趙世光	
Zhao Zichen	趙紫宸	
Zhi Liang Zhi	致良知	Extension of the innate knowledge of the good
Zhi Xing He Yi	知行合一	Unity of knowing and acting
Zhong Yong	中庸	The Doctrine of the Mean
Zhou Ji	周積	
Zhou Zhiyu	周志禹	
Zhu Guishen	竺規身	
Zhu Xi	朱熹	
Zi Gong	子貢	

Bibliography

Aikman, David. 2003. *Jesus in Beijing: How Christianity is Transforming China and Changing the Global Balance of Power*. Washington DC: Regenry Pub.

Allen, Barbara, and William Lynwood Montell. 1981. *From Memory to History: Using Oral Sources in Local Historical Research*. Nashville, TN: The American Association for State and Local History.

Arias, Mortimer, and Alan Johnson. 1992. *The Great Commission: Biblical Models for Evangelism*. Nashville, TN: Abingdon Press.

Atkinson, Robert. 1998. *The Life Story Interview, Qualitative Research Methods*. Thousand Oaks, CA: Sage Publications.

Avolio, Bruce J. 1999. *Full Leadership Development: Building the Vital Forces in Organizations*. Thousand Oaks, CA: Sage Publications Inc.

Baker, C., J. Wuest, and P.N. Stern. 1992. Method Slurring: The Grounded Theory / Phenomenology Example. In *Grounded Theory: 1984-1994*, edited by B. G. Glaser. Mill Valley, CA: Sociology Press.

Bartell, Sherrie R.. 1982. In Support of Grounded Theory: One Researcher's Experience. In *Grounded Theory: 1984-1994*, edited by B. G. Glaser. Mill Valley, CA: Sociology Press.

Bass, Bernard M. 1985. *Leadership and Performance Beyond Expectations*. New York, NY: The Free Press.

———. 1990. From Transactional to Transformational Leadership: Learning to Share the Vision. *Organizational Dynamics* 18 (3):19-31.

———. 1997. Does the Transactional-transformational Leadership Paradigm Transcend Organizational and National Boundaries? *American Psychologist* 52 (2):130-139.

Bass, Bernard M., and Bruce J. Avolio, eds. 1994. *Improving Organizational Effectiveness Through Transformational Leadership*. Thousand Oaks, CA: Sage Publications.

Bass, Bernard M., and Ronald E. Riggio. 2006. *Transformational Leadership*. 2nd ed. New Jersey, NJ: Lawrence Erlbaum Associates, Publishers.

Bass, Bernard M., and Ralph Melvin Stogdill. 1981. *Stogdill's Handbook of Leadership: Theory, Research, and Managerial Applications*. Revised and expanded edition. New York, NY: Free Press.

Bays, Daniel H. 1993. Christian Revival in China, 1900-1937. In *Modern Christian Revivals*, edited by E. L. Blumhofer and R. Balmer. Chicago, IL: University of Illinois Press.

———. 1995. Indigenous Protestant Churches in China, 1900-1937: A Pentecostal Case Study. In *Indigenous Responses to Western Christianity*, edited by S. Kaplan. New York, NY: New York University Press.

———, ed. 1996. *Christianity in China: From the Eighteenth Century to the Present*. Stanford, CA: Standford University Press.

Becker, Howard S. 2006. Problems of Inference and Proof in Participant Observation. In *Case Study Research*, edited by M. David. London: Sage Publications.

Beckhard, Richard. 1996. On Future Leader. In *The Leader of the Future: New Visions, Strategies, and Practices for the Next Era*, edited by F. Hesselbein, M. Goldsmith and R. Beckhard. San Francisco, CA: Jossey-Bass.

Bennis, Warren G., and Burt Nanus. 1985. *Leaders: The Strategies for Taking Charge*. New York, NY: Harper & Row.

Bernard, H. Russell. 2006. *Research Methods in Anthropology: Qualitative and Quantitative Approaches*. Lanham, MD: Altamira Press.

Blackaby, Henry, and Richard Blackaby. 2001. *Spiritual Leadership: Moving People on to God's Agenda*. Nashville, TN: B&H Publishing Group.

Blanchard, Ken, and Phil Hodges. 2005. *Lead Like Jesus: Lessons from the Greatest Leadership Role Model of All Time*. Nashville, TN: Thomas Nelson.

Blanchard, Ken, and Margret McBride. 2008. *The 4th Secret of the One Minute Manager: A Powerful Way to Make Things Better*. New York, NY: William Morrow.

Block, Peter. 1987. *The Empowered Manager: Positive Political Skills at Work*. San Francisco, CA: Jossey-Bass Publishers.

Bloor, Michael, and Fiona Wood. 2006. *Keywords in Qualitative Methods*. London: Sage Publications.

Borchert, Gerald L. 1996. *John 1-11*. Edited by E. R. Clendenen. Vol. 25A, *The New American Commentary*. Nashville, TN: Broadman & Holman Publishing Group.

Bosch, David J. 1991. *Transforming Mission: Paradigm Shifts in Theology of Mission*. New York, NY: Orbis Books.

———. 1991. *Transforming Mission: Paradign Shifts in Theology of Mission*. New York, NY: Orbis Books.

Broomhall, Marshall. 1934. *To What Purpose?* Edinburgh: R & R Clark Ltd.

Bruce, Alexander Balmain. 1930. *The Training of the Twelve: or, Passage out of the Gospels, exhibiting the Twelve Disciples of Jesus under discipline for the Apostleship*. 3rd ed. New York, NY: R.R. Smith.

Bruce, F.F. 1979. *Jesus Past, Present & Future: The Work of Christ*. 1st ed. Downers Grove, IL: InterVarsity Press.

———. 1986. *Jesus: Lord & Savior*. Edited by M. Green. 1st ed, *The Jesus Library*. Downers Grove, IL: InterVarsity Press.

Burke, Wyatt Warner. 1963. Leadership Behavior as a Function of the Leader, the Follower, and the Situation. Dissertation, Experimental Psychology, University of Texas, Austin.

Burns, James MacGregor. 1979. *Leadership*. New York, NY: Harper & Row.

———. 2003. *Transforming Leadership: A New Pursuit of Happiness*. New York, NY: Grove Press.

Ceng, Wewu (曾文武). 1989. 天安門六四事件紀實 (A Documentary of the June-Fourth Incident in Tiananmen). *The Mirror*, 49-50.

Cha, Shihchieh (查時傑). 1983. 中國基督教人物小傳 (*Concise Biographies of Important Chinese Christians*). Taipei: Chinese Evangelical Seminary Press.

Chaleff, Ira. 1995. *The Courageous Follower: Standing up To and For our Leaders*. San Francisco, CA: Berrett-Koehler Publishers.

Chan, Wingtsit. 1963a. *A Source Book in Chinese Philosophy*. Princeton, NJ: Princeton University Press.

———. 1963b. *Instructions for Practical Living and Other Neo-Confucian Writings*. New York, NY: Columbia University Press.

Chan, Wingtsit (陳榮捷). 1983. 王陽明傳習錄詳註集評 (*Commentary on Wang Yang-ming's Instructions for Practical Living*), Series of Chinese Philosophy. Taipei: Taiwan Xue Sheng Shu Ju.

Chao, Jonathan (趙天恩). 1988. 1929 年至 1927 年間非基督教運動壓力下興起的中國基督教的本色化運動 (A Study of Protestant Response to the Anti-Christian Movement During the 1924-1927 Period). In 基督教與中國本色化 (*Indigenization of Christianity in China*), edited by Z. Lin (林治平). Taipei: Cosmic Light.

Charmaz, Kathy. 1994. The Grounded Theory Method: An Explication and Interpretation. In *More Grounded Theory Methodology: A Reader*, edited by B. G. Glaser. Mill Valley, CA: Sociology Press.

———. 2006. *Constructing Grounded Theory: A Practical Guide Through Qualitative Analysis*. London: Sage Publications.

Chen, Lai (陳來). 1991. 有無之境: 王陽明哲學的精神 *(The State of Yu and Wu: The Spirit of the Wang Yangming's Philosophy)*. Beijing: Ren Min Chu Ban She.

Chen, Xiaoqing (陳孝卿). 2005. 我在新疆六十年 (My Sixty Years in Xinjiang). 新疆中華基督教會建立六十周年感恩特刊 *(The Xinjiang Chinese Christian Church 60th Anniversary Special Thanksgiving Issue)*, August 28, 2005, 9-13.

Chen, Yaonan (陳耀南). 2007. 從自力到祂力 *(From Self Effort to His Effort)*. Hong Kong: Cosmos Books Ltd.

Chen, Yicheng (陳以誠). 1989. 賈玉銘與中國基督教靈修學院在四川 (Jia Yuming and Chinese Christian Spiritual Institute in Sichuan). 金陵神學誌 *(Chinese Theological Review)* 11 (2):121-123.

Cheng, Bor-Shiuan (鄭伯壎), Li-Fang (周麗芳) Chou, Min-Ping (黃敏萍) Huang, Jiing-Lih (樊景立) Farh, and Si-Qing (彭泗清) Peng. 2003. 家長式領導的三元模式: 中國大陸企業組織的證據 (A Triad Model of Paternalistic Leadership: Evidence from Business Organizations in Mainland China). 本土心理學研究 *(Indigenous Psychological Research in Chinese Societies)* (20:12), http://www.airiti.com/ceps/ec_en/ecjnlarticleView.aspx?jnlcattype=0&jnlptype=0&jnltype=0&jnliid=373&issueiid=10818&atliid=156856.

Cheng, Chung Ying. 1979. Practical Learning in Yen Yuan, Chu Hsi and Wang Yang-ming. In *Principle and Practicality: Essays in Neo-Confucianism and Practical Learning*, edited by W. T. de Bary and I. Bloom. New York, NY: Columbia University Press.

Ching, Julia. 1973. Beyond Good and Evil : the Culmination of the Thought of Wang Yang-ming, 1472-1529. *Numen* 20 (2):125-134.

———. 1976. *To Acquire Wisdom: The Way of Wang Yang-ming, Studies in Oriental Culture*. New York, NY: Columbia University Press.

———, ed. 1972. *The Philosophical Letters of Wang Yang-ming, Asian Publication Series*. Columbia, SC: University of South Carolina Press.

Ching, Julia (秦家懿). 1987. 王陽明 *(Wang Yang-ming), World Philosophers Series*. Taipei: Dong Da Tu Shu Gong Si.

Clarke, Andrew D. 2000. *Serve the Community of the Church -- Christians as Leaders and Ministers, First-century Christians in the Graeco-Roman world*. Grand Rapids, MI: W. B. Eerdmans Publishing Company.

Cliff, Norman H. 1998. Building the Protestant church in Shandong, China. *International Bullentin of Missionary Research* 22 (April: 2):62-68.

Clinton, J. Robert. 1988. Leadership Development Theory: Comparative Studies among High Level Christian Leaders. Dissertation, Intercultural Studies, Fuller Theological Seminary, Pasadena.

———. 1989. *Leadership Emergence Theory: a Self-study Manual for Analyzing the Development of a Christian Leader*. Altadena, CA: Barnabas Resources.

———. 1990. *The Making of a Leader*. 3rd ed. Colorado Springs, CO: Navpress.

———. 1992a. *A Short History of Leadership Theory*. Altadena, CA: Barnabas Publishers.

———. 1993b. *Leadership Perspectives: How to study the Bible for Leadership Insights*. Altadena, CA: Barnabas Publishers.

———. 1995. *Focused Lives: Inspirational Life Changing Lessons from Eight Effective Christian Leaders who Finished Well*. Altadena, CA: Barnabas Publishers.

———. 1997. *Having a Ministry that Lasts: Becoming a Bible Centered Leader*. 1st ed. Altadena, CA: Barnabas Publishers.

———. 2003. *1 and 2 Corinthians: Problematic, Apostolic Leadership, Clinton's Biblical Leadership Commentary Series*. Altandena, CA: Barnabas Publishers.

Clinton, J. Robert, and Richard W. Clinton. 1991. *The Mentor Handbook: Detailed Guidelines and Helps for Christian Mentors and Mentorees*. Altadena, CA: Barnabas Publishers.

Cohen, Paul A. 1965. The Roots of the Anti-Christian Tradition in China. In *Christian Missions in China -- Evangelists of What?*, edited by J. G. Lutz. Boston, MA: D.C. Heath and Company.

———. 1984. *Discovering History in China: American Historical Writing on the Recent Chinese Past*. New York, NY: Columbia University Press.

Coleman, Robert E. 1993. *The Master Plan of Evangelism*. 2nd ed. Grand Rapids, MI: Fleming H. Revell.

Conger, Jay A. 1989. *The Charismatic Leader: Behind the mystique of Exceptional Leadership*. San Francisco, CA: Jossey-Bass.

Conger, Jay A., and Rabindra N Kanungo. 1987. Toward a Behavioral Theory of Charismatic Leadership in Organizational Settings. *The Academy of Management Review* 12 (4):637-647.

Covey, Stephen R. 1989. *The 7 Habits of Highly Effective People: Restoring the Character Ethic*. New York, NY: Simon & Schuster.

Culbert, Samuel A. 1996. *Mind-Set Management: The Heart of Leadership*. New York, NY: Oxford University Press.

Culpepper, Charles L. 1968. *The Shantung Revival*. Dallas, TX: General Baptist Convention of Texas.

Dansereau, F., and G. Graen. 1975. A Vertical Dyad Linage Approach to Leadership within formal Organizations. *Organizational Behavior and Human Performance* 13 (1):46.

De Bary, WM. Theodore, Wing-tsit Chan, and Burton Watson, eds. 1960. *Sources of Chinese Tradition*. Edited by W. T. De Bary. Vol. 1, *Introduction to Asian Civilizations*. New York, NY: Colombia University Press.

De Bary, WM. Theodore, Wing-tsit Chan and Burton Watson, ed. 1960. *Sources of Chinese Tradition*. Edited by W. T. De Bary. 1 ed. Vol. 1, *Introduction to Asian Civilizations*. New York, NY: Colombia University Press.

De Pree, Max. 1992. *Leadership Jazz*. New York, NY: Dell Publishing.

———. 2004. *Leadership is an Art*. New York, NY: Doubleday.

Denzin, Norman K., and Yvonna S. Lincoln, eds. 2005. *The Sage Handbok of Qualitative Research*. 3rd ed. Thousand Oaks, CA: Sage Publications, Inc.

Drucker, Peter F. 2005. *Managing the Non-profit Organization: Practices and Principles*. First Collins Business ed. New York, NY: Harper Collins.

———. 2006. *The Effective Executive: The Definitive Guide to Getting the Right Things Done*. New York, NY: Harper Collins.

Edgar, Brian. 2004. *The Message of the Trinity*. Edited by D. Tidball, *The Bible Speaks Today*. Leicester: InterVarsity Press.

Editor. 1950. 揭穿帝國主義的假仁假義 (To Unveil the Hypocrisy of Imperialism). *Tien Feng (天風)* 9 (80).

———. 1950. 傳教士與帝國主義 (Missionary and Imperialism). *Tien Feng* (天風) 10 (6).

Editorial. 2009. 倪柝聲 (Watchman Nee). In *Biographical Dictionary of Chinese Christianity*, edited by G. Doyle, Wright. Charlottesville: Global China Center.

Edwards, Mark. 2004. *John, Blackwell Bible Commentaries*. Oxford: Blackwell Publishing

Ellingworth, Paul. 1998. Translating the Language of Leadership. *The Bible Translator* 49 (1):126-138.

Evans, Craig A. 2003. *Matthew-Luke, The Bible Knowledge Background Commentary*. Colorado Springs, CO: Cook.

Fairbank, John K., ed. 1974. *The Missionary Enterprise in China and America*. Cambridge: Harvard University Press.

Fallman, Fredrik. 2008. *Salvation and Modernity: Intellectuals and Faith in Contemporary China* Revised Edition ed. Lanham, MD: University Press of America.

Fan, Cenquang (範晨光). 2005a. 壯哉此行 (A Spectacular Trip). 新疆中華基督教會建立六十周年感恩特刊 *(The Xinjiang Chinese Christian Church 60th Anniversary Special Thanksgiving Issue)*, August 28, 2005, 20-22.

Farh, Jiing-Lih (樊景立), and Bor-Shiuan (鄭伯壎) Cheng. 2000. 華人組織的家長式領導: 一項文化觀點的分析 (A Cultural Analysis of Paternalistic Leadership in Chinese Organization). 本土心理學研究 *(Indigenous Psychological Research in Chinese Societies)* (13:6), http://www.airiti.com/ceps/ec_en/ecjnlarticleView.aspx?jnlcattype=0&jnlptype=0&jnltype=0&jnliid=373&issueiid=10819&atliid=157092.

Fay, Ron C. 2008. Greco-Roman Concepts of Deity. In *Paul's World*, edited by S. E. Porter. Boston, MA: Brill.

Fernando, Ajith. 2002. *Jesus Driven Ministry*. Wheaton, IL: Crossway Books.

Fetterman, David M. 1998. *Ethnography: Step by Step*. 2nd ed. Vol. 17, *Applied Social Research Methods Series*. Thousand Oaks, CA: Sage Publications, Inc.

Fiedler, Fred E. 1978. Situational Control and a Dynamic Theory of Leadership. In *Managerial Control and Organizational Democracy*, edited by B. King, S. Streufert and F. E. Fiedler. Washington, D.C.: V. H. Winston & Sons.

Fletcher, Holly, and Jayshree Bajoria. 2008. The East Turkestan Islamic Movement (ETIM). *CFR Newsletter*, July 31, 2008.

Fuchs, Toni-Carl. 2007. Situational Leadership Theory: An Analysis within the European Cultural Environment. Dissertation, School of Business & Technology, Capella University, Minneapolis.

Fulton, Brent. 2007. Toward a Typology of Christian Leaders in China. *China Source* 9 (1):6-9.

Fung, Yulan. 1983. *A History of Chinese Philosophy Vol. II: The Period of Classical Learning*. Translated by D. Bodde. Princeton, NJ: Princeton University Press.

Gardner, Daniel K. 2007. *The Four Books: The Basic Teachings of the Later Confucian Tradition*. Indianapolis, IN: Hackett Publishing Company, Inc.

Gardner, William L., and Bruce J. Avolio. 1998. The Charismatic Relationship: A Dramaturgical Perspective. *Academy of Management Review* 23 (1):32-58.

Gerson, Lloyd. 2008. Plotinus. In *The Stanford Encyclopedia of Philosophy*, edited by E. N. Zalta.

Gibb, Cecil A. 1947. The Principles and Traits of Leadership. *The Journal of Abnormal and Social Psychology* 42 (3):267-284.

Gini, Al. 1998. Moral Leadership: An Overview. In *Contemporary Issues in Leadership*, edited by W. E. Rosenbach. Boulder, CO: Westview Press.

Glaser, Barney G, and Anselm L. Strauss. 1994. Case Histories and Case Studies. In *More Grounded Theory Methodology: A Reader*, edited by B. G. Glaser. Mill Valley, CA: Sociology Press.

Glaser, Barney G. 1992. *Basics of Grounded Theory Analysis*. 1st ed. Mill Valley, CA: Sociology Press.

―――, ed. 1994. *More Grounded Theory Methodology: A Reader*. Mill Valley, CA: Sociology Press.

―――, ed. 1995. *Grounded Theory: 1984-1994*. Vol. 1. Mill Valley, CA: Sociology Press.

Glaser, Barney G., and Anselm Strauss. 1967. *The Discovery of Grounded Theory: Strategies for Qualitative Research*. Chicago, IL: Aldine Pub. Co.

Graen, G., and James F. Cashman. 1975. A Role-Making Model of Leadership in Formal Organizations: a Developmental Approach. In *Leadership Frontiers*, edited by J. G. Junt and L. L. Larson. Kent: The Kent State University Press.

Granberg-Michaelson, Wesley. 1982. *The Servant as Religious Leader*. Peterborough: Center for Applied Studies.

Green, Joel B. 1997. *The Gospel of Luke*. Edited by N. B. Stonehouse, F. F. Bruce and G. D. Fee, *The New International Commentary on the New Testament*. Grand Rapids, MI: William B. Eerdmans Publishing Co.

Green, Michael. 2003. *The Message of Matthew*. Edited by J. Stott. 3rd ed, *The Bible Speaks Today*. London: InterVarsity Press.

Greenleaf, Robert K. 1973. *The Servant as Leader*. Cambridge: Center for Applied Studies.

―――. 1996a. *On Becoming a Servant-Leader*. Edited by D. M. F. a. L. C. Spears. San Francisco, CA: Jossey-Bass Publishers.

―――. 1996b. *Seeker and Servant: Reflections on Religious Leadership*. Edited by A. T. F. a. L. C. Spears. San Francisco, CA: Jossey-Bass Publishers.

―――. 2002. *Servant Leadership: A Journey into the Nature of Legitimate Power and Greatness*. 25th Anniversary Edition ed. New York, NY: Paulist Press.

Gunton, Colin E. 1998. *The Triune Creator: A Historical and Systematic Study*. Vol. III, *New Studies in Constructive Theology*. Grand Rapids, MI: William B. Eerdmans Publishing Co.

Hamel, Jacques, Stephane Dufour, and Dominic Fortin. 1993. *Case Study Methods, Qualitative Research Methods Series*. Newbury Park, CA: Sage Publications.

Harris, R. Geoffrey. 2004. *Mission in the Gospels*. London: Epworth Press.

Hattaway, Paul. 2000. *Operation China: Introducing all the Peoples of China*. Pasadena, CA: William Carey Library.

Hedin, Norma. 2010. Experiential Learning: Theory and Challenges. *Christian Education Journal* 7 (1):254.

Hengel, Martin. 1981. *The Charismatic Leader and His Followers*. Translated by J. Greig. New York, NY: Crossroad.

Henke, Frederick G. 1964. *The Philosophy of Wang Yang-ming*. 2nd ed, *Paragon Reprint Oriental Series*. New York, NY: Paragon Book reprint Corp.

Hesselbein, Frances, Marshall Goldsmith, and Richard Beckhard, eds. 1996. *The Leader of the Future: New Visions, Strategies, and Practices for the Next Era*. San Francisco, CA: Jossey-Bass.

Hollander, Edwin P. 1992. The Essential Interdependence of Leadership and Followership. *Current Directions in Psychological Science* 1 (2):71-75.

Holstein, James A. , and Jaber F. Gubrium. 1995. *The Active Interview, Qualitative Research Methods series*. Thousand Oaks, CA: Sage Publications Inc.

Hopper, Linda. 2008. Courageous Followers, Servant-Leaders, and Organizational Transformations. In *The Art of Followership*, edited by R. E. Riggio, I. Chaleff and J. Lipman-Blumen. San Francisco, CA: Jossey-Bass.

Horsley, Richard A. 2003. *Jesus and Empire: The Kingdom of God and the New World Disorder*. Minneapolis, MN: Fortress Press.

Howell, Jane M., and Boas Shamir. 2005. The Role of Followers in the Charismatic Leadership Process: Relationships and their Consequences. *Academy of Management Review* 30 (1):96-112.

Howell, Jon P., and Maria J. Mendez. 2008. Three Perspectives on Followership. In *The Art of Followership*, edited by R. E. Riggio, I. Chaleff and J. Lipman-Blumen. San Francisco, CA: Jossey-Bass.

Huang, Qingzhi (黃清治). 2005. A Brief History on Xinjiang Urumqi City Church (新疆烏魯木齊市基督教簡史). *The Xinjiang Chinese Christian Church 60th Anniversary Special Thanksgiving Issue* (新疆中華基督教會建立六十周年感恩特刊), August 28, 2005, 3-4.

Huang, Tsung-hsi. 1987. *The Records of Ming Scholars: A Selected Translation*. Edited by J. Ching. Honolulu, HI: University of Hawaii Press.

Hughes, Richard L., Robert C. Ginnett, and Gordon J. Curphy. 2009. *Leadership: Enhancing the Lessons of Experience*. 6th ed. Boston, MA: McGraw-Hill.

Jia, Yuming (賈玉銘). 1914. 中華全國長老會聯合總會之成立 (The Establishment of United Chinese National Congress of Presbyterian Church). 中華基督教會年鑑 *(Annual Report of Chinese Christian Church)* 1:22-25.

———. 1926b. 教牧學 *(Pastoral Theology)*. 2 vols. Vol. 1. Nanjing: Ling Guang.

———. 1926c. 教牧學 *(Pastoral Theology)*. 2 vols. Vol. 2. Nanjing: Ling Guang.

———. 1935. 路得記之靈訓 *(The Spiritual Lessons from the Book of Ruth)*. Nanjing: Ling Guang Bao She.

———. 1959. 聖經要義 *(The Essential Meaning of the Bible)*. 6 vols. Vol. 1. Hong Kong: The Bellman House Publishers.

———. 1981a. 聖經要義 *(The Essential Meaning of the Bible)*. 5 ed. 6 vols. Vol. 2. Hong Kong: The Bellman House Publishers.

———. 1981b. 聖經要義 *(The Essential Meaning of the Bible)*. 5 ed. 6 vols. Vol. 3. Hong Kong: The Bellman House Publishers.

———. 1981c. 聖經要義 *(The Essential Meaning of the Bible)*. 5 ed. 6 vols. Vol. 4. Hong Kong: The Bellman House Publishers.

———. 1981d. 聖經要義 *(The Essential Meaning of the Bible)*. 5 ed. 6 vols. Vol. 5. Hong Kong: The Bellman House Publishers.

———. 1987. 完全救法 *(A Perfect Salvation)*. 3rd ed. Hong Kong: The Bellman House Publishers.

———. 1988. 聖經要義 *(The Essential Meaning of the Bible)*. 6 vols. Vol. 6. Hong Kong: The Bellman House Publishers.

———. 1990. 基督聖蹟 *(The Life and Teaching of Jesus Christ)*. Hong Kong: The Bellman House Publishers.

———. 1992a. 神道學 *(Systematic Theology)*. 2nd ed. 4 vols. Vol. 1. Taipei: Gan Lan Shei Ye Ji Jin Hui.

———. 1992b. 神道學 *(Systematic Theology)*. 2nd ed. 4 vols. Vol. 2. Taipei: Gan Lan Shei Ye Ji Jin Hui.

———. 1992c. 神道學 *(Systematic Theology)*. 2nd ed. 4 vols. Vol. 3. Taipei: Gan Lan Shei Ye Ji Jin Hui.

———. 1992d. 神道學 *(Systematic Theology)*. 2nd ed. 4 vols. Vol. 4. Taipei: Gan Lan Shei Ye Ji Jin Hui.

Jin, Ze, and Yonghui Qiu, eds. 2010. *Annual Report on China's Religions (2010)*. Beijing: Chinese Academy of Social Science.

Johnson, McKinley. 2006. *Natural Leadership Development*. Lake Mary: Creation House.

Jones, Laurie Beth. 1995. *Jesus, CEO: Using Ancient Wisdom for Visionary Leadership*. New York, NY: Hyperion.

Jorgensen, Danny L. 1989. *Participant Observation : a Methodology for Human Studies*, *Applied Social Research Methods Series*. Newbury Park, CA: Sage Publications.

Kellerman, Barbara. 2004. *Bad Leadership*. Boston, MA: Harvard Business Press.

―――. 2008. *Followership: How Followers are creating Change and Changing Leaders*. Boston, MA: Harvard Business Press.

Kelley, Robert E. 1988. In Praise of Followers. In *Harvard Business Review*: Harvard Business School Publication Corp.

―――. 1992. *The Power of Followership: How to Create Leaders People want to Follow and Followers who Lead Themselves*. New York, NY: Doubleday.

―――. 2008. Rethinking Followership. In *The Art of Followership*, edited by R. E. Riggio, I. Chaleff and J. Lipman-Blumen. San Francisco, CA: Jossey-Bass.

Kenner, Craig S. 1997. *Matthew*. Edited by G. R. Osborne, *The IVP New Testament Commentary Series*. Downers Grove, IL: InterVarsity Press.

Kezar, Adrianna, and Rozana Carducci. 2009. Revolutionizing Leadership Development: Lessons from Research and Theory. In *Rethinking Leadership in a Complex, Multicultural, and Global Environment: New Concepts and Models for Higher Education*, edited by A. Kaezar. Sterling, VA: Stylus Publishing.

Kim, Heup Young. 1996. *Wang Yang-ming and Karl Barth: A Confucian-Christian Dialogue*. New York, NY: University Press of America, Inc.

Kinnear, Angus I. 1973. *Against the Tide: The Story of Watchman Nee*. Eastbourne: Victory Press.

Komives, Susan R., Nance Lucas, and Timothy R. McMahon. 1998. *Exploring Leadership: for College Students who want to Make a Difference*. San Francisco, CA: Jossey-Bass Publisher.

Köstenberger, Andreas J. 2004. *John, Baker Exegetical Commentary on the New Testament*. Grand Rapids, MI: Baker Academic.

Kouzes, James M., and Barry Z. Posner. 1993. *Credibility: How Leaders gain and lose it, Why People demand it*. San Francisco, CA: Jossey-Bass.

―――. 1995. *The Leadership Challenge: How to Keep Getting Extraordinary Things Done in Organizations*. San Francisco, CA: Jossey-Bass.

Kuhnert, Karl W., and Philip Lewis. 1987. Transactional and Transformational Leadership: A Constructive/Developmental Analysis. *The Academy of Management Review* 12 (4):648-657.

Kung, Hans, and Julia Ching. 1989. *Christianity and Chinese Religions*. 1st ed. New York, NY: Doubleday.

Kwok, Wailuen (郭偉聯). 1997. 靈意與正解: 解玉銘釋經方法初探 (Spiritualization and Interretation: A Study on Jia Yu-ming's Hermeneutics). 建道學刊 *(Jian Dao: A Journal of Bible & Theology)* (7):191-233.

———. 2001. 中國教會合一運動與基要主義: 以賈玉銘為個案的研究 (The Ecumenical Movement and Fundamentalism in Chinese Churches: A Case Study on Chai Yuming). Dissertation, Alliance Bible Seminary, HongKong.

———. 2002. 反對合一? 賈玉銘、基要主義與合一運動的糾結 (Advocating separatism? Chia Yuming, Fundamentalists and their Difficulties in Chinese Church Union Movement). Hong Kong: Tien Dao.

———. 2003. Salvation and Life: A Reflection on Chia Yu Ming's Christocentric Theology (救恩與生命: 賈玉銘以基督為中心的神學論述). *CGST Journal* (34):55-91.

———. 2003. 救恩與生命: 賈玉銘以基督為中心的神學論述 (Salvation and Life: A Reflection on Chia Yu Ming's Christocentric Theology). *CGST Journal* (34):55-91.

Lam, Wing-hung (林榮洪). 2001. 華人神學三大路線 (The Three Major Routes of Chinese Theology). In 基督教與中國文化的相遇 *(Encounter between Christianity and Chinese Culture)*, edited by L.-k. 盧. Lo. Hong Kong: Chung Chi College, The Chinese University of Hong Kong.

———. 2003. 屬靈神學: 倪柝聲思想的研究 *(The Spiritual Theology of Watchman Nee)*. 3rd ed. Hong Kong: China Alliance Press.

Lam, Winghung (林榮洪). 1982. 王明道與中國教會 *(Wong Ming-Tao and the Chinese Church)*. Hong Kong: China Graduate School of Theology.

———. 1990. 風潮中奮起的中國教會 *(Chinese Theology in Construction)*. 3rd ed. Vol. 2, *CGST Theological Series*. Hong Kong: Tien Dao Publishing House, Ltd.

———. 1998. 中華神學五十年: *1900-1949 (A Half Century of Chinese Theology 1900-1949)*. Hong Kong: China Graduate School of Theology.

Lambert, Tony. 2009. "The What Purpose?" The Life and Death of Emil Fischbacher. *China Insight* (March-April):1-4.

Latour, Sharon M., and Vicki J. Rast. 2004. Dynamic Followership. In *Air & Space Power Journal*: Superintendent of Documents.

Latourette, Kenneth Scott. 1969. *Christianity in a Revolutionary Age: A History of Christianity in the 19th and 20th Centuries*. Vol. 5. Grand Rapids, MI: Zondervan Publishing House.

———. 1973. *A History of Christian Missions in China*. Taipei: Ch'eng Wen Publishing Company Ltd.

Lau, D.C., ed. 2002. *The Analects* 2nd ed. Hong Kong: The Chinese University Press.

Lee, Maocheng (李茂政). 1989. 典型在夙昔: 華人教會領袖塑造過程之比較 *(The Comparison of the Leadership Selection Processes among Four Chinese Leaders)*. Taipei: Chinese Evangelical Seminary Publishing House.

Lee, Samuel Mau-Cheng. 1985. A Comparative Study of Leadership Selection Processes among four Chinese Leaders. Dissertation, School of World Mission, Fuller Theological Seminary, Pasadena.

Leung, Kalun (梁家麟). 1997. 徘徊於耶儒之間 *(Wondering between Christianity and Confucianism)*. Taipei: Cosmic Light Publishing House.

———. 1999a. 華人傳道與奮興佈道家 *(Evangelists and Revivalists of Modern China)*. Vol. 8, *CCCRC Occasional Paper*. Hong Kong Alliance Bible Seminary.

———. 2001b. 他們是為了信仰: 北京基督徒學生會與中華基督徒佈道會 *(By Faith they did it: Beijing Christian Student Association and Chinese Christian Evangelistic Band)*. Vol. 10, *CCCRC Occasional Paper*. Hong Kong: Alliance Bible Seminary.

———. 2003a. 倪柝聲的榮辱升黜 *(Watchman Nee: His Glory and Dishonor)*. Vol. 12, *CCCRC Occasional Paper*. Hong Kong: Alliance Bible Seminary.

———. 2003b. 超前與墮後: 本土釋經與神學研究 *(Far Ahead and Lagging Behind: Studies in Contextual Hermeneutics and Theology)*. Vol. 13, *CCCRC Occasional Paper*. Hong Kong: Alliance Bible Seminary.

Leung, Yuensang (梁元生). 2006. 基督教與中國 *(Christianity and China)*. Vol. 20, *Essays for the 200th Anniversary of Robert Morrison coming to China*. Taipei: Cosmic Light.

Li, Jinqiang (李金強). 2006. 聖道東來: 近代中國基督教史之研究 *(A Study on Modern Chinese Church History)*. 30 vols. Vol. 10, *Essays for the 200th Anniversary of Robert Morrison coming to China*. Taipei: Cosmic Light.

Li, Nanxiong (李南雄). 1989. 動亂裡的中國: 評天安門廣場屠殺學生事件 (China in Turmoil: Comments on the Massacre of Students in Tiananmen Square). *Mingpao Monthly* 24 (7):54-57.

Li, Yading (李亞丁). 2009. 楊紹唐 (Yang Shaotang). In *Biographical Dictionary of Chinese Christianity*, edited by G. Doyle, Wright. Charlottesville: Global China Center.

———. 2009. 賈玉銘 (Jia Yuming). In *Biographical Dictionary of Chinese Christianity*, edited by G. Doyle, Wright. Charlottesville: Global China Center.

Lindars, Barnabas. 1981. *The Gospel of John, The New Century Bible Commentary*. Grand Rapids, MI: Wm. B. Eerdmans Publishing Co.

Lingenfelter, Judith E. and Sherwood G. Lingenfelter. 2003. *Teaching Cross-Culturally: An Incarnational Model for Learning and Teaching*. Grand Rapids, MI: Baker.

Lipman-Blumen, Jean. 1996. *The Connective Edge: Leading in an Interdependent World*. San Francisco, CA: Jossey-Bass Publishers.

———. 2005. *The Allure of Toxic Leaders*. New York, NY: Oxford University Press.

Liu, Shu-Hsien. 1972. The Confucian Approach to the Problem of Transcendence and Immanence. *Philosophy East & West* 22 (1):45-52.

Liu, Shuxian. 1998. *Understanding Confucian Philosophy: Classical and Sung-Ming*. Westport: Greenwood Press.

Lord, Robert G., and Douglas J. Brown. 2004. *Leadership Processes and Follower Self-Identity*. London: Lawrence Erlbaun Associates Publishers.

Lundin, Stephen C., and Lynne C. Lancaster. 1990. Beyond Leadership: The Importance of Followership. *Futurist* 24 (3):18-22.

Luo, Guanzhong(羅冠中), ed. 2003. 前事不忘後事之師: 帝國主義利用基督教侵略中國史實評述 *(Learning from the History of the Past: Comments of the Invastions of Imperialism through Christianity in China)* Beijing: Religion and Culture Publishing House.

Lutz, Jessie G., ed. 1965. *Christian Missions in China -- Evangelists of What?* Boston, MA: D.C. Heath and Company.

Lyall, Leslie T. 2000. *Three of China's Mighty Men*. Fearn: OMF.

Lyall, Leslie T. (賴恩融). 2003. 中國教會三巨人 *(Three of China's Mighty Men)*. Translated by Z. Lin. 4 ed. Taipei: Gan Lan Wen Hua Shi Ye Ji Jin Hui.

Maccoby, Michael. 2008. What Kind of Leader Do People Want to Follow? In *The Art of Followership*, edited by R. E. Riggio, I. Chaleff and J. Lipman-Blumen. San Francisco, CA: Jossey-Bass.

Malina, Bruce J. 1996. *The Social World of Jesus and the Gospels*. London: Routledge.

Malphurs, Aubrey. 2004. *Values-Driven Leadership : Discovering and Developing Your Core Values for Ministry* 2nd ed. Grand Rapids, MI: Baker Books.

Maroosis, James. 2008. Leadership: A Partnership in Reciprocal Following. In *The Art of Followership*, edited by R. E. Riggio, I. Chaleff and J. Lipman-Blumen. San Francisco, CA: Jossey-Bass.

Marshall, I.H. 1992. Church. In *Dictionary of Jesus and the Gospels*, edited by J. B. Green and S. KMcKnight. Downers Grove, IL: InterVarsity Press.

Maxwell, John C. 1995. *Developing the Leaders Around You* Nashville, TN: Thomas Nelson.

———. 1998. *The 21 Irrefutable Laws of Leadership: Follow them and People will Follow You*. Nashville, TN: Thomas Nelson.

———. 2005. *The 360-degree Leader: Developing Your Influence from Anywhere in the Organization*. Nashville, TN: Thomas Nelson.

———. 2007. *The Maxwell Leadership Bible*. Nashville, TN: Thomas Nelson.

Maxwell, John C., and Jim Doman. 1997. *Becoming a Person of Influence: How to Positively Impact the Lives of Others*. Nashville, TN: Thomas Nelson.

Maxwell, Joseph A. 2005. *Qualitative Research Design: An Interactive Approach*. 2nd ed. Vol. 41, *Applied Social Research Methods Series*. Thousand Oaks, CA: Sage Publications Inc.

McKinney, Carol V. 2000. *Globe-Trotting in Sandals: A Field Guide to Cultural Research*. 1st ed. Dallas, TX: SIL International.

McLeod, G. Alexus. 2010. Why Can't Nanzi Catch a Break? In *Unpolished Jade: A Chinese Philosophy Blog*.

Miller, Georgy A. *WordNet: A Lexical Database for the English Language*. Princeton University, May 24, 2009 2006. Available from http://wordnet.princeton.edu/.

Morgan, G. Campbell. 1931. *The Gospel According to Luke*. New York, NY: Fleming H. Revell Company.

———. 1933. *The Gospel According to John*. New York, NY: Fleming H. Revell Company.

Morris, Leon. 1992. *The Gospel According to Matthew*. Grand Rapids, MI: William B. Eerdmans Publishing Co.

———. 1994. Disciples of Jesus. In *Jesus of Nazareth: Lord and Christ: Essays on the Historical Jesus and New Testament Christology*, edited by J. B. Green and M. Turner. Grand Rapids, MI: William B. Eerdmans Publishing Company.

———. 2008. Luke: An Introduction and Commentary. In *Tyndale New Testament Commentaries*, ed L. Morris. Downers Grove, IL: InterVarsity Press.

Mouw, Richard J. 2006. Leadership and the Three-fold Office of Christ. In *Traditions in Leadership: How Faith Traditions Shape the Way we Lead*, edited by R. J. Mouw and E. O. Jacobsen. Pasadena, CA: The De Pree Leadership Center.

Murren, Doug. 1997. The Leader as Change Agent. In *Leaders on Leadership*, edited by G. Barna. Ventura, CA: Regal Books.

Nanus, Burt. 1992. *Visionary Leadership: Creating a Compelling Sense of Direction for your Organization*. San Francisco, CA: Jossey-Bass Publishers.

Nee, Watchman (倪柝聲). 教會的正統 *(The Orthodoxy of the Church)* (3rd). Taiwan Gospel Book Room Ltd. 1967.

Neuschel, Robert P. 1998. *The Servant Leader: Unleashing the Power of Your People*. East Lansing, MI: Visions Sports Management Group, Inc.

Ng, Esther Yue L. (吳羅瑜). 1996. 義僕君王: 馬太福音注釋 *(一)(Righteous Servant and King: A Commentary on the Gospel of Matthew I)*. Hong Kong: China Graduate School of Theology.

Nivison, David S. 1953. The Problem of "Knowledge" and "Action" in Chinese Thought Since Wang Yang-Ming. In *Studies in Chinese Thought*, edited by A. F. Wright. Chicago, IL: The University of Chicago Press.

Northouse, Peter G. 2007. *Leadership: Theory and Practice*. 4th ed. Thousand Oaks, CA: Sage Publications.

Nouwen, Henri J.M. 1996. *In the Name of Jesus: Reflections on Christian Leadership*. New York, NY: Crossroad.

Olson, Roger E., and Christopher A. Hall. 2002. *The Trinity*. Grand Rapids, MI: William B. Eerdmans.

Osiek, Carolyn. 1992. *What are they Saying about the Social Setting of the New Testament?* Rev. and expanded ed. Mahwah, NJ: Paulist Press.

People's Daily Online. 2010. *Xinjiang Uygur Autonomous Region* 2010 [cited January 25, 2010]. Available from http://english.peopledaily.com.cn/data/province/xinjiang.html.

Perkins, Pheme. 1990. *Jesus as Teacher*. Edited by H. C. Kee. 1st ed, *Understanding Jesus Today*. Cambridge: Cambridge University Press.

Portelli, Alessandro. 1998. What makes Oral History Different. In *The Oral History Reader*, edited by R. Perks and A. Thomson. London: Routledge.

Potter III, Earl H., William E. Rosenbach, and Thane S. Pittman. 1998. Followers for the Times. In *Contemporary Issues in Leadership*, edited by W. E. Rosenbach and R. L. Taylor. Boulder, CO: Westview Press.

Pye, Lucian W. 1985. *Asian Power and Politics: the Cultural Dimensions of Authority*. Cambridge: Belknap Press.

Robeck, Cecil M. Jr. 2006. A Pentecostal Perspective on Leadership. In *Traditions in Leadership: How Faith Traditions Shape the Way we Lead*, edited by R. J. Mouw and E. O. Jacobsen. Pasadena, CA: The De Pree Leadership Center.

Rosenau, James. 2004. Followership and Discretion. *Harvard International Review* 26 (3):14-17.

Sanders, E.P. 1993. *The Historical Figure of Jesus*. London: Penguin Group.

Sanders, J. Oswald. 1994. *Spiritual Leadership: Principles of Excellence for every Believer*. 2nd Revision ed. Chicago, IL: Moody Press.

Schein, Edgar H. 2004. *Organizational Culture and Leadership*. 3rd ed. San Francisco, CA: Jossey-Bass.

Sergiovanni, Thomas J. 1986. Leadership as Cultural Expression. In *Leadership and Organizational Culture: New Perspective Theory and Practice*, edited by T. J. Sergiovanni and J. E. Corbally. Urbana, IL: University of Illinois Press.

Shen, Ruhuai (沈如槐). 2004. 清華大學文革記事 *(Records of Events during Cultural Revolution in Qing Hua University)*. Hong Kong: Trendy Arts Publishing House.

Shi, Meiling (施美玲). 2001. 六十三年──與王明道先生窄路同行 *(Sixty Three Years—Walking on the Narrow Road with Mr. Wang Ming Dao)*. Washington: Spiritual Rock Publishers.

Shim, Seung Hwan. 2007. *Two Model Teachers: Jesus and Confucius*. Bloomington, IN: Xlibris Corporation.

Smart, Ninian. 1974. *Mao*. Glasgow: William Collins Sons & Co. Ltd.

Spencer, F. Scott. 2008. *The Gospel of Luke and Acts of the Apostles, Interpreting Biblical Texts*. Nashville, TN: Abingdon Press.

Spradley, James P. 1979. *The Ethnographic Interview*. New York, NY: Rinehart and Winston.

Stambaugh, John E., and David L. Balch. 1986. *The New Testament in its Social Environment*. Philadelphia. PA: Westminster Press.

Stanton, Graham N. 1989. *The Gospels and Jesus*. New York, NY: Oxford University Press.

Stech, Ernest L. 2008. A New Leadership-Followership Paradigm. In *The Art of Followership*, edited by R. E. Riggio, I. Chaleff and J. Lipman-Blumen. San Francisco, CA: Jossey-Bass.

Stogdill, Ralph Melvin. 1950. Leadership, Membership and Organization. *Psychological Bulletin* 47 (1):1-14.

Strong, Kendrick. 1978. *All the Master's Men: A Study of Human Insufficiency Made Sufficient through Faith*. New York, NY: Christian Herald Books.

Sun, Po-ling (孫寶玲). 2007. 道可道: 約翰福音中的宣講與神學*(The Word in Words: Preaching and Theology in the Gospel of John)*. Hong Kong: Tien Dao Publishing House Ltd.

Szeto, Paul Cheuk-Ching. 1980. Suffering in the Experience of the Protestant Church in China (1911-1980), School of World Missions, Fuller Theological Seminary, Pasadena.

Tang, Junyi (唐君毅). 1974. 說中華民族之花果飄零 *(That the Fruit of the Chinese Nation Falling)*. Taipei: San Min Book Co. Ltd.

———. 1977. 生命存在與心靈境界 *(The Existence of Human Life and the Realm of the Spirit)*. 2 vols. Taipei: Student Book.

———. 1988. 中國人文精神之發展 *(The Development of Chinese Humanity)*. Vol. 6, 唐君毅全集 *(Complete Works of Tang Yunyi)*. Taipei: Taiwan Xue Sheng Shu Ju.

Tang, Kailin (唐凱麟), and Huaicheng (張懷承) Zhang. 1999. 成人與成聖: 儒家道德精粹 *(On Becoming a Man and a Sage: A Summary on Confucian Moral Values)*. Edited by K. Tang, 中國傳統倫理道德文化叢書 *(Traditional Chinese Moral Cultural Series)*. Cheungsha: University of Hunan Press.

Tang, Qing (湯清). 2001. 中國基督教百年史 *(The First Hundred Years of Protestant Mission in China)*. 2nd ed. Hong Kong: Taosheng Publishing House.

Tao, Feiya (陶飛亞). 2006. 衝突的解釋: 基督教與近代中國政治 *(The Explanation of Conflicts: Christianity and Modern Chinese Politics)*. 30 vols. Vol. 22, *Essays for the 200th Anniversary of Robert Morrison coming to China*. Taipei: Cosmic Light.

Tasker, R.V.G. 2000. *The Gospel according to St. John: An Introduction and Commentary*. Edited by R. V. G. Tasker. Reprint ed, *Tyndale Bible Commentaries Series*. Grand Rapids, MI: InterVarsity Press.

Team, Editorial. 2009. 王明道 (Wang Mingdao). In *Biographical Dictionary of Chinese Christianity*, edited by G. Doyle, Wright. Charlottesville: Global China Center.

The Party History Research Centre of Beijing, (中共北京市委黨史研究室), ed. 1989. 北京革命史大事記: *1919-1949 (The History of Revolutionary Events in Beijing: 1919-1949)*. Beijing: Zhong Gong Dang Shi Zi Liao Chu Ban She.

The Special Committee on Survey and Occupation China Continuation Committee, (中華續行委辦會調查特委會) ed. 1985. 中華歸主: 中國基督教事業統計 *1901-1920 (The Christian Occupation of China: a General Survey of the Numerical Strength and Geographical Disctibution of the Christian Forces in China 1901-1920)*. Edited by M. T. Stauffer. 3 vols. Vol. 1. Beijing: Zhong Quo She Hui Ke Xue Chu Ban She.

———, ed. 2007. *The Christian Occupation of China (1901-1920* 年中國基督教調查資料*)*. Edited by M. T. Stauffer. Revised ed. Beijing: Zhong Quo She Hui Ke Xue Chu Ban She.

Thompsett, Fredrica Harris. 2006. Episcopal Images of Leadership Shaped in Community. In *Traditions in Leadership: How Faith Traditions Shape the Way we Lead*, edited by R. J. Mouw and E. O. Jacobsen. Pasadena, CA: The De Pree Leadership Center.

Thompson, Paul. 1998. The voice of the Past. In *The Oral History Reader*, edited by R. Perks and A. Thomson. London: Routledge.

Titon, Jeff Todd. 2006. The Life Story. In *Case Study Research*, edited by M. David. London: Sage Publications.

Tsou, Tang (鄒讜). 1994. 二十世紀中國政治—宏觀歷史與微觀行動角度看 *(Twentieth Century Chinese Politics)*. Hong Kong: Oxford University Press.

Tu, Wei-ming. 1976a. *Centrality and Commonality: An Essay on Chung-Yung*. Hawaii, HI: The University Press of Hawaii.

———. 1976b. *Neo-Confucian Thought in Action: Wang Yang-ming's Youth (1472-1509)*. Berkeley: University of California Press.

———. 1979. *Humanity and Self-Cultivation: Essays in Confucian Thought*. Berkeley: Asian Humanities Press.

———. 1985. *Confucian Thought: Selfhood as Creative Transformation*. Albany: State University of New York Press.

Tu, Wei-ming (杜維明). 2008. 儒教 *(Confucianism)*. Shanghai: Shanghai Chinese Classics Publishing House.

Unknown. 2010. *Confucius and his Love Story* 2010 [cited October 10, 2010]. Available from http://www.faithandfilmcritics.com/confucius-and-his-love-story.

Urumqi China Christian Council, ed. 2005. 新疆中華基督教會建立六十周年感恩特刊 *(The Xinjiang Chinese Christian Church 60th Anniversary Special Thanksgiving Issue)*. Urumqi: Urumqi China Christian Council.

Van Vugt, Mark. 2006. Evolutionary Origins of Leadership and Followership. In *Personality & Social Psychology Review (Lawrence Erlbaum Associates)*: Lawrence Erlbaum Associates.

———. 2009. Despotism, Democracy, and the Evolutionary Dynamics of Leadership and Followership. In *American Psychologist*.

Van Vugt, Mark, Robert Hogan, and Robert B. Kaiser. 2008. Leadership, Followership, and Evolution: Some Lessons From the Past. In *American Psychologist*.

Vansina, Jan. 1965. *Oral Tradition: A Study in Historical Methodology*. Translated by H. Wright, M. Chicago, IL: Aldine Publishing Company.

———. 1985. *Oral Tradition as History*. Madison, WI: The University of Wisconsin Press.

Vroom, Victor Harold, and Philip W. Yetton. 1973. *Leadership and Decision-Making*. Pittsburgh, PA: University of Pittsburgh Press.

Wang, Hebin (王鶴濱). 2007. 我在毛澤東身邊的日子 *(The Days I Worked for Mao Zedong)*. Taipei: Xin Chao She.

Wang, Juichen (王瑞珍). 2003. 神國俠侶: 西域宣教傳奇 *(Silk Route Mission: Story of a Heroic Couple)*. Taipei: Campus Evangelical Fellowship.

Wang, Mingdao. 1983. *Spiritual Food*. Translated by A. Reynolds. Southampton: Mayflower Christian Books.

Wang, Mingdao (王明道). 1977a. 靈食 *(Spiritual Food)*. Edited by C. Wang (王正中). 7 vols. Vol. 3, 王明道文庫 *(Collected Writings of Wang, Mingdao)*. Tai Zhong: China Baptist Press.

———. 1977b. 餘糧 *(Surplus Grain)*. Edited by C. Wang (王正中). 7 vols. Vol. 4, 王明道文庫 *(Collected Writings of Wang, Mingdao)*. Tai Zhong: China Baptist Press.

———. 1978. 天召 *(Calling)*. Edited by C. Wang (王正中). 7 vols. Vol. 5, 王明道文庫 *(Collected Writings of Wang, Mingdao)*. Tai Zhong: China Baptist Press.

———. 1984a. 窄門 *(Narrow Door)*. Edited by C. Wang (王正中). 7 vols. Vol. 1, 王明道文庫 *(Collected Writings of Wang, Mingdao)*. Tai Zhong: China Baptist Press.

———. 1984b. 小徑 *(Trail)*. Edited by C. Wang (王正中). 7 vols. Vol. 2, 王明道文庫 *(Collected Writings of Wang, Mingdao)*. Tai Zhong: China Baptist Press.

———. 1984c. 借鏡 *(Reference)*. Edited by C. Wang (王正中). 7 vols. Vol. 6, 王明道文庫 *(Collected Writings of Wang, Mingdao)*. Tai Zhong: China Baptist Press.

———. 1984d. 衛道 *(Apologetics)*. Edited by C.-c. Wang (王正中). 7 vols. Vol. 7, 王明道文庫 *(Collected Writings of Wang, Mingdao)*. Tai Zhong: China Baptist Press.

———. 1997. 王明道日記選輯 *(Selections from Wang's Diaries)*. Hong Kong: Spiritual Rock Publishers.

———. 2005. 五十年來 *(The Fifty Years)*. 12th ed. Hong Kong: Bellman House Publishers.

Wang, Xue (王雪). 2007. 基督教與陝西 *(Christianity and Shaanxi)*. Beijing: Chinese Academy of Social Science.

Wang, Yangming (王陽明). 1992. 王陽明全集 *(Complete Works of Wang Yang Ming)*. 2 vols. Shanghai: Shanghai Gu Ji Chu Ban She

Wang, Zhixin (王治心). 1925. 中國本色教會的討論 (A Discussion on Indigenous Churches in China). 青年進步 *(Progressive Youth)* 79 (1).

———. 1998. 中國基督教史綱 *(History of Christianity in China)*. 5th ed. Hong Kong: Chinese Christian Literature Council Ltd.

Weigh, K.H. (魏光禧), ed. 1974. 倪柝聲弟兄三次公開的見證 *(Watchman Nee's Testimony)*. Hong Kong: Hong Kong Church Book Room Ltd.

Whitacre, Rodney A. 1999. *John*. Edited by G. R. Osborne, *The IVP New Testament Commentary Series*. Downers Grove, IL: InterVarsity Press.

Wickeri, Philip L. 2007. *Reconstructing Christianity in China: K. H. Ting and the Chinese Church*. New York, NY: Orbis Books.

Wilcock, Michael. 1979. *The Message of Luke: The Saviour of the World*. Edited by J. Stott, *The Bible Speaks Today*. Leicester: InterVarsity Press.

Wilkes, C. Gene. 1998. *Jesus on Leadership*. Carol Stream, IL: Tyndale.

Wilkins, M.J. 1992. Disciples. In *Dictionary of Jesus and the Gospels*, edited by J. B. Green and S. KMcKnight. Downers Grove, IL: InterVarsity Press.

Wilkinson, Bruce, and David Kopp. 2001. *Secrets of the Vine: Breaking through to Abundance*. Sisters, OR: Multnomah.

Wood, Richard J. 2006. Christ has come to Teach his People Himself: Vulnerability and the Exercise of Power in Quaker Leadership. In *Traditions in Leadership: How Faith Traditions Shape the Way we Lead*, edited by R. J. Mouw and E. O. Jacobsen. Pasadena, CA: The De Pree Leadership Center.

Woodside, Arch G. 2010. *Case Study Research: Theory, Methods, Practice*. Bingley: Emerald Group Publishing Limited.

Wright, Walter C. 2000. *Relational Leadership: A Biblical Model for Influence and Service*. Carlisle: Paternoster Press.

———. 2004. *Mentoring: the Promise of Relational Leadership*. Bucks: Paternoster Press.

———. 2009. *Relational Leadership: A Biblical Model for Influence and Service*. Revised and Expanded ed. Colorado Springs, CO: Paternoster Press.

Xie, Longyi (謝龍邑). 1995. 委曲求全? 吳耀宗的生平與救國情懷 *(Tolerance for the Sake of Survival? Christianity, China's Reconstruction and Y.T. Wu)*. Hong Kong: Logos Publishers Ltd.

———. 2008. 基督人: 賈玉銘的靈命神學 *(Christ Man: the Spiritual Theology of Chia Yuming)*. Taipei: China Evangelical Seminary.

Yang, Brother (楊弟兄). 2009. 死在耶穌前、活在耶穌前: 回憶我的父親楊紹唐牧師 *(Die before Jesus, Live before Jesus: In the Memories of my father Yang Shaotang)* 2004 [cited October 13, 2009]. Available from http://jesus.bbs.net/bbs/05/34.html.

Yang, Huijie (楊慧傑). 1981. 天人關係: 中國文化一個基本特徵的探討 *(A Theory on the Relationship of Heaven and Humanity)*. Taipei: Dalin Publishing House.

Yang, Kuo-Shu. 2000. Monocultural and Cross-cultural Indigenous Approaches: The Royal Road to the Development of a Balanced Global Psychology. *Asian Journal of Social Psychology* 3 (3):241-264.

Yang, Shaotang (楊紹唐). 1939. 教會與工人 *(The Church and the Worker)*. Tianjin: The Kwang Hsueh Publishing House.

———. 1941. 華東傳道人員退修會講道紀錄 *(The Record of Sermons of the East China Patoral Retreat)*. Shanghai: Zhong Hua Shen Xue Yuan.

———. 1961. 神的工人 *(God's Workmen)*. Hong Kong: Christian Witness Press.

———. 1998. 得勝與得賞 *(Victory and Reward)*. Shanghai: China Christian Council.

———. 2005a. 教會路線・教會的成長 *(The Course of the Church and Church Growth)*. Hong Kong: Found Treasure Publishing House.

———. 2005b. 聖經綱要: 靈修講題 *(The Outline of the Bible: The Devotional Topics)*. Hong Kong: Found Treasure Publishing House.

Yao, Minquan (姚民權), and Weihong (羅偉虹) Luo. 2000. 中國基督教簡史 *(A Brief History of Christianity in China)*. Beijing: Religious and Culture Publishing House.

Ye, Zude (葉祖德). 2006a. 天國的信息 *(The Messages of the Heavenly Kindgom)*. 2 vols. Vol. 1. Fuzhou: Fujian China Christian Council.

———. 2006b. 天國的信息 *(The Messages of the Heavenly Kindgom)*. 2 vols. Vol. 2. Fuzhou: Fujian China Christian Council.

Yeh, Solomon (葉仁昌). 1987. 近代中國的宗教批判: 非基運動的再思 *(Religious Critcism in Modern China)*. 3rd ed. Taipei: Christian Arts Press.

Yeung, Jason King-kau (楊慶球). 1996. 成聖與自由: 王陽明與西方基督教思想的比較 *(Sanctification and Freedom: A Comparative Study on the Thought of Wang Yang-ming and Christianity)*. Vol. 2, *CCCRC Occasional Paper*. Hong Kong: Alliance Bible Seminary.

Yeung, Linda. 2006. *The Gentle Pastor with Rock Solid Faith, Living Faith Series*. Hong Kong: Christian Communications Ltd.

Yin, Robert K. 2003. *Applications of Case Study Research*. 2nd ed. Vol. 34, *Applied Social Research Methods Series*. London: SAGE Publications.

———. 2009. *Case Study Research : Design and Methods* 4th ed. Vol. 5, *Applied Social Research Methods Series*. Thousand Oaks, CA: Sage Publications.

Ying, Fuktsang (邢福增). 1997. 基督仰信與國實踐――二十世紀前前的個案研究 *(Christian Doctrine and the Praxis of National Salvation: A Case Study of the First Half of 20th Century China)*. Vol. 3, *Chinese Study Series*. Hong Kong: Alliance Bible Seminary.

———. 2001. 中國基要主義者的實踐與困境: 陳崇桂的神學思想與時代 *(Praxis and Predicament of a Chinese Fundamentalist: Chen Chonggui (Marcus Cheng)'s Theological Thought and his Time)*. Vol. 5, *Chinese Study Series*. Hong Kong: Alliance Bible Seminary.

———. 2006. 衝突與融合: 近代中國基督教史研究論集 *(Conflict and Integration: Essays on Modern Chinese Christian Historical Research)*. 30 vols. Vol. 11, *Essays for the 200th Anniversary of Robert Morrison coming to China*. Taipei: Cosmic Light.

———. 2008. 內聖外王: 從華人教會歷史角度看教牧職事 (Inner Saint and Outer King: A Study on Pastoral Ministry from the Chinese Church History Perspective). In 華人教會處境中的教牧職事 *(Defining Pastoral Ministry in the Chinese Church Context)*, edited by Y. 李. Lee. Hong Kong: The Divinity School of Chung Chi College.

Yip, Kache. 1980. *Religion, Nationalism, and Chinese Students: The Anti-Christian Movement of 1922-1927*. Vol. 15, *Studies on East Asia*. Bellingham, WA: Western Washington University.

Yu, Leekung (于力工). 2006. *Western Missionary Movement and the Rise of the Chinese Church* (西方宣教運動與中國教會之興起). Berkeley: Gan Lan Chu Ban She.

———. 2006. 西方宣教運動與中國教會之興起 *(Western Missionary Movement and the Rise of the Chinese Church)*. Berkeley: Gan Lan Chu Ban She.

Yukl, Gary A. 1989. *Leadership in Organizations*. 2nd ed. Englewood Cliffs, NJ: Prentice Hall.

———. 2010. *Leadership in Organizations*. 7th ed. Upper Saddle River, NJ: Prentice Hall.

Zaccaro, Stephen J., Cary Kemp, and Paige Bader. 2004. Leader Traits and Attributes. In *The Nature of Leadership*, edited by J. Antonakis, Cianciolo, Anna T. and Sternberg, Robert J. Thousand Oaks, CA: Sage Publications.

Zhang, Guanru (張冠儒). 2009. *The Rock and Living Water (*靈磐活水*)*. Revised ed. Xian: Shaanxi China Christian Council.

Zhao, Junying (趙君影). 1981. 漫談五十年來中國的教會與政治 *(The Chinese Churches and Politcs in the past 50 Years)*. Taipei: Chinese for Christ, Inc.

Zhao, Shilin (趙士林). 1993. 心靈學問: 王陽明心學 *(Wang Yang-ming's Theory of Heart-mind)*. Hong Kong: Chung Hua Book Co. Ltd.

Zhu, Meng(朱夢), ed. 2001. 大風暴: 毛澤東與紅衛兵 *(Mao Zedong and the Red Guards)* Urumqi: Xinjiang People's Publishing House.

Zhuo, Kou (拙口). 2009. 賈玉銘牧師的慘痛教訓—(看這些人) (二) *(The Bitter Lessons of Rev. Jia Yuming—Look at these Men II)* 2008 [cited October 13, 2009]. Available from http://blog.haleluya.com.tw/nobody/archives/9384.html.

———. 2009. 賈玉銘牧師的慘痛教訓—(看這些人) 三 *(The Bitter Lessons of Rev. Jia Yuming—Look at these Men III)* 2008a [cited October 13, 2009]. Available from http://blog.haleluya.com.tw/nobody/archives/9385.html.

Zou, Shuhua (鄒淑華). 2005. 一粒麥子—記西北靈工團團長張谷泉牧師 (A Seed of Grain: In the Memory of the President of Northwest Spiritual Movement, Rev. Zhang Guquan). 新疆中華基督教會建立六十周年感恩特刊 *(The Xinjiang Chinese Christian Church 60th Anniversary Special Thanksgiving Issue)*, August 28, 2005, 23-25.

Zuck, Roy B. 1995. *Teaching as Jesus Taught*. Grand Rapids, MI: Baker Books.

Index

Aikman, David 5, 136, 295
Allen, Barbara 15, 295
Analects 83, 87, 89, 98, 105, 138, 143, 292, 306
Anti-Christian Movement 111, 116, 117, 119, 120, 124, 127, 178, 297, 317
apprentice 160, 162, 164, 165, 179, 230, 231, 232, 233, 234, 236, 250
Arias, Mortimer 39
Atkinson, Robert 15, 295
attributes 36, 47, 48, 49, 50, 51, 52, 53, 54, 56, 60, 62, 69, 71, 74, 76, 77, 95, 100, 103, 145, 153, 156, 158, 160, 169, 170, 173, 181, 221, 250, 254, 255, 259, 317
Avolio, Bruce J. 64, 71, 295, 301
back to Jerusalem xvii, 5, 192, 230, 283
Bader, Paige 50, 52, 317
Baker, C. J. Wuest 18, 295, 305, 308, 318
Bartell, Sherrie R. 18, 295
Bass, Bernard M. 50, 52, 53, 58, 62, 64, 65, 295, 296, 299, 302, 303, 305, 308, 309, 311
Bays, Daniel H. 12, 114, 115, 120, 121, 122, 127, 296
Becker, Howard S. 17, 296
Bennis, Warren G. 53, 65, 296
Bible centered leader 36, 299
Blanchard, Ken 52
Block, Peter 63
Bloor, Michael 13, 14, 16, 296
Bosch, David J. 9, 296

Bruce, F. F. 28, 30, 34, 37
Buddhism 84, 86, 101, 112, 131, 156
Burns, James MacGregor 53, 61, 64, 65, 74, 297
Carducci, Rozana 76, 305
CCC xvii, 126, 189, 193, 194, 196, 201, 205, 206, 228, 238, 242, 283, 285, 288, 313, 316, 317
Ceng, Wewu 2, 143, 291, 297
Chaleff, Ira 70, 297, 303, 305, 308, 311
Chao, Tianen 118, 291
charismatic leadership 51, 61, 64, 69, 70, 71, 223, 299, 303
Charmaz, Kathy 18, 19, 297
Cheng, Bor-shiuan 72
Ching, Julia 82, 84, 298
Christ-human 150, 151, 155, 156, 158, 174, 179, 180, 249, 256
Christian Communications Ltd. xvii, 3, 16, 316
Church Assembly Hall xvii, 120, 121, 123, 134, 185, 203, 204, 205, 206, 208, 209, 217, 218, 224, 225, 236, 240, 241, 242
Clarke, Andrew D. 26, 27, 40, 298
Clinton, J. Robert 9, 25, 36, 38, 42, 44, 53, 109, 110, 137, 299
Cohen, Paul A. 12, 117, 299
Coleman, Robert E. 24
collectivism 49, 72, 79, 176, 181, 219, 222, 244
Confucianism xiii, xv, 3, 4, 7, 8, 9, 10, 11, 15, 19, 47, 49, 58, 69, 77, 79, 80, 81, 82, 83, 84, 85, 86, 87, 88, 89, 90, 92, 93, 94, 96, 98, 99, 100, 101, 102, 103,

105, 106, 109, 112, 128, 129,
130, 131, 132, 135, 137, 138,
139, 140, 142, 143, 144, 145,
146, 147, 150, 152, 154, 155,
156, 158, 172, 173, 174, 175,
177, 178, 179, 181, 187, 200,
208, 211, 212, 219, 220, 221,
222, 234, 244, 248, 251, 252,
255, 256, 259, 263, 264, 270,
271, 272, 287, 301, 305, 307,
308, 312, 313
Confucius 6, 10, 11, 19, 23, 24, 80,
81, 87, 89, 93, 94, 98, 105,
138, 143, 229, 291, 311, 313
Conger, Jay A. 51, 71, 299
contextualization 3, 4, 6, 95, 178,
217, 247, 270, 307
Covey, Stephen R. 51, 299
Culbert, Sammuel A. 51
cultural revolution 1, 8, 10, 16, 61,
126, 188, 199, 201, 204, 209,
212, 226, 227, 240, 264, 273,
281, 283, 285, 287, 289, 311
culture
  Asian 45, 69, 72, 73, 74, 77, 79,
  160, 256, 259
  Chinese 2, 3, 5, 6, 7, 8, 11, 15,
  48, 49, 62, 73, 79, 80, 81, 100,
  103, 105, 109, 117, 118, 119,
  130, 131, 135, 137, 161, 163,
  173, 175, 176, 220, 222, 223,
  253, 254, 255, 258, 263, 271
  humanistic 80, 101, 178
  organizational 49, 58, 59, 60, 77
  paternalistic 66, 72, 74, 77
Curphy, Gordon J. 57, 60, 63, 303
De Bary, WM. Theodore 10, 87, 88,
300
De Pree, Max 65, 68, 300, 309, 310,
313, 315

Denzin, Norman K. 13, 300
Ding, Guangxun 126, 270, 291
disciple 1, 7, 8, 10, 23, 24, 25, 26, 28,
29, 30, 31, 32, 33, 34, 35, 36,
37, 38, 39, 40, 41, 42, 43, 44,
45, 81, 86, 87, 99, 131, 143,
146, 149, 156, 236, 258, 297,
309, 315
Drucker, Peter F. 51, 300
Dufour, Stephane 13, 302
empowerment 39, 40, 44, 63, 75, 251
experiential learning 37, 47, 219,
229, 244, 250, 251, 257, 258,
303
Fairbank, John K. 12, 300
Farth, Jing-lih 72
Fernando, Ajith 32, 36
Fetterman, David M. 17, 301
Fiedler, Fred E. 56, 301
Fischbacher, Emil 191, 231, 306
followership 48, 63, 65, 71, 74, 77,
175, 177, 303, 305, 306, 308,
310, 311, 313
Fortin, Dominic 13, 302
Fujian 14, 85, 203, 205, 206, 207,
242, 243, 289, 316
Fulton, Brent 4, 301
fundamentalism 111, 113, 114, 115,
116, 117, 124, 125, 132, 133,
136, 137, 146, 167, 178, 218,
239, 255, 270, 306, 317
Fung, Yulan 92
Fuping 198, 199, 200, 202, 213
Fuzhou 16, 121, 185, 186, 187, 189,
203, 204, 206, 207, 209, 211,
217, 222, 223, 224, 227, 236,
244, 254, 259, 268, 269, 272,
289, 316
Gardner, William L. 71
Gibb, Cecil A. 54

Ginnett, Robert C. 57, 60, 63, 303
Glaser, Barney G. 18, 295, 297, 302
gospel 7, 8, 10, 24, 25, 28, 30, 31, 32, 37, 39, 41, 132, 192, 199, 241, 279, 297, 302, 307, 308, 309, 310, 311, 312, 315
Green, Michael 35
Greenleaf, Robert K. 51, 302
guanxi 222, 257
Gubrium, Jaber F. 16, 303
Hamel, Jacques 13, 302
Harris, R. Geoffrey 39
Hattaway, Paul 207
Heaven 3, 30, 40, 42, 79, 80, 87, 89, 90, 92, 93, 97, 100, 101, 103, 104, 105, 106, 131, 139, 140, 141, 144, 145, 152, 155, 156, 158, 170, 173, 174, 177, 241, 250, 257, 292, 316
  mandate of 80, 87, 89, 90, 91, 93, 98, 100, 101, 102, 103, 104, 105, 144, 173, 174, 177, 250, 292
  principles of 80, 91, 97, 140
Henke, Frederick G. 82
Holstein, James A. 16, 303
Horsley, Richard A. 26, 303
Huang, Zongxi 96, 99, 291
Hughes, Richard L. 57, 60, 63
human nature 10, 42, 69, 78, 79, 81, 82, 86, 87, 88, 90, 91, 92, 93, 95, 96, 97, 98, 100, 101, 102, 135, 144, 145, 151, 155, 158, 174, 177, 182, 236, 244, 255, 256, 270, 271, 293
indigenization xv, 1, 2, 7, 8, 15, 18, 106, 109, 111, 117, 118, 119, 120, 121, 122, 123, 127, 129, 130, 142, 146, 175, 177, 179, 185, 192, 195, 197, 203, 208, 215, 217, 218, 254, 258, 264, 265, 266, 267, 272, 296, 297, 298, 301, 314, 316
innate knowledge 80, 81, 85, 88, 89, 91, 92, 95, 96, 98, 102, 106, 131, 154, 292, 293
inner life 5, 35, 36, 37, 44, 47, 77, 105, 106, 114, 115, 130, 150, 155, 158, 163, 165, 169, 170, 173, 177, 221, 222, 237, 244, 249, 250, 255, 256, 265, 266
inter-faith dialogues 3
interpersonal relationships 50, 56, 181, 252
investigation of things 83, 84, 85, 86, 91, 96, 98, 291
Jen xvi, 10, 87, 88, 89, 100, 143, 291
Jesus, of Nazareth 6, 7, 8, 10, 19, 23, 24, 25, 26, 27, 28, 29, 30, 31, 32, 33, 34, 35, 36, 37, 38, 39, 40, 41, 42, 43, 44, 45, 47, 81, 101, 106, 114, 120, 147, 148, 149, 156, 169, 172, 180, 212, 213, 221, 236, 250, 253, 258, 271, 295, 296, 297, 301, 303, 304, 308, 309, 310, 311, 315, 318
Jia, Yuming 111, 112, 113, 114, 115, 119, 120, 121, 122, 123, 124, 125, 126, 127, 132, 133, 134, 135, 146, 147, 148, 149, 150, 151, 152, 153, 154, 155, 156, 157, 158, 160, 169, 172, 174, 177, 179, 180, 192, 218, 227, 249, 256, 264, 272, 279, 291, 298, 303, 305, 307, 318
Johnson, Alan 39, 295
Johnson, McKinley 212
Jorgensen, Danny L. 17, 304
Junzi 10, 80

Kanungo, Rabindra N. 51
Kellerman, Barbara 66, 67, 68, 69, 304
Kelley, Robert E. 50, 59, 67, 69, 305
Kemp, Cary 50, 317
Kezar, Adrian 76
Kim, Heup Young 82
Komives, Susan R. 75
Kung, Hans 305
Kwok, Wailuen 134, 180
Latour, Sharon M. 65
Latourette, Kenneth Scott. 12, 112, 117, 120, 123, 306
leader-centric 50, 63, 65, 71
leadership traits theory 48, 50, 53, 254
Lee, Maucheng 109, 110
Leung, Kalun 94, 131, 137, 140
Li, Jinqiang 13
liang zhi 81, 85, 87, 88, 89, 90, 95, 96, 98, 99, 100, 101, 102, 131, 141, 154, 257
Lincoln, Yvonna S. 13, 138, 300
Lingenfelter, Judith 33
Lipman-Blumen, Jean 69, 71, 303, 305, 308, 311
Liu, Shuxian 3, 80, 173
Liu, Zongzhou 99, 292
Lucas, Nance 75, 305
Luo, Guanzhon 118
Lutz, Jessie G. 117
Lyall, Leslie T. 134
Maccoby, Michael 72
Malphurs, Aubrey 51
Mao, Zedong 1, 10, 16, 61, 311, 314, 318
Mather, Percy 191, 231
Maxwell, John C. 51, 52
Maxwell, Joseph A. 309
McKinney, Carol V. 14, 16, 309
McMahon, Timothy R. 75, 305
Mencius 11, 81, 83, 85, 86, 87, 88, 90, 91, 93, 95, 97, 152, 155, 292
mentor xiii, 43, 44, 64, 74, 112, 162, 164, 165, 179, 230, 231, 232, 233, 234, 235, 236, 237, 250, 251, 267, 268, 299
mentoring 5, 8, 42, 44, 72, 135, 158, 160, 161, 162, 164, 165, 170, 171, 172, 179, 229, 230, 232, 234, 235, 236, 238, 251, 258, 267, 268, 269, 315
Messiah 26, 31, 39
messianic expectation 26, 30, 31, 45
mission
  cross cultural 1, 5, 9, 20, 38, 248
  missionary xvii, 111, 118, 122, 127, 277, 298, 300, 317
  missionary society xvii, 2, 3, 112, 113, 133, 191, 192, 195, 197, 203, 217, 218, 230, 281, 283, 285
modeling 23, 24, 51, 64, 73, 74, 77, 83, 94, 95, 101, 103, 106, 126, 139, 147, 149, 151, 156, 158, 161, 162, 163, 164, 165, 166, 174, 176, 179, 180, 202, 208, 212, 213, 216, 219, 220, 226, 227, 229, 230, 231, 232, 233, 236, 237, 238, 240, 244, 249, 250, 251, 252
Montell, William Lynwood 15, 295
moral leadership 64, 69, 74, 76, 100, 103, 105, 130, 140, 158, 173, 175, 178, 221, 255, 256
moral perfection 62, 81, 89, 93, 102, 103, 145, 152, 153, 154, 156, 158, 174, 177, 256
Mouw, Richard J. 59

Index

Nanus, Burt 51, 53, 65, 296, 309
Nee, Watchman 94, 95, 110, 115, 119, 120, 121, 123, 133, 134, 140, 203, 204, 205, 206, 217, 237, 242, 289, 292, 300, 305, 306, 307, 310, 315
nei sheng wai wang 130, 150, 158
Neo-Confucianism 10, 81, 82, 84, 86, 90, 98, 173, 297, 298, 313
Ng, Esther 35
Normative Model 55
North China Seminary 115, 192
Northouse, Peter G. 53, 310
Osiek, Carolyn 26, 310
Perkins, Pheme 23
Portelli, Alessandro 15, 16, 310
pragmatism 98, 105, 141, 145, 172, 173, 175, 251, 257
Pye, Lucian 73, 310
Rabbi 27
Rast, Vicki J. 65, 306
red guards 1, 10, 16, 201, 318
redemption 114, 147, 148, 151, 256
research method 1, 11, 13, 14, 18, 269, 295, 296, 301, 302, 303, 304, 309, 316
    case study 11, 12, 13, 14, 17, 18, 190, 197, 203
    ethnographic interviewing xvii, 12, 13, 14, 15, 16, 18, 187, 311
    grounded theory 12, 18, 295, 297, 302
    historiography 11, 12
    life story 11, 13, 14, 15, 16, 17, 82, 132, 187, 295, 313
    multiple 13
    oral history 12, 14, 15, 310, 313
    participant observation xvii, 12, 13, 14, 17, 18, 187, 272, 296, 304

    qualitative 11
Robeck, Cecil M. 59
Rosenau, James 58, 71, 310
sage 93, 292, 295, 296, 297, 300, 301, 302, 303, 304, 309, 310, 312, 313, 316
salvation 146, 147, 148, 156, 300, 304, 306, 316
sanctification 82, 131, 135, 142, 144, 145, 146, 147, 148, 149, 150, 151, 152, 153, 154, 155, 156, 157, 158, 174, 179, 180, 181, 249, 250, 316
Sanders, E. P. 28
Sanyuan 19, 185, 186, 187, 188, 189, 197, 198, 199, 200, 201, 202, 208, 209, 211, 213, 220, 221, 222, 223, 226, 227, 234, 235, 239, 244, 252, 253, 257, 259, 268, 269, 272, 287, 288
self-cultivation 77, 94, 96, 100, 101, 105, 144, 175, 176
servant leadership 25, 36, 38, 51, 101, 149, 169
Seung, Hwan Shim 24
Shaanxi 14, 197, 198, 199, 201, 234, 283, 287, 288, 314, 317
sheng ren 80
situational theory 49, 54, 55, 56, 57, 58, 77, 109, 258
Smart, Ninian 311
Song, John 110, 113, 114, 115, 119, 134, 180, 200, 208, 218, 285, 287, 291
spirit-life 148, 150, 155
Spiritual Action Team 112, 115, 120, 123, 160, 161, 162, 170, 253, 281
Spiritual Institute 115, 120, 123, 125, 126, 192, 227, 279, 298

spiritual leadership 25, 36, 76
Spradley, James P. 311
Stern, P. N. 18, 295
Stogdill, Ralph M. 50, 52, 58, 62, 295, 311
Strauss, Anselm L. 18, 302
Strong, Kendrick 23
suffering 5, 31, 88, 159, 169, 170, 171, 212, 213, 240, 244, 248, 264, 311
Tang, Junyi 3, 89, 292
Tang, Qing 12, 111
Taoism xvi, 58, 84, 86, 101, 131, 216
team leadership 29, 32, 34, 43, 76, 159, 165, 223, 224, 225, 226, 253
Thompsett, Fredrica H. 59
Three Self Patriotic Movement xvii, 9, 11, 110, 118, 124, 125, 126, 127, 132, 133, 136, 142, 178, 189, 190, 193, 194, 199, 201, 204, 205, 206, 214, 215, 217, 218, 228, 238, 242, 255, 259, 263, 264, 266, 267, 270, 271, 277, 281, 283, 285, 288, 289
Titon, Jeff Todd 14, 313
training 1, 3, 4, 5, 6, 17, 24, 29, 37, 41, 42, 50, 52, 113, 115, 120, 122, 123, 125, 127, 129, 132, 133, 149, 153, 160, 165, 166, 167, 169, 170, 171, 179, 197, 201, 205, 206, 207, 216, 217, 228, 232, 234, 236, 238, 239, 240, 241, 242, 243, 244, 254, 264, 265, 274, 275, 297
  curriculum 4, 37
  program 4, 123, 130, 205, 216, 234, 264, 265, 274
transactional leadership 64, 65
transformational leadership 61, 64, 65
Tu, Weiming 82, 94
Urumqi 16, 19, 185, 186, 187, 188, 189, 190, 191, 192, 193, 194, 195, 196, 197, 202, 208, 209, 211, 215, 216, 217, 220, 222, 223, 224, 227, 228, 229, 230, 231, 232, 233, 234, 236, 239, 240, 242, 244, 251, 252, 253, 257, 259, 268, 269, 272, 283, 285, 303, 313, 318
Vansina, Jan 15, 313
Vroom, Victor H. 55, 313
Vugt, Mark Van 57, 313
Wang, Mingdao 19, 110, 112, 113, 115, 119, 120, 121, 123, 124, 125, 130, 132, 133, 134, 135, 136, 137, 138, 139, 140, 141, 142, 143, 144, 145, 146, 158, 169, 172, 174, 175, 176, 177, 178, 179, 180, 181, 214, 218, 229, 248, 251, 264, 272, 277, 292, 312, 314
Wang, Yangming 10, 80, 81, 82, 83, 84, 85, 86, 87, 88, 89, 90, 91, 92, 95, 96, 97, 98, 99, 100, 101, 102, 105, 140, 142, 145, 176, 181, 219, 251, 258, 271, 292, 298, 314
Wang, Zhixin 12, 118
Watson, Burton 87, 88, 122, 300
Wood, Fiona 13, 14, 16, 296, 315
Wood, Richard J. 60
Woodside, Arch G. 13, 315
Wright, Walter C. 42, 160
Xie, Longyi 134, 146
Xinjing 14
Yang, Shaotang 19, 110, 112, 113, 115, 116, 119, 120, 123, 124,

125, 127, 132, 133, 134, 135,
158, 159, 160, 161, 162, 163,
164, 166, 167, 168, 169, 170,
172, 176, 177, 178, 179, 180,
181, 218, 229, 252, 253, 264,
272, 281, 293, 307, 315, 316
Yetton, Philip W. 55, 313
Yeung, Jason xiii, 82
Ying, Fuktsang xiii, 115, 130
Yu, Leekung 119, 162, 293
Yukl, Gary A. 48, 52, 75, 317
Zaccaro, Stephen J. 50, 52, 317
Zhongzhou 19, 257
Zhu Xi 81, 83, 85, 86, 90, 96, 98,
175, 293
Zuck, Roy B. 23

Vita

Otto Lui was born in Hong Kong in 1969. He was educated in Catholic elementary and high schools. He did not become Catholic even though he was educated under Catholic background. Rather, he went to a Christian church with his elder brothers and sisters. Otto became a Christian when he was a teenager. In 1989, Otto was shocked by the June-Fourth Incident in Tiananmen Square. He realized the value and importance of freedom and found his mission to become a bridge between Christian faith and Chinese culture. He then chose to study religion and philosophy in Hong Kong Baptist University in 1989.

After Otto graduated from university and got his bachelors degree, he wanted to enrich his life experiences before furthering his studies. He worked in a political party called Meeting Point in 1992 which later merged and renamed as the Democratic Party. After a year of political experience, Otto decided to pursue a masters degree at the University of Science and Technology. His research focus was Process Philosophy of Norman Whitehead. However, due to the changes of the faculty after one year, Otto did not finish his masters and quit. He joined Christian Communications Ltd. (CCL) in 1995 and began his ministry in China ministry.

As a ministry director, Otto travelled extensively in China. Between 1997 and 2003, Otto spent six years to acquire a theological degree: Master of Divinity from Lutheran Theological Seminary in Hong Kong. In 1977, his first daughter was born, and he had to keep travelling at the same time. God called Otto to serve him in China. In addition, God wanted him to finish his unfinished dream, to be a bridge between Christianity and Chinese culture. As a result, together with his wife, Yvonne, and two daughters, Jurita and Jackie, Otto came to Fuller Theological Seminary in 2007. Otto was a full-time student and ministry director of CCL at the same time during his studies.

In 2010, Otto and his family moved back to Hong Kong to continue his dissertation writing. Meanwhile, he was assigned to be the Associate General Secretary (Development) of CCL in 2011. He continues his ministry in developing Chinese church leaders in both Hong Kong and mainland China in CCL.

www.ingramcontent.com/pod-product-compliance
Lightning Source LLC
Chambersburg PA
CBHW070233240426
43673CB00044B/1770